H

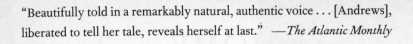

"Beautifully told in a remarkably natural, authentic voice . . . [Andrews], liberated to tell her tale, reveals herself at last." —*The Atlantic Monthly*

"Immensely readable." —*The Los Angeles Times*

"Forthright and fascinating." —*USA Today*

"Winningly humble." —*Vogue*

"Refreshing and authentic in its wide-eyed wonder . . . Andrews honestly and often humorously recounts the seminal moments of her early career . . . Her generous nature shines through every word." —*BookPage*

"Clearly and elegantly presented." —*Kirkus Reviews*

"Brims with eloquently told anecdotes . . . A lucidly told and engaging autobiography." —*The Orange County Register*

"*Home* carries little earthy charges of delight . . . A smoothly narrated story." —*The New York Observer*

"So sad—and so lovely . . . Andrews shares each detail in a voice as direct and crystal-clear as the four-octave soprano that shot her to stardom." —*The Buffalo News*

"Full of insights and wisdom, expressed with cultivated eloquence." —*The Philadelphia Enquirer*

"An extraordinary look at the beginning of an extraordinary career, and a wonderful insider's view of show business from the fading days of English vaudeville to London's West End, to the era of Boston and New Haven tryouts before Broadway openings." —*The East Hampton Star*

HOME

Julie Andrews

HOME

A MEMOIR

OF

MY EARLY YEARS

HYPERION

NEW YORK

For Emma,

with all my love

Silver tinsel on the ground.
River, streams. A round
water tower. Shining sun
flooding woods and meadows. Spun
gold and steel. Clouds punctuate
the hills and valleys and great
white cliffs of Dover.
Sea and ships. And, crossing over,
my heart soars like this aeroplane,
and I know I'm going home again.

JULIE ANDREWS

HOME

ONE

I AM TOLD THAT the first comprehensible word I uttered as a child was "home."

My father was driving his secondhand Austin 7; my mother was in the passenger seat beside him holding me on her lap. As we approached our modest house, Dad braked the car to turn onto the pocket-handkerchief square of concrete by the gate and apparently I quietly, tentatively, said the word.

"Home."

My mother told me there was a slight upward inflection in my voice, not a question so much as a trying of the word on the tongue, with perhaps the delicious discovery of connection . . . the word to the place. My parents wanted to be sure they had heard me correctly, so Dad drove around the lanes once again, and as we returned, it seems I repeated the word.

My mother must have said it more than once upon arrival at our house—perhaps with satisfaction? Or relief? Or maybe to instill in her young daughter a sense of comfort and safety. The word has carried enormous resonance for me ever since.

Home.

THE RIVER THAMES begins as a trickle just above Oxford in an area referred to in old literature as "Isis." The trickle has become a fair river and fordable by the time it reaches the great university city, and from there it winds its way through the English countryside, changing levels from time to time, spewing through the gates of some exquisitely pretty locks, passing old villages with lovely names like Sonning, Henley, Marlow, Maidenhead, and Bray.

It flows on through Windsor and Eton. Wicked King John signed the Magna Carta at a picturesque stretch of the Thames called Runnymede. It progresses through the county of Surrey, past Walton—the village where I was born—past the palace of Hampton Court where Sir Thomas More boarded the water taxis that carried him downriver after his audiences with Henry VIII, and continues through the county town of Kingston, on to Richmond and Kew. Finally it reaches London, gliding beneath its many bridges, passing the seat of British government, the Houses of Parliament, before making its final journey toward Greenwich and the magnificent Thames Estuary into the North Sea.

Because of the Thames I have always loved inland waterways—water in general, water sounds—there's music in water. Brooks babbling, fountains splashing. Weirs, waterfalls; tumbling, gushing. Whenever I think of my birthplace, Walton-on-Thames, my reference first and foremost is the river. I love the smell of the river; love its history, its gentleness. I was aware of its presence from my earliest years. Its majesty centered me, calmed me, was a solace to a certain extent.

The name "Walton" probably derives from the old English words *wealh tun* (Briton/serf and enclosure/town). Remnants of an ancient wall were to be found there in my youth. Walton is one of three closely related villages, the others being Hersham and Weybridge. When I was born, they were little more than stops on the railway line leading out of London into the county of Surrey. Hersham was the poor relative and had once been merely a strip of woodland beside another river, the Mole. It was originally occupied by Celts, whose implements were found in large numbers in the area. The Romans were there, and Anglo-Saxons were the first settlers. Hersham was very much a fringe settlement. Walton, slightly better off, was a larger village; Weybridge was altogether "upmarket."

Walton's small claim to fame was its bridge over the Thames. A very early version was painted by Canaletto; J. M. W. Turner painted a newer bridge in 1805. The span was reconstructed again long ago, but in my youth the bridge was so old and pitted that our bones were jarred as we rattled over it, and I was able to peer through the cracks and see the river flowing beneath. Driving across, away from the village, usually meant that I was leaving home to go on tour with my parents. Crossing back, though, was to know that we were in familiar territory once again. The river was our boundary; we could leave the busy world behind us and our front door was only moments away.

To this day, when I am flying into England, it is the view of the river that I search for as we descend toward Heathrow. And suddenly, I see it—stately, sparkling, winding through the meadows, forever soothing, forever serene.

I WAS NAMED after my two grandmothers—Julia Elizabeth.

Julia, my mother's mother, was the eldest daughter of William Henry Ward. He was a gardener, and met my great-grandmother, Julia Emily Hearmon (always referred to as Emily), when they joined the staff of a large house in Stratford-upon-Avon. Great-Granny Emily was a "tweeny," which is the name given to the poor unfortunate who gets up even before the servants and lights their fires so that they, in turn, can see to the comforts of the household. She was eleven years old when she went into service.

Some years later, she and Great-Grandpa William married and moved to Hersham, where their first daughter, my maternal grandmother, Julia Mary Ward, was born in 1887. There was to be a barren lapse of nine years before the rest of the family came along at two-year intervals, in a vain effort to produce a son. Four daughters were born, who were collectively known as "the girls," all bearing highfalutin names, starting with Wilhelmina Hearmon, followed by Fenella Henrietta, Nona Doris, and finally, Kathleen Lavinia. Mercifully, they were all shortened, to Mina, Fen, Doll, and Kath. Finally, the longed-for son arrived—William Henry, shortened to Harry and then to Hadge, by which time Julia, being the eldest, had married . . . and soon after, gave birth to my mother, Barbara Ward Morris, in July 1910. This meant that my mum had an uncle only a few years older than she, and therefore a built-in playmate.

I remember meeting my Great-Granny Emily Ward when she was in her eighties. Great-Grandpa had died, and she was living with her daughter Kath. Great-Granny was small and round like a barrel, with flawless skin and fine, pure white hair. She always smelled of fresh lavender and called me "dearie."

She had a sweet smile and a soft voice that sounded as if it were coming from a great distance. She loved canaries, and kept an aviary in the back of Auntie Kath's house in Hersham. I have loved canaries ever since.

Aunt Mina, Aunt Kath, and the other great-aunts were wonderful ladies, great characters all. Uncle Harry—or "Hadge"—was the black sheep of the family, and an alcoholic. I always felt there was something a little rough and dangerous about him, though he could be kind and had a playful sense of humor. Like his father, he had a magical touch with the land, and he eventually became our gardener. Things flourished when Hadge was in charge. My mother had a soft spot in her heart for him, and he was so competent when he was sober that she always wanted to keep him around. I used his image for the character of the gardener in my first children's book, *Mandy*.

My sense of the family history is somewhat sketchy, because my mother kept a great deal to herself. She spoke of her early years when pressed, but she never volunteered much—other than to speak lovingly of her mother, my namesake, Julia. Mum always took primroses to her grave in Hersham on Primrose Day, April 19, which was Granny Julia's birthday. Clearly, she missed her mother very much. The earliest recollections I have are of my mother's sadness at losing her. She must have carried her grief with her for many years in order for me to pick up on something like that.

It was left to my father and my aunt Joan, my mother's younger sister, to fill in what little I do know about my grandparents.

Grandmother Julia was apparently a sweet mouse of a woman. Sensitive, shy, of a retiring nature, yet a lover of music—my aunt told me she sang quite well. She wanted no more of life than to look after and love her children. I was told that my grandfather Arthur found this state of affairs suffocating and that her obvious attempts to please irritated him.

Unlike my mother, Aunt Joan spoke rather scathingly about Granny Julia, putting her down as being inferior to their father in intellect and breeding. Piecing the details together, I have concluded that my maternal grandmother was uneducated, pretty, hardworking, troubled; and that her husband, Grandfather Arthur Morris, was angry, talented, a womanizer, a bully, a drunkard, and illegitimate.

Arthur Morris was conceived at a time when it boded ill to be born "on the wrong side of the blanket," even if sired by a "Sir." Being tall—over six feet—of good countenance, and brainy, he apparently had an arrogant personality, but if he desired, he could be a great charmer. His own childhood was unhappy to say the least, as he was banished to the scullery most of the time, for his mother eventually married and his stepfather couldn't bear the sight of him.

As soon as he was of age, Arthur ran away to join the army and became a Grenadier Guard. Here he learned music and gained a promotion into the brass band, where he played the trumpet. He also excelled at the piano.

While stationed at Caterham Barracks, Surrey, Arthur met Granny Julia. They started seeing each other at every opportunity, and according to family rumor, Arthur "took advantage of" Julia in a field and she became pregnant. They dutifully married on February 28, 1910, at the Register Office, Godstone.

My mother, Barbara Ward Morris, was born on July 25, 1910. Five days later, Arthur did the unthinkable and deserted his regiment. The small family seemed to disappear into thin air for a time, but two years later Arthur was identified by a policeman as being on the army's missing list and was arrested, tried, and sentenced to sixty-three days in military prison for desertion. His superiors may have recognized that Julia was a new wife with a young child and that she needed her husband, for pleadings were made on his behalf, and after only twenty-nine days in prison, Arthur was formally discharged.

Julia and Arthur made a fresh start. They traveled to Kent, where Arthur became a member of the recently established Kent coal-mining community. On June 30, 1915, another daughter was born to them—my aunt Joan. After her birth, Arthur "deserted" again for a while, this time leaving his family. He was subject to bouts of depression, but it may simply have been that he went to the more lucrative mining area of South Yorkshire to search out new prospects for himself—for not long afterward, the Morrises moved again, to the pit village of Denaby, where Arthur was hired as a deputy at the local colliery.

The girls were both enrolled at Miss Allport's Preparatory School for Boys and Girls, and later they attended the village school in nearby Old Denaby. According to school records, my mother was very popular, very attractive. Aunt Joan was more reserved, always nervous. She depended on my mother a great deal. Both girls were striking, with alabaster complexions and glorious auburn hair.

It was during the period at Denaby that Arthur started composing and publishing poetry, which was quite well received and which earned him the moniker "The Pitman's Poet."

He also used his musical skills to entertain the villagers at cricket club functions, "smoking concerts" (men-only evenings), fund-raisers, and other parties around town. Arthur began teaching my mother to play the piano. Temperamentally, they were very much alike, being both self-willed and used to getting their own way. According to my aunt, many a shouting match was heard culminating with the sound of a sharp slap and a box on the ear.

Mum's version of these events was a little harsher; she claimed that her father hit her across the hands with a ruler. Either way, Arthur seems to have been a tyrannical and cruel parent. Eventually Mum took private lessons from a Miss Hatton and built her piano skills to a very high standard. In July of 1920, at the age of ten, she passed the first stage of the London College of Music curriculum. Her father is referred to in the announcement as "Mr. Arthur Morris, the well-known entertainer."

Years later, my aunt wrote this of her father: *"People would come up to our mother and congratulate her on being married to such a fun-loving man. Little did they know of his dark moods of despair, when he would sit in his chair and speak not a word for days, and I would take the longest way round when crossing the room to avoid going near him. After these bouts, he would go away for a while, and return laden with gifts for us."*

It seems that desertion continued to be a theme in Arthur's life.

Toward the end of 1921, he left the Denaby Colliery and the family moved a few miles away, to Swinton. Mum was eleven at the time, and Auntie was six. As Arthur became increasingly busy with his poetry, music, and entertaining, my mother became more accomplished at the piano—and in 1924, at the age of fourteen, she left school to pursue her piano playing full-time with a private tutor, and just a year and a half later she had passed the London College of Music's senior-level exams.

Mum now often accompanied her father on his tours, playing at many provincial concerts. She took part in several early radio broadcasts from Sheffield, and by the time she was sixteen, she was teaching music. Listed among her students for that year is my aunt, though the lessons didn't last long for several reasons—one being an acute sibling rivalry. My aunt was proficient at the piano, but music inspired her in other ways, namely to dance. Though untrained, she used every opportunity as a young child to dress up in her mother's clothes to improvise and to dance whenever possible.

All this information came not from my mother, but from my aunt and from research. Other than telling me she had passed her exams at an early age—she gained her LRAM and ALCM degrees—my mother never spoke about those years. How she felt about her studies remains a mystery, and I do not know where she took her exams. Given that the family was so poor, I cannot imagine who paid for her lessons in those days. Even if she had a scholarship, which I believe she did, I never saw her actual diplomas: she never displayed them, never had them framed.

IN THE SUMMER of 1926, Granny Julia took my mum and my aunt to Hersham to visit her own mother, sweet Great-Granny Emily Ward. This was apparently a bucolic holiday for the girls, and they discovered the joys of the countryside and all that it had to offer compared to the mining towns where they lived.

Great-Granny Emily took in washing for the more affluent villagers. The tradition of "wash day" was backbreaking, rigorous work and was typical of the hardship and poverty the family endured in those times. Weather permitting, washing was done outside in the garden. Two enormous tubs with washboards and the requisite bars of yellow carbolic soap were set on trestle tables. Buckets of boiling water were constantly carried to and from the house. Sheets, pillowcases, towels, etc., were set in heaps on the ground. Whites went into one vat, colored items in the other, all to be soaked, scrubbed, then set in baskets while the tubs were emptied of their foamy suds and filled with fresh hot water for the rinsing process. Clothes were pegged on lines strung between two apple trees. Sheets were laid out on convenient bushes. In the evenings, the sweet-smelling laundry was brought indoors and made ready for ironing the next day.

My aunt recalled the fun of bringing in frozen shirts and pajama tops sparkling with a silver sheen of frost, the sleeves stiff and straight, which she used as dancing partners while she cavorted over the frozen cabbage stumps.

The following morning, sheets were carefully folded and set on the kitchen table to be used as a soft base for the ironing of clothes. No ironing boards then, and the irons themselves were heavy and had to be constantly reheated on trivets that swung over the fireplace.

ARTHUR, MEANWHILE, WAS performing for club audiences in various towns in the north of England. He bought a set of drums, which he taught himself to play, and when he thought he was proficient, he hired the local church hall. With my mother playing the piano and her mother at the entrance collecting the admission money, he began to run a series of profitable dances.

This new era meant that he was invited to many social gatherings. Granny Julia became hopelessly out of her depth in this more sophisticated company, so Arthur started going alone.

He was seldom home, and one morning, predawn, Julia tiptoed out of the house with her girls and left Arthur, probably because of his infidelities and alcoholism. They took the first train, returning to Hersham to stay permanently with Great-Granny Emily Ward.

Granny Julia quickly found a job as a maid for a Mr. Mortimer, who allowed her and the children to live in. Arthur remained in Swinton, but then tragedy struck: his new lifestyle had driven a wedge between him and his family, and his casual liaisons with women resulted in his contracting syphilis. He traveled down to Hersham, and perhaps realizing that she was unhappier without him than she was with him, or knowing that he was ill and in need of care, Julia took him back and the family was reunited for a time. Arthur's vitality quickly dwindled, however, and he became thin and lethargic. He was admitted to the Brookwood Sanatorium in Woking on November 16, 1928. He died the following August, at the age of forty-three, with the cause of death given as "Paralysis of the Insane."

I think my mother mentioned this period in their lives just once, giving me only the bare facts. Later, I begged my aunt Joan to write about it, but she shuddered and said, "Why would I write about something so terrible? That place, the stench, the people . . . screaming, demented." She must have been traumatized, given that she was only thirteen at the time, but I sensed she was also ashamed and loath to discuss this with me. Syphilis was certainly not "genteel." The heartbreaking consequence of Arthur's actions was that he infected Julia, and shortly thereafter she, too, became ill and died just two years later. In retrospect, it's not surprising that my mother's grief was so transparent and lasted so long.

TWO

O VERNIGHT, CHILDHOOD ENDED for the girls and the business
of survival began. The early demise of their parents changed forever the course of my mother's career, for she now became mother as
well as sister to Aunt Joan, assuming the role of full-time caretaker and
thus cementing what had always been present—their larger-than-life
sibling rivalry and a total dependency on each other.

They moved from Mr. Mortimer's house and took a bed-sitting-room
to be closer to Great-Granny Ward, who provided them with lunch, ensur-
ing they had one good meal a day. Finding the room was comparatively
easy, until they mentioned they would be bringing a piano and a set of
drums. It was only after a great deal of cajoling and the promise that Mum
would teach the daughter of the house to play the piano that they finally
got the room. All they needed now was some money. They calculated
their assets and decided they couldn't sell the piano. But what should they
do about the drums?

My mother said, "Right Joan. It's obvious you must learn to play them.
You watched Dad often enough, so let's give it a try."

They launched themselves on the local Women's Institute. The sight
of a skinny fifteen-year-old girl, clad in pink velvet, black stockings, with
long red hair secured by a white ribbon à la *Alice in Wonderland* playing
the drums was apparently too tantalizing and people closed in, staring
curiously.

When my aunt complained about this, my mother said, "Play louder—

bang everything you've got!" And it worked. The money started rolling in.

The girls began to play a number of highly improbable gigs, from genteel afternoon and evening parties to a rather risqué nightclub in a once-venerable old mansion called Mount Felix. When eventually one of the flats in this building became vacant, they were able to rent it. It soon became apparent that most of the turnover for the club was acquired by providing drinks after hours, and one Saturday night the place was raided and they were all driven off to the police station in the local Black Maria, the police van.

Aunt was still attending school, and when the kindly headmistress learned the girls were trying to survive on their own, she arranged a scholarship for Aunt. Other employments included a stint in the chapel of a local convalescent home, where Mum played the harmonium and Aunt worked the bellows—Mum often exhorting Auntie to "Pump harder!" They often laughed at the contrast between their pious pursuits at the beginning of the day and their sleazy nightclub occupations in the evenings.

A dear friend once described them to me: "You cannot imagine the impact those two girls had on the sleepy villages of Walton and Hersham. They were a sensation! They had a strange Northern dialect, they were marvelously attractive, vital, self-confident, with this wonderful red hair—and each brilliant in her field."

One of their employers suggested that my aunt should be taught to dance properly, and kindly offered a letter of introduction to a good school in Wimbledon. Somehow my mother got my aunt to the audition, where she was asked what she could do.

"Well, I don't actually do anything special," Joan replied. "I express what the music seems to be saying."

"Then we'd better have some music, hadn't we?" the auditioner suggested, and commissioned my mother to play.

It was decided that though Aunt was very late starting, especially for ballet, she had ability and could make a good all-rounder. Terms were discussed, and in exchange for arriving at 10:30 A.M. to tidy up the studio, dust and plump the cushions, attend to the cleanliness of the cloakrooms, wash up, serve tea to guests in the afternoons between classes, and be a general dogsbody, Aunt received her tuition, doing so well that after a few weeks she was dispatched to Balham in South London to teach a tap class on behalf of the school. Mum was also to play for two afternoons a week.

The year before their father had died, the girls had come to the attention of two decent young men: one, Edward Charles ("Ted") Wells, my father; the other, Arthur Cecil ("Bill") Wilby, later to be Joan's husband. My dad was two years older than my mum, which would have made them just nineteen and seventeen when they first met. After the girls were orphaned, the lads pitched in to provide them with a fish and chips supper twice a week, with Lyons French Cream Sandwiches for "afters," often explaining that they'd bought too much food and needed someone to share it with.

MY FATHER'S UPBRINGING was equally impoverished. His paternal grandfather, David Wells, had been a coachman for a Lady Tilson of Guildford, Surrey, and later he'd been a caretaker for the Wesleyan Chapel there. He and his wife, Fanny Loveland Wells, were natives of Middlesex and Surrey, respectively.

Fanny's relatives had a shop in Hersham called Loveland's, which made deliveries around town with a pony and trap. Fanny and David had one son, David Wilfred Wells. Young David, my grandfather, was a carpenter/joiner. He was one of the first to be on the City and Guild's list of qualified carpenters, and builders would give him jobs around the village. During a bad period of unemployment he cycled from Hersham to Wales—about sixteen hours away—in order to find work.

Dad's maternal grandfather, Mr. Charles Packham, was a skilled gardener. He and his wife, Elizabeth, raised six children: Mary, Susan, Charles, Ellen, Caroline, and Elizabeth Packham.

The youngest, Elizabeth, was a kindergarten teacher when she met and married David Wilfred Wells, my paternal grandfather. David and Elizabeth Wells had four children: Frank, the eldest; Ted, my father; Robert (Uncle Bob); and a daughter, yet another Elizabeth, but always known as Betty.

Frank, I was told, was a dear man and a magnificent craftsman, but he died at the age of thirty from meningitis and I never met him. In addition to being a carpenter, Frank was a teacher, which eventually influenced my dad to become a teacher himself. Bob, the third son, was thought to be the "brains" of the family, and became leader of a research team in a firm called Hackbridge Electric in Hersham, which made huge transformers.

Betty, the youngest and the only daughter, was born mentally handicapped. I don't know the exact cause, but it was said that her mother, my Granny Elizabeth Wells, had tried to abort her. The child was a terrible burden on the family. Though apparently pretty, she couldn't speak and was given to fits and rages. My father could never have friends over to the house because of her disruptive nature. At a young age she was placed in a home for the handicapped, but when Granny Wells went to visit her, she was filled with such remorse that she brought the child back home. Betty eventually died at the age of twenty-seven. It's my belief that Betty had a powerful impact on my father, coloring forever his perceptions of women as being somewhat needy and fragile.

After the 1914–18 war, there was a subsidy scheme for young people wanting to buy houses. My grandfather, David, applied for and received a grant of £70. He bought a plot in Pleasant Place, Hersham, and with his sons and some builder friends he built a two-story house he called "Deldene." It was primitive: three small bedrooms upstairs, plus a living room, scullery, and an outside toilet. Fireplaces were the only source of heat, and the one in the living room had a trivet, which swung into or away from the fire, upon which a kettle was placed for boiling water or cooking. Next to it was a cast-iron baking oven, which, as I recall, was also heated by the fire. There was a bath of sorts—a pump took water from the copper tank downstairs and conveyed it to a tub—but the water was only lukewarm. My dad and his brothers preferred to swim in the rivers Mole, Thames, and Wey for their ablutions. Having covered themselves in soap, they would plunge into the river and rinse the suds away.

Dad received a scholarship to go to Tiffin Grammar School in nearby Kingston, and he enjoyed his time there very much. His first job was at the Hackbridge Electric Factory, presumably before his brother Bob made his way up the corporate ladder there. Dad disliked Hackbridge intensely. It was hot, dirty, noisy—there was no fresh air and he felt trapped indoors. He began drifting around building sites, working as a journeyman/craftsman with his father. Sadly, Dad's father, David, died at the age of forty-five, from colon cancer.

After a while Dad had to return to factory work because there was much unemployment and it was hard to get building jobs. He became a mechanic, but took evening classes at Kingston Tech in order to obtain his building certificate. Later, when his mother suggested he should follow in Frank's footsteps and earn more money, he passed his teacher's qualification finals with distinction. He became a full-time teacher at age twenty-four on Boxing Day, December 26, 1932. On the very same day, at St. Peter's Church in Hersham, he and my mother were married.

My mother once told me that Granny Julia had said to her on her deathbed, "Whatever you do, don't marry Ted Wells." It was probably because he was so very poor. Mum also told me that she married Dad because he was a rock, because he adored her, and because it was safe.

Dad was officially a "practical handicrafts teacher," giving lessons in woodwork, metalwork, basic construction, engineering, and so on, but he subbed for other teachers—teaching math, English literature, and grammar. The schools weren't big enough to employ a full-time specialist teacher, so he spent one day a week at each of various schools, bicycling some two hundred miles a week from Hersham to other villages in Surrey. He taught evening classes as well. At one time he owned a motorcycle, but he sold it in order to help my mother and Aunt Joan keep a roof over their heads after the death of their father.

Part-time and substitute teachers were only paid by the hour. At the end of the 1932 term, he took home the princely sum of £11, which had to last until the end of the following month—two months in all. Eventually he was offered a full-time position at the school in Shere. His pupils were between the ages of fourteen and sixteen; boys, who were old enough to be responsible handling dangerous equipment, but who, in many cases, were mere country lads with plenty of natural teenage aggression. Dad was good with them all. Being an amateur boxer, he could take on any one of them, and a couple of times he almost had to. He played football with them, kept them interested. He earned their respect and was a popular teacher.

My mother augmented their meager income by giving piano lessons and performing. Aunt Joan, ever-present, had started her own dancing school at a place in Walton, which was Miss LeMarchand's Primary School by day, but accommodated her classes in the afternoons and evenings. She, too, added to the coffers by moving in with my parents when they rented a small house called "Threesome"—so named perhaps because of their joint occupancy.

How they managed I'll never know, but somehow they were even able to take the odd vacation—usually on the South Coast around Bognor. More often than not, "Uncle Bill" Wilby went along, too. The old car was stacked high with a tent, cooking utensils, a Primus stove, collapsible beach chairs, food, blankets, and pillows. There are hilarious family stories of their adventures, including the time when the Austin 7 took a countryside humpbacked bridge a little too fast. It sailed into the air and landed hard, breaking an axle and bringing most of the contents down about my father's shoulders, pinning his face to the wheel. They were only halfway to their destination, and I gather my mother was none too pleased, sitting on the luggage at the side of the road and complaining mightily. My father flagged a ride for Mum, Aunt, and Uncle Bill and sent them on ahead, after which he trudged several miles to the local garage to seek help.

I WAS BORN on October 1, 1935, at Rodney House, Walton-on-Thames's maternity hospital.

The very first thing that I can recall was when I was perhaps two or three. I remember standing in the middle of the staircase, neither up nor down, and telling my mother that I wanted to go to the bathroom.

"Well, come on down," she said, to which I replied, "No."

"Go on up then," she said.

Again, "No."

I obviously wanted her to come and attend to me.

"Well stay there, then," she said. So I did. And I peed in my pants.

I was wearing a little brown woolen outfit, which quickly became extremely uncomfortable. I think I had a tantrum, so nothing about the incident was successful.

THERE ISN'T AN awful lot about my mother that I recall from my earliest years, other than it seemed to me she was away quite often.

I do, however, remember very specific things about my dad . . . wonderful things. He treated me and my siblings as his beloved companions, never dismissing or talking down to us. When one or other of us provoked, he only had to say "Look, Chick—" in a patient, weary voice, and we would understand and back off. He told me later in his life that he had once whacked my brother Johnny—and when the boy said, pleadingly, "No more, Daddy, please," he had been devastated and vowed never to do it again. And he didn't.

Throughout our childhood, he exposed us to the wonders of nature. One of my earliest memories was his taking me outside to view a large ants' nest, which he had discovered under a stone while gardening.

"See, Chick, how the ants carry things from here to there? Look how busy they are." I saw them working within their little tunnels, hauling whatever they needed—and we pored over this nest for a good hour or more.

Another time, I remember Dad waking me from sleep. It must have been ten or eleven o'clock at night.

"I want to show you something, Chick," he said, and he carried me downstairs. "We found a little hedgehog on the doorstep."

He explained how hedgehogs curl themselves into a ball for protection, and I saw this round spiky object that was lying on the floor in the kitchen.

Dad said, "If I put some milk out, it will eventually uncurl itself and go lap it up . . . ," which it did. By morning the milk was gone, and the hedgehog was safely returned to the garden.

Dad was not a religious man, and he once said to me that he didn't think he would believe in God at all were it not for the existence of two things: trees—and man's conscience. He said that without trees, we would not survive on this planet, for they feed us, clothe us, shelter us, make oxygen. Without a conscience, man would probably never have developed beyond a primitive state.

But Dad was fond of church music, and always listened to the Sunday services on the BBC radio. He had a light, "bathroom baritone" voice of which he was somewhat proud. He sang any hymn or song right through to the end, his diction precise, relishing every note and every word. Certain ballads would crop up often in his repertoire: "Has Anyone Seen My Lady as She Went Passing By?" and "Where E'er You Walk" by Handel. He was a good whistler, too.

More important to him than singing was poetry. All his life he committed poems to memory, reasoning he could then return to them anytime he wished. One of the first books Dad bought me was Palgrave's *Golden Treasury of English Poems*.

My love of water probably stems from my father, because he adored rivers and lakes. Dad enjoyed hiring a skiff and taking my brother and me for a boat ride on the Thames. Before we left the shore, he'd carefully explain, "Now listen, both of you. This can tip very easily, so keep low as you get in or get out. Do *not* stand up."

He would let us take an oar beside him and teach us how to feather it across the top of the water. But mostly Johnny and I would sit side by side on the cane-backed double seat, proudly, in charge of the rope on the rudder, watching as he evenly and easily worked on the oars, dipping them in, pulling them out. Wherever we went, he pointed out the beauty of nature: the majesty of a cliff face; the blossoms, the wildflowers. He knew the name of every tree, whether in bloom or in silhouette.

He seemed to know a lot about a lot of things. He loved language and grammar and math. He loved to study, and would sit at his desk, one hand to his brow, as he pored over the pages. Study, for him, was essential.

"If you don't have a God-given talent," he said, "it's your duty to stimulate your brain for as long as possible in life." At age seventy-four, he enrolled in his local college to study German and sat for the exams.

Dad was not demonstrative. He rarely pulled me to him or hugged me or sat me on his knee. Yet I never doubted his love for me. He expressed his affection in so many small ways, like sharing the poems, or reading to me, or giving the gift of his companionship, going for walks together.

"I often wonder, " Dad said to me once, "what the point of my life was. So many children passed through my hands, but I seldom knew the result of my teaching. There was never much closure."

He felt that what he did had no significance. Yet many pupils came back in later years and told him what a difference he'd made to them, and every one of us in the family treasured his ability to communicate a sense of wonder and awe. He treated all children the same way: we were young minds to be accorded dignity, to be nurtured. In retrospect it is amazing how clearly he conveyed to me that I was loved.

Someone once asked me which parent I hated the most. It was a provocative question and an interesting one, because it suddenly became apparent to me which one I loved with all my being . . . and that was my father. My mother was terribly important to me and I know how much I yearned for her in my youth, but I don't think I truly trusted her.

THREE

WHEN I WAS two and a half, my brother John was born. Mum, Dad, Johnny, and I (with Auntie of course) moved to another rented house called "Kenray" in Thames Ditton—again, not too far from the river.

Kenray was slightly bigger than Threesome. It had a fair-sized front garden with a big tree in it. I did not like the place. There seemed to be a large number of spiders—pale brown with dark spots—that would weave their webs in autumn between the wilting irises and gladioli along the front path. I remember the dead flowers, sodden and drooping in the rain, and the frost outlining the stalks as winter arrived.

My first really vivid memory of Johnny is on my fourth birthday. I had been given a beautiful little stuffed doll with a china head and eyes that opened and closed. I'd only had it a few hours, and my brother picked it up and swung it in a haphazard fashion. The next thing I knew, that lovely little china head had been smashed to pieces. My childhood rage was so huge—I wanted him out of my life forever!

Aunt Joan was still teaching at Miss LeMarchand's School, and I began attending pre-school there in the mornings and Aunt's dancing classes in the afternoons. Once a year, Aunt put on shows with her pupils at the local Walton Playhouse. My father built the scenery and my mother supplied the music. Aunt choreographed and designed the costumes. Her beau, Uncle Bill Wilby, helped Daddy backstage.

My father created some marvelous sets, like a complete airplane, which took up the entire width of the proscenium—twenty children could stand on it, ten on each wing—with a pilot in the cockpit, fronted by a whirling propeller. Another time he made a mock-up of the ocean liner *Queen Mary*, using false perspective to great effect. This time sailors waved through the portholes and the captain stood aloft on the bridge. His pièce de résistance was a complete carousel seating eight children on wooden horses, which revolved to the tune of "Come to the Fair."

My very first stage appearance was in one of these shows. I performed "Wynken, Blynken and Nod" when I was three and a half, with two other girls. One, named Patricia ("Trish") Waters, has remained a friend to this day. When we danced a polka together onstage, Trish's hat fell over her eyes—and apparently I continued to guide her around the stage so that she wouldn't fall. It seems I already knew that the show must go on!

Once, Aunt staged "A Day at the Races," with herself as the front legs and me the back of the winning horse. We did a ridiculous dance, performed blindly on my part since my head was buried against Aunt's posterior. The papier-mâché head was held together with strong-smelling glue, and there was no air circulating in that confined space. We muddled through the dance, but upon stepping out of the contraption, Auntie completely passed out.

MY MOTHER AND my father's mother did not get on. Granny Elizabeth was apparently a fine mathematician and had been a good teacher, but she had precious little tenderness or grace about her. She was bone thin, her face was lined, and she could be sharp of tongue. She once told my mother that she would never conceive children, that she'd be barren. There was no love lost between them.

Granny lived alone when I knew her. Her sons visited her from time to time, and Dad would occasionally take me along with him.

Deldene, the house her husband and sons had built for her, smelled of mice, urine, dust and dirt, and that acrid smell of people who don't wash often. I remember her bed was behind a drawn curtain in the living room. She lived in the one room and didn't bother about the upstairs. The lavatory, in a little concrete-roofed enclosure connected to the back door, was primitive and filthy.

Dad would take me outside into the garden at some point, which was laid out like an allotment, with rows of runner beans, peas, and potatoes. He did it, I think, to get me away from the stench and acrimony.

On one of my first visits to the house, Dad's sad, demented sister, Betty, was there. I don't know what precipitated it, but she suddenly had a terrible fit. I remember my father and his mother and someone else arm-wrestling this shrieking, drooling creature through the living room, up the stairs, and into her bedroom, locking the door after her because she was so out of control. Her screams, her rage, her inability to convey her dilemma were terrifying to me—and I was quickly taken home.

Though I only saw her the once, I dwelled on the incident for many years.

MY MOTHER STARTED going away for periods of time, working more regularly, mostly playing at concert parties. A concert party was much like a vaudeville show, usually performed in an open-air theater on a seaside pier, or sometimes on the beach itself. Performance times would be posted on a big sign stuck in the sand, with the caveat: "weather and tide permitting."

In the summer of 1939, Mum played a series of concert parties for the Dazzle Company in the seaside town of Bognor Regis. It was there that she became an accompanist for a young Canadian tenor by the name of Ted Andrews, who had just arrived in England.

Apparently this tenor rather foolishly—perhaps teasingly—mentioned that Mum played the piano "like a virgin." My mother was outraged—she was, in fact, proud that her playing strength was comparable to a man's. She had great technique, could transpose anything, and was highly skilled.

When she returned home from rehearsals that fateful day, she told my aunt what Ted Andrews had said to her.

"Can you believe the *gall* of that man?" she railed. "How *dare* he!"

My aunt later said she felt her skin prickle, and knew instantly that this was more than plain rage—that my mother was attracted to the singer, and the incident was much bigger than she was revealing.

THAT SEPTEMBER, World War II broke out.

Hitler concentrated his forces on invading Poland and then, in the spring of 1940, Norway and Denmark. This period was known as "The Phony War." Although Germany and the European allies had officially declared war on one another, neither side had launched a significant attack. This gave England a very slight margin of time in which to build up its defenses. America had not yet entered the conflict, so little England attempted to prepare for the German advance on its own.

The national spirit rose to the fore. Every able-bodied person was mobilized to help, and the populace worked incredibly hard. Uncle Bill joined the air force, but my father, because of his engineering skills, was considered necessary to the defense effort at home, and was refused for combat. Instead, he joined the Home Guard.

"If the Germans do invade," he explained to me, "we're the ones who'll be in the trenches, the last to fight to the death for our country."

He was issued a helmet, a khaki uniform, a gas mask, a gun, and six rounds of ammunition. The Home Guard was small in number and made up mostly of older men. I've often wondered how long they could have held out—and what would have happened if the Germans' vast army had, in fact, landed on British soil.

My father came home one day with gas masks for the whole family. After World War I, mustard gas had become the great threat. Dad showed us what we had to do and made us try them on.

Made of heavy rubber, the gas masks were the strangest, ugliest things. They had a snout, two goggle-like eyes much like an alien's, and one had to pull the whole thing over one's face. There was no fresh air inside; it smelled awful and I wanted to rip it off my face immediately. I doubt I would ever have been able to keep it on for more than a few seconds.

Life was entirely focused around the war. It was ever-threatening, ever-present. All Hitler had to do was to cross the English Channel . . . Our air force was smaller than the Luftwaffe, but we had a fine Royal Navy, which protected our coastline for the time being. However, the seas were patrolled by German U-boats, and they were so effective that convoys bringing vital supplies to Britain were often sunk. In January of 1940, food rationing began.

"You cannot imagine what it was like to live in prewar days," my mother once said. "The world seemed so carefree."

In order to keep the Royal Air Force supplied with new planes, all kinds of unlikely buildings were turned into factories. Pots and pans were donated by housewives for the metal they contained; railings and gates from London's famous parks and squares were removed and melted down.

The Esher Filling Station, a local garage not too far from where we lived, had several work sheds, and they were soon made ready for the war effort. Equipment was brought in to manufacture parts for Spitfire fighter aircraft, and Dad was hired as the shop manager because of his knowledge of tools and lathes.

He worked day and night. Sometimes he would go home and crash for an hour, or he'd catnap at work on a narrow bench and then get up and continue on, because continuing, no matter what, was so vitally important.

Once in a rare while, he would take me down to the riverside pub at Thames Ditton. Being underage, I couldn't go inside, but he would get his beer and bring me out a lemonade and some crisps, and we would sit together. I didn't understand why people liked to congregate just to drink, but I sensed that for my dad it was a welcome break.

My mother was now often away with Ted Andrews. They were billed as "The Canadian Troubadour, with Barbara at the Piano." Johnny and I remained with Dad and Aunt Joan.

Early in 1940, my mother signed on for ENSA, or the Entertainments National Service Association—jokingly referred to as "Every Night Something Awful." This was an organization set up to provide recreation for British armed forces personnel during the war. She went off with Ted to entertain the troops in France. There were two children at home who needed her, but I think the compulsion to go with Ted was overwhelming.

One particular day before she left is seared upon my memory.

Mum took me out for a walk, which was unusual since she never had time to take walks with me. We strolled through the village, hand in hand, past the shops—and I saw a child's dress in a window. It was over-the-top, fluffy and pink, but I thought it the prettiest I had ever seen. A day or so later, I came home from some outing and as I entered the house, I realized it was empty and that she had gone. She had not said good-bye. Though she had been away before, I sensed, the way that children can, that she was not coming back.

Feeling terribly sad, I went upstairs to my bedroom and discovered the pink fluffy dress spread out on the bed with a note. Nothing special—just *"With love, from Mummy"* or some such thing. My heart full to bursting, I ached for her, loved her, missed her, knew that she had thought of me as she left—and I wept.

It occurs to me now that she may have wanted to say something during our walk together. Did she *not* say anything because I was babbling on too happily, glad to be skipping along beside her, just the two of us? Perhaps her heart told her she could not hurt me at that moment. I can only wonder at the strength of my mother's passion, and what it must have cost her to go. I think she felt guilty about her decision for the rest of her life.

Soon after that, I had my first nightmare. I dreamed that an ugly goblin walked through the open door of my bedroom and stood in front of me. At first I thought he might be a friend, or a new toy, but then he took out a knife and I knew he intended to cut me.

I woke in the dark, terrified, convinced of his presence. I had to find my father, and summoning a desperate courage, I made a panicked dash for his room, sure that on the way I would be attacked.

My father was asleep, with Johnny curled beside him in the big bed. He instantly understood my wailing terror and folded me into warm covers and the safety of his arms. But even then I could not communicate the dread that seemed rooted in my soul.

FOUR

O N MAY 10, 1940, the same day that Winston Churchill became our prime minister, Germany invaded France, Belgium, and Holland in what was known as the "Blitzkrieg." Hitler pushed through France, encountering resistance all the way, and he eventually succeeded in reaching Paris. On June 23, he paraded his victorious troops down the Champs Elysées, marching them through the Arc de Triomphe. He had been expecting to find all the treasures of the Louvre Museum waiting for him but, in a brief space of time, they had all been removed, spirited away and hidden in chateaux and caves across France. The fact that Hitler never found them is miraculous.

The might of the German Army was such that the British troops (and some of their French allies) were forced to retreat to the English Channel beaches of Dunkirk, where they were constantly strafed by the Luftwaffe and a great many died. But some 340,000 men were rescued from the beaches by every civilian yacht, fishing vessel, barge, and motorized boat that could sail across the Channel from England, all of whom had been called to action by Churchill.

Some years later, my mother mentioned that she and Ted had been entertaining the troops in France when Hitler invaded, and they had been lucky to catch one of the last ferries to England before the borders closed; if they hadn't, they would have been interned. I realized that had things been different, I might not have had a mother at all, and I felt a deeper sense of appreciation for her.

Finally, Hitler turned his attention to Britain and began to prepare for an invasion. In order to be successful, he needed to achieve air superiority—so he charged his Luftwaffe with destroying the British air and coastal defenses first. The result was the Battle of Britain, which lasted from July to October of 1940, and was the first battle to be fought solely in the air.

JUST BEFORE THE Blitz began in earnest, Mum sent for me to come to London to live with her and the new man in her life, Ted Andrews. Though my father had custody of Johnny and me and could have contested it, he didn't—perhaps because he felt a little girl needed her mother, perhaps because he couldn't afford to keep us both. Whatever the details of this decision, the result was that I went with my mother, and Johnny stayed behind with Dad.

London was an awakening of some sort—as if I suddenly grew up, child to adult-child in a matter of days. In retrospect it seems I had been half-asleep until then, safely cradled in the warmth of a home and my father's love. I remember little snippets of early history before I was five, but afterward the memories are solid.

My first impression of the city was that it was full of soot and black. The trunks of the trees were black; their branches were bare and black—with limbs reaching toward an unforgiving sky. The buildings were black, the streets were black. There was seldom any sun. It was foggy, damp, and cold, the kind that gets into your marrow. It must have been a winter month, for I remember a dusting of snow, like dandruff on the hard lumps of brown grass in some little square or park.

I don't remember how I was brought to London, just that I suddenly came to live in a tiny ground-floor apartment in Mornington Crescent, Camden Town. It was in a building shaped somewhat like a flatiron, on the corner of a curving street that bracketed an old cigarette factory. Two pantherlike statues stood at the entrance, and it was aptly named the Black Cat Factory. With the advent of the war, it had been converted to the manufacture of munitions, and soon thereafter became a target for German bombs.

Camden Town in those days had nothing to recommend it—just a main street coming from Euston and going north to Chalk Farm, the traffic merely passing along it. These days it is increasingly upmarket, and the factory building has been turned into offices. But in 1940 it was a very shabby area.

The apartment was dark, no color that I recall. In the kitchen a dusty window with bars on it overlooked a small, bare inner courtyard. There was a bedroom and a bit of a living room. And there was Ted Andrews—a new shadow in my life.

I don't recall that I met him before coming to London. I didn't want to acknowledge his presence, and in truth I only have a vague memory of him at Mornington Crescent. It was as if by focusing on my mother and our genetic bond I could exclude him, deny that he had anything to do with us. I blanked him out, trying to make him disappear. But he didn't.

Compared to my father, this Ted was a big man. Compact, powerful, a sort of bullet head, and fast-receding sandy hair. For the theater he wore a toupee, blending the hairline with color. He had a florid complexion—everything about him seemed a little pink or red, even at times his eyes. He dressed smartly for the era—he often wore a fedora, and his suit jackets were double-breasted, with two open seams at the back, which created a flap.

"So you can lift it up and enjoy what's underneath," my mother would say in the bawdy voice she used when she wanted to convey what a lusty wench she was. She always claimed that she loved a good backside . . . and teapots, things with spouts. It made people laugh. (And she did indeed have a small collection of bizarre-looking teapots.)

Ted had been the black sheep of his family and had apparently endured a miserable and abused childhood. I know nothing about his parents, although in later years I did meet one sister, Mabel, and her children. He ran away from home when he was twelve, and later traveled from Canada to London to seek his fortune. He played the guitar and had a fine tenor singing voice.

He was ill at ease with me. His occasional overtures were met with shyness or outright derision on my part. My father and mother had not yet divorced—that would take three years. But Mum became pregnant, though I'm not sure even that registered with me at first.

Someone moved in with us—a mother's helper, I think. There wasn't space enough for us all to sleep in the apartment, so a room in the basement of the building at Mornington Crescent was taken over. It was a utility room of some sort. Pipes ran across the ceiling and there was an old iron boiler. Certainly it was hot, even stifling. Two barred windows revealed a wall mere inches behind them. The place was freshened up with a coat of whitewash, and cots were brought in for this "someone" and me. After the first twenty-four hours, we kept the lights on all night, as rats would emerge and creep along the pipes.

My mum and Ted continued to go away at times, performing various gigs. They were probably just overnight trips—but life seemed empty and I felt very alone. I missed my brother and the countryside, and thinking about Dad made me unbearably sad. I don't recall what I did with myself at the beginning ... except for one day.

It was close to Christmas, and I think the promise of the holiday had been talked up by my mother in her desire to cheer me and give me something to look forward to.

With no one around, I let myself into their cold apartment (which was never locked during the day), and began to search for hidden Christmas packages. I rifled through a chest of drawers, peeking under clothes that I didn't recognize. There were satin and lace cami-knickers that seemed too luxurious and indulgent to be my mother's, but were obviously hers. I opened closet doors and poked about and even looked in the kitchen cabinets. I felt sick and guilty, and knew that if I discovered anything tantalizing it would diminish the pleasure of it on Christmas Day. But the compulsion to search for some concrete proof of love was strong. I was careful to leave everything as I found it, and came away empty-handed.

THE WAR SUDDENLY came into focus for me. Air raid sirens wailed often, especially after dark. The warden came around.

"Put that light out!" he would shout at the smallest chink of brightness escaping through the blackout curtains.

The basement room became my shelter, and I prayed that my mother would be safe in the flat above.

As the bombing raids increased, we were often forced to retreat into the Underground stations for safety, joining the streams of people doing the same thing. I had never been in a subway before. I remember going down long escalators to the station platform and inhaling that unforgettable smell of baked dust. Cots were stacked in tiers against the platform walls, pushed as far away as possible from the black pit and the terrifying electric rail—so powerfully alive that it would kill you if you fell on it.

There was a tremendous sense of unity in the subway shelters. Night after night people survived, and bonded. They gathered in groups to socialize and smoke. They tended to their kids, changing little ones' nappies or sitting them on their potties. They cooked on small Bunsen burner stoves and drank hot tea. The really exhausted ones slept under coarse blankets, even when the trains roared through. It all looked exactly as depicted by Henry Moore in his extraordinary sketches that I came to admire later in life.

One night when the Blitz was particularly bad, we had just stepped off the escalator when Ted suddenly said, "Jesus, I forgot the guitar!" It was a precious and important belonging, for half the vaudeville act would have been ruined if the instrument had been destroyed. He raced back up and out into the dark night to retrieve it, and it seemed to us below that he was away far too long. Every once in a while we heard the ominous crunch of a bomb decimating some building. My mother was terribly worried. When Ted finally reappeared down the escalator, triumphantly holding the guitar aloft, a great cheer went up from the crowd. He responded by entertaining everyone with his songs, which pleased the crowd and took their minds off the horrors going on above.

Another time, another air raid, my mother and Ted returned late from entertaining somewhere. The warden came around, knocking on every door in the apartment building, saying that an incendiary bomb had been dropped in the area. The trouble with incendiaries was that sometimes they would not explode until hours after they had been dropped. This one could not be found. Everyone was told to evacuate.

My mother and stepfather were so exhausted that they decided not to respond to the call. I believe they were the only ones left in the building, and they quietly crept into bed. Upon getting up in the morning and going into the kitchen to make a cup of tea, my mother pulled back the blackout curtains and gasped—for there, snugly settled in the concrete square of the courtyard, was the incendiary bomb. They had slept by it all night long.

On November 14, nine hundred incendiary bombs were dropped in a period of ten hours on the city of Coventry, razing it to the ground. It was a terrible blow to the nation, and morale was badly shaken.

AUNT JOAN SENT a terse telegram: *"Married Bill in Gretna Green yesterday. Love Joan."*

Gretna Green is a romantic spot in Scotland, famous for providing quick weddings to lovers who elope there.

The news came as a shock to my mother. She believed (probably correctly) that Joan was angry with her for abandoning her and my father, and that Joan only married Bill to spite her. I got the impression that she was also very sad about the marriage and felt it foolish: that Bill was a good sort, but rather weak. Caught up in the confusion and demands of her new life and what must have been a chaos of emotions, it may have been the first time my mother reflected on the consequences of her actions. Aunt's marriage was the closing of another door, perhaps one that Mum hadn't anticipated.

Some forty years later, Aunt told me that my father had offered to marry her for the sake of us children. After Mum left, it had been up to him and to Auntie to look after Johnny and me, and though it must certainly have been difficult with Dad working and Aunt teaching, they coped brilliantly. Aunt confided that Dad said that he could never love her; it would be a marriage of convenience only. I think Aunt secretly always loved *him*, and years later she clung to him as a lifeline—which drove my father nuts! Needless to say, they did not marry.

After Auntie married Bill, Dad moved with Johnny from Kenray to a small flat in Hinchley Wood, near Esher, Surrey.

SOME TIME IN 1941, my mother's helper took me to the Bedford Theatre on the High Street in Camden Town. It was my first visit ever to a theater. I don't remember what I saw, but everything I did then was unfocused and anxiety-ridden. Several days later my head began to itch dreadfully. My mother examined my hair. I had lice. She scrubbed me raw, then rinsed with vinegar, which on my lacerated skin was a form of torture. I screamed a lot—but it did the trick.

Also around this time, I remember being taken to a specialist for what my mother referred to as my "wandering eye." A condition now known as "strabismus," it was probably inherited—my daughter, and later her son, had the same problem when they were young. At that time it was thought to be due to a weak muscle, and the theory was that if strengthened with exercise, the eye would straighten up. So my mother found a woman who specialized in eye massage.

I underwent several excruciatingly painful treatments. I had to lie down and submit to the therapist sticking her thumb in my tear duct and working the muscle with enormous pressure. I could hardly bear it—the tears simply poured out—but since I was told it was necessary, I tried to comply. I don't believe the treatments did me any good at all.

Ted Andrews bought me a new book called *The Art of Seeing* by Aldous Huxley. It was the first gift he ever gave me. It contained eye exercises, such as holding a pencil and following it with one's eye to the right or left, and wearing a bow pinned to one's shoulder so that the offending eye could be attracted toward it. I was made to do these exercises religiously, and maybe they worked, or maybe I simply outgrew the strabismus, for today I don't seem to have it—except perhaps when I'm very, very tired.

A YOUNG WIDOW named Winifred Maud Hyde came to work at the Esher Filling Station factory. Her husband had been a bomb disposal specialist named Pat Birkhead. They had been married only fourteen months when Pat was killed defusing a bomb. Despite her grief, Win had to find a job. She was hired as a capstan lathe operator, doing twelve-hour shifts at Dad's plant. I met her there once, and I remember the snood that she wore to keep her hair clean and tidy and away from the machinery. She was a handsome woman with lovely eyes, and she seemed kind and real. My father and Win became friends, and when time and the war effort permitted, they would go up to London for an outing.

The radio at the filling station was always on, and often the workers would listen to Mum and Ted performing on a program called *Workers' Playtime*. One day, Dad heard Ted Andrews dedicate a song to "my wife Barbara and baby son Donald." This was extremely disturbing to Dad—particularly since he and Mum weren't divorced, and she hadn't yet told him that a baby had arrived.

Donald Edward Andrews came into the world on July 8, 1942, at Rodney House, the Walton-on-Thames maternity hospital, where Johnny and I had been born.

While Mum was there, I stayed in Walton with Uncle Bill Wilby's mother and stepfather, Aunt Paula (always called "Auntie Caula") and Uncle Fred. Auntie Joan and Uncle Bill had moved to a flat in Belgravia, so Uncle Bill's parents were the only relatives I could stay with. It was convenient because I could be near my mother and could occasionally visit her.

I don't remember what Uncle Fred did for a living, but he left early in the morning and only came home in time for dinner. Auntie Caula was utterly dour. All day long she moaned about her aches and pains, and though she was kind to me, the entire cadence of her voice had a downward inflection. It wasn't until Uncle Fred came home in the evening that things became more cheerful. He was a complete contrast to his wife: a short fellow, with sparkling eyes and a cheery demeanor. He always announced his presence in the evening by whistling. We heard his familiar trilling just before the garden gate clicked open. He'd come up the garden path calling out for his "girls," and knowing Uncle Fred was home at last, my spirits would lift.

Their house was immaculate with not a speck of dust. They only lived in the kitchen and the parlor, though there was a front drawing room, where everything was covered in white dust sheets, includng a billiard table. There were stacks and stacks of *National Geographic* magazines, which I found wonderfully interesting.

I slept in a guest room upstairs, on an enormous four-poster bed, the obligatory white china piss pot tucked beneath it. With the perfectly starched sheets and the huge feather mattress, the whole experience made me feel hugely comfortable, and unbearably lonely.

I stayed there for two weeks while Mum recuperated from Donald's birth. (In those days one always stayed that long in the hospital after childbirth, even if complication-free.) I was taken a couple of times to visit the maternity hospital, but because of my age, I was told I was not allowed to go inside. Ted Andrews took me to the back of the building, where I stood in a rose bed and looked through the window of her room. My mother held up the baby, smiled, and waved. I missed her very much.

I later learned that Dad, not wishing to get divorced, had offered to adopt Donald if only Mum would return to him. It was one more act of chivalry on his part—but of course it didn't happen.

FIVE

S OON AFTER DONALD'S birth, we moved from Camden Town to
Clarendon Street in Victoria. It was another ground-floor flat, slightly
better—with a sitting room and bedroom on the street level, and a kitchen,
bathroom, and living area below. Windows in the basement looked out
onto a rectangle of concrete set beneath a grid in the pavement, on the
other side of which were three arched storage areas with black painted
doors. One of these became our air raid shelter, one was used for storage,
and one became my bedroom. It had a whitewashed curved ceiling, much
like a crypt, and no windows at all. I remember lying in bed listening to
the crunch of bombs dropping during the night raids, and though scared,
feeling oddly safe being under the road. But to this day I have a fear of
explosions: fireworks, guns, balloons—anything volatile and out of my
control.

My mother often put baby Donald outside in his pram during the day
to give him some fresh air. Since we had no garden, she would tie the
pram with a padlock and chain to the railing outside our front door. One
morning, I was in the basement kitchen looking up through the grid and
I suddenly saw a strange woman lift Donald out of his pram and walk
away with him.

I ran to tell Mum, and the police were notified and came around to
question us. It was presumed that the woman could not have gone far, and
after a search of the neighborhood they found the misguided soul, who
had probably lost her own child or was unable to have one and, seeing this
baby unattended, had taken it for herself. Happily, Donald was perfectly

fine, but he had in fact been kidnapped for about four hours—and my mother was, understandably, distraught.

In September of 1942, Johnny and I were evacuated to Wrecclesham Farm, in Farnham, Surrey, about thirty miles south of London. With Uncle Bill away in the Royal Air Force, Aunt Joan came along also—presumably to look after us, since I was only six and Johnny was four. We should really have gone to the west or north of England, where many other children were being sent.

Why my mother chose Wrecclesham Farm, I don't know—but I think she and Ted had once stayed with the owners, a family by the name of Gardener, when they had been doing a concert in the Farnham area.

"Auntie Gardener" was a dear lady and the matriarch of a family that seemed to bicker a lot. She had a very stern husband, Wilfred "Pop" Gardener, and a physically attractive son, Phil, whose use of the English language seemed mostly limited to loud expletives.

The farmhouse was big, old, and comfortable, with the most enormous fireplace I'd ever seen. One could actually walk inside it, and sit in either side of the hearth under the square of the chimney. This was fascinating to me, definitely a place where Santa Claus could manage an entrance. It was also practical because its heat was the main source of warmth in the house. In spite of its charm, the farmhouse was incredibly damp.

Auntie Joan and I shared a large bedroom, and Johnny had a closet-sized room down the corridor. Our room did have a small electric heater, and we used stone hot water bottles in the big bed at night. But the sheets were so moist that steam almost rose from them when touched by a warm body, and they smelled horribly of mildew.

The farm had a lot of acreage. It was also a popular riding school, with stables and several horses. I loved the smell of the tack room, the leather saddles, bridles, and the whole sensory experience of the animals. Johnny and I would help one of the local farm girls lather and clean the tack, and feed the horses and bring them in from the fields at night. I saw the smithy work on the horses' hooves. And, of course, I learned to ride.

When I went out with Pop Gardener, I was perfectly fine. But every time I went out with Phil, I was so nervous about his bluster and his cussing that I always managed to fall off. Somehow, as soon as we began to trot I would feel myself slipping, tilting sideways. I would put my hand on the horse beside me—usually Phil's—to steady myself, but the horse would naturally move aside as it felt the pressure and I would topple between the two. Phil was always exasperated.

"Christ, Julia, get back up!"

Occasionally my gray pony, Trixie, would jerk her head down to eat grass and I would slide right down her neck and suddenly be looking up her nostrils. I remember feeling very silly much of the time . . . sensitive, scared, foolish. I was a complete wimp.

The loose hay in the barn was always piled very high, and Johnny and I used to climb the stacked bales and jump into the soft mound below. It was a delicious game, safe and free, and we screamed and laughed, having fun together for the first time in ages. Phil bawled us out for damaging the horses' feed, and that pleasure was curtailed.

Phil and Aunt Joan were certainly having fun. They were immediately attracted to each other, and often sparred playfully. One time Phil picked Auntie up, she screaming and protesting with delight, and dumped her in the water trough. I was dreadfully upset.

"You leave my auntie alone!" I yelled, pummeling him with my fists. Years later, Aunt often said that Phil was the love of her life, and she should have married him.

Even though we were protected from the worst of the Blitz and the ravages of the war in London, there were still occasional air raids in Farnham, and when the sirens sounded we would go down through a trap door into the basement for safety.

Rationing continued, and even at Wrecclesham Farm, with its chickens and produce, everything was scarce. Butter, milk, cheese, and sweets were in short supply. The equivalent of one T-bone steak had to feed an entire family for a week, and peaches and bananas were extremely rare. To this day, they still feel like a luxury to me.

Once or twice a week, Johnny and I would share a boiled egg for breakfast. I would have the yolk one day and he would have the white. The next day he would have the yolk and I the white. Why no one thought to make a scrambled egg, I don't know. Fortunately, there was plenty of bread and cereal. The black market sprang up around this time, too, and certain hard-to-get items like real nylon stockings could only be bought at a premium price when funds allowed. Regular stockings were mostly made of lisle, and were rather thick.

At lunchtime, which was the main meal of the day in the farmhouse, everyone gathered in the living room. There was a huge oval dining table in the center, and as we ate, we would listen to the midday news on the radio. If anyone dared make a sound, Pop Gardener would bellow, "QUIET!"

The newscasters had serious names like Alvar Liddell and Bruce Belfrage, and in their serious, well-cadenced voices they read the news with careful precision and crisp diction. We would listen to Churchill speak, hanging onto his every word.

I enjoyed my time at the farm. I was back in the countryside again, and Johnny and I were together. But we didn't have Dad, and we didn't have Mum. Once in a while, one of them would come to visit, and I would always beg, "Couldn't you stay?" But they couldn't, of course, both being so busy—Dad with the war effort, and Mum and Ted entertaining and helping to keep morale high. Thank God Auntie was there. For a great deal of my life she was a surrogate mother, vivacious and fun, and Johnny and I depended on her completely. Little Johnny once cried, "Oh, Auntie! Don't take me out without you!," which became a beloved family phrase.

IN THE SPRING of 1943, there was a momentary lull in the war. I was reunited with my mother and Ted Andrews at Clarendon Street, and Johnny went to live with Daddy once again in Hinchley Wood.

Two things happened at this point. I was enrolled in school, and Ted Andrews decided to give me singing lessons. Aunt departed from Wrecclesham as well, and took a one-room flat in London. She was teaching dance at the Cone-Ripman School, a conservatory for the performing arts, which had academic classes in the morning and all kinds of dance lessons in the afternoon. This was the school I attended. It seemed huge and I felt lost at first; I was only seven years old.

I don't know why Ted started giving me singing lessons. It was often reported that my voice was "discovered" when singing to the family in the air raid shelters, but that was a publicity gimmick—dreamed up by my stepfather or the press. More probable is that I was horribly under-foot with nothing to do, and he decided to give me lessons to keep me quiet, so to speak. Or perhaps it was an effort on his part to get to know this new stepdaughter who was intimidated by him and who didn't like him. Whatever the case, it seems that he and my mother were surprised to discover that my singing voice was quite unique. It had phenomenal range and strength, which was unusual at such a young age.

It was decided that I should go visit a throat specialist to ascertain that I was doing no harm to my vocal cords. Our cleaning lady at the time was a smoker, and when my parents were away or out on business, she would ask me to go down to the local stationer at the corner and buy her a fresh packet of Player's Weights or Woodbines. I'd bargain that I'd only do it if she let me try a cigarette when I returned, which she very foolishly agreed to.

Cigarette in hand, I'd go behind the bathroom door, open the windows so the smell wouldn't linger, and rather guiltily puff away. I absolutely hated it, but it seemed the thing to do at the time.

When she learned that I was to visit a throat specialist, this silly girl panicked.

"Lord help me!" she cried. "The doctor is going to look into your throat and he'll see it's black like a chimney from the cigarettes. He's going to know you've been smoking!"

I was so anxious by the time I went that it was all the poor man could do to pry my mouth open and take a look inside. I gagged and retched from the instruments thrust down my throat. Of course my vocal cords were perfectly healthy . . . but I never smoked again, thank heavens. In retrospect, it was a godsend—everyone was smoking in those days, including my dad, my mother, and Ted Andrews. The specialist declared that I had an almost adult larynx and that there seemed no harm in con-tinuing my singing lessons.

*

IT WAS AT Clarendon Street that I began really to love reading. My father had taught me to read when I was very young, and it became my salvation. I would curl up in a chair and read for hours. Oddly, my mother would call me on it, saying, "That's quite enough for one day!" or "You're being lazy, wasting your time away!" Perhaps she had a legitimate reason; maybe I needed to help with the washing up, or maybe she was worried about my strabismus or something, but I took it rather badly, resenting her for not allowing me that lovely escape. There was a period of time when I did not read for quite a while. I felt guilty at loving it so much. It wasn't until later, when a tutor encouraged me to read some of the classics, that I enjoyed it once again.

DURING THE MOMENTARY lull in the war, Mum and Ted decided to move out of London. They bought a house on Cromwell Road, Beckenham, Kent, which became our home for the next five years.

Kent is often known as "the garden of England" because of its orchards and fruit trees, and parts of it are beautiful. However, it is the county in southeast England that abuts the English Channel, and as such it was right in the middle of the flight path between Germany and London. Any bombs that weren't dropped on London were dumped on us as the Luftwaffe returned home.

Just before we moved, my parents' divorce came through, and my mother and Ted married immediately in a civil ceremony on November 25, 1943. In later years, Mum told me that she had hoped to wait a while before remarrying, but Ted Andrews had been insistent—and of course there was Donald.

One day, not long afterward, my mother and I were crossing the high street in Beckenham when she suddenly suggested that we find an appropriate name for me to call Ted. It should not be "Daddy"— because Daddy was my daddy—but something that would signify he was sort of my *second* daddy. Up to this point I had been calling him "Uncle Ted." I didn't like the conversation at all, but my mother proposed that I call him "Pop." I disliked the name, but she thought it a good idea, and thus Ted became "Pop" from then on.

It was also at this time that my name was officially changed from Julia Elizabeth Wells to Julie Andrews. I presume that Mum and Pop wished to spare me the outside feeling of being a stepchild. They felt that "Julia Andrews" did not flow well, so I became a Julie. I didn't have any say in the matter, and I don't think my father did either. He must have been hurt.

Our new house was a modest step up for the family. There was a front room, a kitchen, a dining room, and a parlor at the back with a small, enclosed loggia, which led into the garden. We'd had a piano—an upright spinet—in our flat at Clarendon Street, but in Beckenham Mum splurged on a baby grand, which was housed in the parlor. At the beginning I shared a bedroom with Donald, which was not a success since I got little sleep, and eventually I was given my own tiny room at the end of the corridor.

The small back garden had a square pond in the center of it, which was home to a few rather sickly goldfish that soon expired. Also in the garden was an Anderson air raid shelter, set beneath a grass mound. There were concrete steps at the side leading to the shelter below. It had two bunks, a stool, an oil lamp, and a few other bits and pieces in case we had to stay down there for any length of time. Whether it would have been any real protection in the face of a direct hit, I don't know, but Andersons were much to be desired in those days, and it was probably one of the selling points of the house.

Once we had settled in Beckenham, I was given a puppy—an adorable English cocker spaniel. It was golden and velvety soft, with sweet breath and pluggy feet. Sadly, this lovely creature contracted a disease that led to Saint Vitus' dance, and for some reason, my stepfather insisted that I go with him to the vet to have the puppy put down. I remember sitting in the car with it jumping and twitching in my lap while I lovingly tried to soothe it. I stayed in the vehicle while Pop took the little bundle inside. I was so sad, I could hardly bear it.

My stepfather actually did several things in an attempt to reach out to me. He built a tiny playhouse in the garden for me, really a shed, with a sloping roof. He added small leaded windows with colored panes. Everything inside was in miniature: little chairs, little desk, little everything.

I was grateful for the gesture, but I wasn't quite sure what to do with the gift. My mother supplied me with tiny cups and saucers to play "house" with, and I occasionally went out there, but it didn't quite work somehow. I didn't have any social life with children my own age, so no friends came to play. I was just out in the garden by myself, feeling a bit damp and cold.

In retrospect, everything was sad around that time. I was aware that Mum was feeling pressured and seemed more than a little out of sorts. What with a new baby, dealing with the divorce, being newly married to Pop and mediating between us, organizing a new house, and her classical talents being largely wasted—it's no wonder she was depressed.

SIX

THE WAR ESCALATED yet again. Barrage balloons, defending against low-flying aircraft, dotted the London horizon. Searchlights crisscrossed the night skies. Amazingly, in spite of the danger, King George VI and Queen Elizabeth stayed on at Buckingham Palace, to support the British public. Though they could easily have chosen to hide away in the country, they never did—and it was one of the things that made them so beloved by the English people. They visited bomb sites, they visited hospitals—they were a constant, comforting presence.

By the summer of 1944, the Germans were sending pilotless aircraft—literally flying bombs—known as "doodlebugs" to England. We would hear the pulsating drone of their approach, then there would be a sudden silence as the engine cut out, followed by an unforgettable whistling sound as the missile hurtled toward the earth. If the aircraft cut out directly overhead, one was reasonably sure of being safe, since the doodlebugs had a habit of veering at the last second. If they cut out some distance away, the danger was considerable.

I remember the nights especially. When the air raid sirens blared, we would either go into the big cupboard under the staircase or out to the shelter for safety. Mum would try to keep me in bed for as long as possible, saying, "No need to come down yet—I'll tell you when!"

After a pause, I'd yell, "Mum! I think I hear the planes coming . . ."

"Yes, I'll call when it's time!"

Eventually we always went out to the shelter, because the raids were so relentless. Near the end of the war, no housewife could finish her laundry, bake a cake, or make a meal without interruption, as the raids occurred day and night. The sirens would wail continuously, and the entire family would run for the shelter and stay there until the all-clear sounded. (To this day, when I hear the local fire station's noon siren, I am reminded of that all-clear sound.)

My mother devised a time-saving idea. I was able to tell the difference between one of our own fighter aircraft and a German doodlebug. The minute the air raid siren went off, I was dispatched to sit on top of our shelter with a beach stool, an umbrella, a tiny pair of opera glasses, and a whistle. The opera glasses were absolutely useless, but I relied on my sense of sound, and the minute I heard the inevitable approach of a doodlebug, I'd blow my whistle. Mum, therefore, had a little more time to do what she had to do. She'd come running at the last possible minute and we'd all pile into the shelter. The bomb would drop, the all-clear would ring out, and we'd start all over again.

The trouble was that all the neighbors began to rely on my whistle, as well. The day came when it was simply teeming with rain and, despite the umbrella, I rebelled. A bomb dropped close by, and later there were quite a few people pounding at our door.

"Why didn't she blow her bloody whistle?" the neighbors demanded.

From then on I *had* to do it.

One day, we were sitting in the shelter when my stepfather clattered down the steps.

"Come and look at this!" he said, and we went outside to witness a huge dogfight, taking place directly above us. It was scary to see it all going on right over our heads.

Sometimes we were in the air raid shelter all night. We would chat quietly, or listen for the airplanes, huddling down there, feeling claustrophobic and wondering if this was the day we were going to be hit. We'd hear the crunch of the bombs, and were truly blessed in that they only dropped in a circle around us.

ON JUNE 3, 1944, Dad and Win got married. For their honeymoon, they went to Brixham on the south Devon coast for a week, with Johnny in tow. They had a single room with a double bed, and Johnny had to sleep with them. Win very nearly quit the marriage that first week for, according to her, Johnny was a "little bugger" and nothing was right. Somehow, they pulled through it. They used a small legacy that Win's father had left her to buy a house in Chessington, Surrey.

I had met Win only once, when she was working at the Esher Filling Station. On my early visits to Chessington, I was resentful of the new woman in my dad's life, but she tried very hard to make my time there special. She was also a marvelous cook.

While Win stayed home to prepare her meals, Dad would take us on expeditions. Johnny, then six, would ride on the back of Dad's bike and I would ride my own. We'd go to the zoo, or we would cycle a fair distance to Surbiton Lagoon—a big, open-air swimming pool that was always perishingly cold. I wasn't used to the outdoor life, and I often felt weak and sickly. Life with Dad and Win and Johnny could seem a bit too robust.

At Surbiton Lagoon, Dad taught me to swim. He was endlessly patient, but every time he let go of me, I'd go under the surface, gasping and taking in great gulps of chlorinated water. Johnny of course swam easily and well. At the end of each lesson Dad would leave Johnny and me in the shallow end while he went off to enjoy his own moment in the pool. He would climb to the topmost diving board in the deep end.

"There goes Dad!" we'd say, waving and feeling so proud as he executed marvelous swan dives, pikes, and jackknives. Dad would then come and fetch us, give us a rough, brisk towel-down—by now we were all goose bumps and blue—and then he'd buy each of us a hot chocolate and a doughnut at the Lagoon Café.

It was a somewhat painful experience: struggling to learn to swim, with the water so cold, being chilled to the marrow. But by the end of the morning, it felt so good to have done it and to have the treat afterward. In spite of the long ride home, it was always worth the effort—quality time with Dad.

I was promised a £5 note the day I learned to swim. In those days, a "fiver" was a large piece of white paper, thin like tissue, engraved with fine, beautiful calligraphy and with a tiny black thread of steel running through it, only visible when held up to the light. I remember the day when my feet finally came up off the bottom of the pool and there I was, swimming alone! Dad was thrilled. I was thrilled. We went home to tell Win the good news and we had a celebration lunch. I was duly given my fiver—it felt like a lot of money—and a great fuss was made over me. From then on, swimming was great.

Bedtime in Chessington was another painful experience. Dad would tuck me into bed and read me a poem or a story, in his precise, beautifully modulated voice. I would lie there, watching as he leaned toward the bedside light, studying his profile, loving him so much, knowing that my return home was imminent and that he was giving me every ounce of himself that he possibly could. I would feel achingly sad, and try not to cry, knowing that my tears would cause him grief. I'd pretend to fall asleep while he was reading, so that I wouldn't have to return his good-night kiss or hug, for a gentle touch would have done me in altogether.

One particular day I was about to return to Beckenham, and feeling utterly miserable, I stood in the tiny dining area attempting to collect myself. There was a thick cut-glass bowl on the sideboard and the sunlight was sending rainbow refractions off the glass. I thought that if I stared at the bowl long enough, hard enough, something about its sharp angles would stop me from crying. I stared and stared, willing the cause of my anguish to come from the crystal and not my head and heart.

Dad would be stoic. He'd say, "Chick, we'll get together again as soon as we possibly can." We didn't speak on the phone much, for that was painful, too. But he kept every promise, and whatever date he said he was coming for me, he came.

AUTUMN ARRIVED, AND lessons at the Cone-Ripman School began in earnest, which meant that I now had to go up to London every day. Aunt was still teaching dance at the school and living in her one-room apartment. Since I was only eight, it was decided that I would stay with her during the week while classes were in session, and go home to Beckenham at the weekends.

Uncle Bill was away in the Air Force, billeted somewhere, and Aunt and I were mostly alone together. I slept on a little cot; she had a single bed. Occasionally, Uncle Bill came home on leave, whereupon a screen was put up in front of my cot. They would cuddle in the single bed, and Auntie, giggling, would call, "Julia, *turn* to the wall!"—a phrase that stuck with us over the years.

I never had the impression that Auntie was really in love with Bill, though she seemed glad whenever he came back. They made a handsome couple. He was a tall, good-looking man, with silver gray hair. He dressed immaculately, always sporting a good tie or cravat, and looking elegant in his beloved cricket sweater and whites whenever he wore them. His trousers had a perfect crease and his old shoes were polished to a shine. He was certainly dashing in his air force uniform; he was a flight engineer, plotting courses, operating the radio. He flew often, making sorties over Germany and France. If Aunt wasn't completely in love with him, they made a good show of it. They both enjoyed ballroom dancing and shared a similar sense of humor.

Meals were pretty simple in Auntie's flat. She was a fair cook, but money and goods were so scarce. I remember toasting bread on a fork in front of the gas fire. It smelled and tasted horrible, but it was better than plain old bread and it was warm in the winter. Because of war rations, we ate a lot of Spam—fried mostly, with a vegetable or potatoes. We had powdered eggs for breakfast sometimes, and Aunt made a good stew when she could.

I remember when I caught a cold, Aunt said, "Ah, the best cure for *that* is a boiled onion." I *hated* onions and protested, but she said, "No, you'll eat it. It will cure you." She bought a huge white Spanish onion, boiled it, and drenched it in butter, salt, and pepper. Lo and behold, it tasted delicious. The butter helped, the salt helped—and to my surprise, the cold disappeared.

Cone-Ripman School kept Auntie and me on a pretty rigorous schedule. There were academic lessons in the mornings and ballet, tap, and character dancing in the afternoons. Miss Grace Cone was the principal ballet teacher and a real martinet, always banging her cane on the floor to emphasize the musical beats. Another teacher, Miss Mackie, was a tough woman and quite cruel. She taught the tap classes, and had no tolerance for anyone timid or unsure. I received the impression from her that I was simply hopeless. For some reason, she seemed to have it in for me. I could tap fairly well—my feet did their stuff—but my arms were stiff and unco-ordinated. I often elected to hide at the back of the class in hopes that she wouldn't pick on me . . . but pick on me she did, and she was relentless.

I think my aunt felt the stress of teaching and of being responsible for me. She sensed I was unhappy. One day, she said, "Why don't we just take some time off and go to the country and have a picnic? You choose when." I chose a day when I would have had a lesson with Miss Mackie. The following morning when I returned to school, Miss Mackie questioned why I had missed the class. Aunt had told me to say that I hadn't been feeling well, but Miss Mackie said, "I don't believe it!" She wouldn't let me off the hook. "Tell me the truth, tell me the truth, tell me the *truth*!" Finally I crumbled, and when I did tell the truth, I became violently ill, threw up, and was sent to the principal's office to lie down. I was dizzy, sweating, and miserable. Miss Mackie came in. Putting her face close to mine, she hissed, "I *hate* liars."

In the spring, just after I turned nine, Mum decided that I was old enough to try living in Beckenham full-time, and to take the train to London and back on a daily basis. Aunt met me at Victoria Station in the mornings, took me to school, and put me on the train home in the evenings. It was a half-hour journey by myself each way, and I soon became exhausted. Not only did I get up early to make it to London and then work at school all day, but after traveling back in the evening, I'd still have homework to do *and* my singing practice.

Not long after I moved back to Beckenham permanently, Auntie suddenly arrived at our door looking absolutely ashen. She was clutching a telegram in her hand, which announced that Bill had been shot down over France. He had evaded capture for twenty-eight days but had been caught and sent to a German prisoner-of-war camp, where he spent the remaining months of the war. It was not one of the more notorious camps, and mercifully, being an officer, he was not put to death. But we were all very concerned for him.

DURING THIS TIME, Pop continued to give me singing lessons. Although he tried everything he could to make friends, I wouldn't have any of it. I was shy, self-conscious, and overwhelmed by his physicality.

He seemed such a big man to me, and powerful. He was not tall, but everything about him was physical—he flexed his muscles, he chewed loudly and juicily, and sometimes breathed through his nose noisily. My father always seemed so gentle; Pop was strange, different, volatile at times. To a certain extent I was able to blank out the fact that I even had a stepfather. I refused to acknowledge that he and my mother were in the same bedroom; it was always just "my mother's room." I tried to live side by side with him, as if he were a temporary guest in the house, and I hated the singing lessons—absolutely *hated* them. He simply worked on basic vocal exercises with me, but I was also required to do a half hour's practice every day on my own.

However, soon thereafter, I was taken to visit Pop's voice teacher. Her name was Lilian Stiles-Allen, but she was always referred to as "Madame." She had coached Pop when he first came to England from Canada, and she still occasionally gave him lessons. She was a short, very stout woman, with thick ankles, an ample backside, and a heavy bosom. There was a sort of "pouter pigeon" look about her. Her belt hung below her belly and was slung in a nice V, a little to the left of center. Always bejeweled, she dressed in long skirts to her ankles, and sensible lace-up shoes on tiny feet that looked too small to support the frame above. She walked with a strong cane and often donned a wonderful velvet cloak and beret. Her pretty face had several jowls, but her eyes were lovely. Though bulging slightly, their long, spiky lashes fanned her cheeks. Occasionally, she put on a fashionable hat of the times, usually with a great sweeping brim or a feather. She was imposing, yet gentle and kind, and she had the loveliest, most mellifluous speaking voice.

I don't recall what I first sang for Madame, but I remember my stepfather being in the room and my mother playing for me. After I finished, Madame gave a low chuckle, then said gravely, "That was just lovely." She counseled my parents, saying that I was so young and that it might be better to allow me to be a child a little longer and bring me back when I was, say, twelve or fourteen years old; plenty of time then to study in earnest with her if I wanted to, and my voice would have matured and would be ready for training.

But my voice developed so rapidly that by the time I was nine and a half, it was pretty obvious that I was going to sing, and sing quite well. Pop went back to Madame and pleaded with her to take me on, and she finally agreed. From then on my lessons were entirely with her and not with Pop, which was a relief to me. Thus my proper singing training began.

SEVEN

I TOOK LESSONS WITH Madame once a week at first. She was living in Leeds, but traveled regularly down to London to teach at
Weeke's Studios in Hanover Square.

The place was fascinating. Walking the corridors to Madame's class-
room, I heard a cacophony of voices and instruments coming from the
different rooms. My own singing with Madame just added to the chorus,
and didn't feel like any big deal. Once our studio door was closed, I felt
pretty much sealed off from the rest—yet part of a special community at
the same time.

Madame played the piano badly, and she had long, pretty fingernails
that clacked away on the ivory keys. She always wore good rings on her
hands to give her something else to look at during the many hours of
teaching. Her accompaniment was mostly only "suggested," so one
filled in the blanks in one's head as one was singing, but it didn't matter
because she was a superb teacher.

She was a dramatic soprano, having been fairly well known for playing
the role of Old Nokomis in Samuel Coleridge-Taylor's *Hiawatha* at the
Royal Albert Hall. She performed many oratorios, concerts, and radio
programs, and had an amazing singing voice, which produced a kind of
flute-like sound, especially in her higher range. Rather than coming out of
her throat, it seemed to pass down her nose. It was a particular technique
that she had perfected, and later, I realized that her voice resembled that of
Kirsten Flagstad, the Norwegian soprano, whom she admired.

Madame would sit at the piano and I would sit or occasionally stand

50

beside her, and we'd work for a long time on technique. She explained to me, "I'm going to give you lots of mental pictures in terms of place-ment. One of these pictures will fall into place one day, and you will have found your vocal position."

We always began our lessons with breathing exercises and then gentle scales, one in particular called the "five-nine-thirteen," which was the notes of any scale sung in chromatic sequence up and back again, first five, then nine, then all thirteen of the full octave. I would sing these scales using assorted vowels, usually a strong B, the "Buh" pulling the voice forward, followed by a long E. These exercises strengthened the voice, placing it behind the teeth and forward off the throat so that one didn't swallow the sound. We worked with "Bay's" and "Bi's," "Mee's" and "Dee's." The "Oo's" and "Oh's" were harder for me to sustain.

Madame said, "Think of a beautiful string of pearls, and each pearl is identical to the next. I want you to bring the high notes down to where you are placing your low notes and bring the low notes up. As you come down, bring the voice *up* and as you go *up*, bring it *down*." I learned what a wonderful long line of sound this technique makes, which is why, I believe, in later years I was able to glissando up two or three octaves, without a break.

Being a young voice in a young throat, my muscles would occasion-ally ache, but little by little, with Madame's tuition and careful guidance, I was able to improve and push one step further. After every lesson I noticed greater strength in my vocal equipment.

After scales were finished, we worked on simple ballads, but as I advanced, we moved on to more complicated pieces—operatic coloratura arias in particular. (By age twelve, I was blazing away at the most difficult technical passages, which seldom bothered me at all.)

We practiced Handel a great deal, using just the exercise vowels at first, then progressing to the words: songs like "I Know That My Redeemer Liveth," and the "Rejoice" from the *Messiah*, and "Oh, Had I Jubal's Lyre." Madame always said, "When in doubt, return to Handel. Handel will never let you down vocally. Anytime, practice Handel." She praised the composer for his knowledge of words that singers can hang onto, to help strengthen a voice without harm. Handel wrote many long passages that required good breath control, and these were invaluable exercises.

Madame also put great emphasis on the ends of phrases. For example, if I was coming to the end of a song and holding the last note, she would say, "Follow it, follow it, follow it—see it going down the road in front of you as far as you can. See it disappearing into the distance. Now just close the mouth on it and finish the sound."

The lyrics at the end of Handel's "Rejoice" are "Behold, thy King cometh unto thee!" and as I sang the word "thee-e-e-e-e-," I'd hold it, hold it, hold it, hold it—but if I wasn't careful, I'd go "thee-uh" as my vocal line finished, and the voice would fall back into my mouth. She'd tell me to "close the sound beyond the breath." Lo and behold, the voice and the word held true.

Many voices have a natural break going from mid-voice into a higher register. I call it "gear shifting." Madame was very adamant that gear shifting was out of the question, and that one should be able to move up or down in a smooth line and without a change in tone. It's required of opera singers, but for musical theater and popular music, it can sound too "proper," too formal a way of singing. She did not let me use a chest voice at all at first, which was extremely good training for me as a youngster. Later, as I sang more and more musical theater, a chest voice became essential at times—and then she actually worked with me on that, too, helping me bridge the gap between chest voice and soprano, using technique and thought.

Madame hoped very much that I would go into opera, but I always sensed that it was too big a stretch for me. My voice was extremely high and thin, and though clean and clear, it never had the necessary guts and weight for opera. Classical singers never use microphones—they soar above and over an orchestra. It's unbelievable to me how they do it. It's full-bore singing, and although in many operas it only amounts to about twenty minutes or so of true, flat-out vocal effort, it's nevertheless a question of lungs and volume and strength.

I could understand why Madame's weight gave her dramatic voice such power, because good singing does come from the whole body— from well-planted feet and a solid stance on strong legs, to diaphragm control and correct vocal placement. The rest is brain/muscle coordination and air passing through vocal cords, combined with a trained ear and true pitch.

Though Madame gave me the best technique I could possibly have had, I think her ambition for me to go into opera and to try to emulate her sound was, finally, impractical. I didn't seem able to find what she called "that special place," though I tried and tried. My attempts usually resulted in a somewhat pinched, nasal sound. Madame's technique was correct and safe—and for her, foolproof—but for me, I felt it didn't allow for a certain reality. I was "lifting" the voice up into the head, which is essential, but the nasal sound never seemed as true for me as a slightly more open, released sound. When I finally found *that* voice, it was an adaptation of everything she'd ever given me. By the time we had worked together for fifteen years or so, I knew enough to know what was correct and what wasn't, though one never stops learning, thinking, feeling, making vocal choices that are as safe as possible. Continued maintenance and "refresher courses" are essential.

Singers seldom take classes with other pupils, and thus lack the opportunity to make comparisons. We don't *see* what we do, as we would in a ballet class in front of a mirror. It is all about sensing, listening, making subtle adjustments, finding out *why* something doesn't work and solving the problem. After all the practice, one relies on the technique to "hold," so that it virtually becomes second nature. Then, one concentrates on the melody, the phrasing, the lyrics—and the joy of giving it to an audience.

The work can be lonely—much like that of a writer, I suspect. But the rewards, when they come, are to render one humble, to bring one to one's knees with gratitude.

MADAME'S TEACHING WAS all about vocal placement. She used lyrics to help give the voice a foundation. She didn't coach me much as to the *meaning* of the lyric—that is something I came to later in life. Occasionally, she would make me *articulate* a word—"beautiful," for example, to convey its loveliness—but time and again she drilled into me that if I was true to my consonants—let's say, the strong B, as in, again, "Behold . . . thy King cometh unto Thee"—then the consonants would pull my voice forward, and keep my vowels true. For Madame, it was the foundation, the technique, that mattered most.

Right from the start, I was expected to practice daily, of course, and I had to really knuckle down. Madame never had any printed pages, though she did mark my music constantly and I took copious notes. My mother followed Madame's notations and helped me remember whatever was marked, especially when I was very young. The exercises were practiced alone, but my mother often came and worked on specific songs with me afterward.

She was a wonderful accompanist. It was a joy to sing with her because, after Madame's terrible piano playing, Mum's music sounded almost fully orchestrated. Having sung technically for so long, I felt uplifted and set free by hearing the composition played the way it was intended.

There were certain songs, however, that I simply could not sing. Songs in the minor key or with a yearning reference, like "Songs My Mother Taught Me" or "O My Beloved Father," from Puccini's *Gianni Schicchi*, for example. I was overwhelmed by the sadness of the lyric combined with the pure sweetness of a melody. I would feel my throat closing as I choked up. Edging behind the piano stool so that Mum couldn't see, I would fight tears for all I was worth, but suddenly the voice would be gone in a mess of emotion. Mum would turn around and see me simply bawling my eyes out.

"Oh, Julia, don't be so *stupid*!" she would say. But I couldn't help it. More often than not, work with my mother ended on a somewhat acrimonious note, because there was no singing once the tears came.

With Madame, I would cry for different reasons. There were tears of fatigue, tears of frustration or rage with myself when I could not get something right. I think there was such a turmoil going on in my breast anyway, sometimes it was a catharsis to just let go.

Madame was always understanding.

"You must never be embarrassed when you are moved by music," she counseled. "It shows that you are a sensitive human being, capable of much feeling." It was one of the reasons she would not let me sing much Puccini. She wouldn't let me try the great arias from *Madame Butterfly* or *La Bohème*—melodies I longed to sing because of their beauty.

"No, you will sing them when you're older and your voice is more mature. Right now it would just pull you to pieces vocally. It's too emotional; too beautiful and sad, and you will be caught up in it and damage the instrument." She was right, of course.

JUST BEFORE THE end of the school term at Cone-Ripman, I took my Grade IV ballet exam and received a decent mark. Then I worked for and took my Grade V, and something magical happened.

I remember standing in a corridor at school and feeling weary—awaiting my turn with the examiner. I could hear the piano music being played for the student ahead of me. I was nervous, I felt unready, and even wondered if I would hold up because of my fatigue. My body seldom felt as strong as I needed it to be. All the other girls seemed so enthusiastic and capable.

My name was called and I hesitantly went into the room. Sunlight was shafting through a big window and the studio was filled with light.

"Come forward, dear," the examiner said pleasantly. "Let me meet you and say hello."

She put me at ease as she asked me to show her my barre work. The pianist played the set piece for my dance quite beautifully, and suddenly, surprisingly, I was inspired. Everything fell into place: my body felt supported, my arms extended and became graceful, my legs worked, the energy came at the right time. Having stood outside in the dark corridor before, feeling so unsure and fearful, I entered this beautiful sunlit room to discover a kind human being, a wonderful pianist, glorious music that uplifted me . . . and I was able to let go, to dance with freedom and pleasure.

When my exam result finally arrived, Mum and Auntie both came to collect me from school, and they told me that I had received a "highly commended." It was a big moment for me, one of the first times that I felt I'd done something really well.

Nonetheless, because of my singing lessons and going to school on the train every day, dancing, doing homework, and singing practice at night, I had become pale and chronically tired. As the summer holidays began, my mother announced, "You're not going back to Cone-Ripman," which was a big relief to me. I was enrolled in Woodbrook, a local girls' school in Beckenham, and would begin classes in the autumn.

EIGHT

O N MAY 8, 1945, peace was declared in Europe. My mother, Pop, Don, and I traveled to Walton-on-Thames to join some friends and to see the festivities, and everywhere there was an incredible sense of celebration: bonfires on the village greens, people spilling out of the pubs, flags waving in all directions. This became known as VE Day—Victory in Europe.

Almost immediately afterward, the newspapers printed the most horrific images of the concentration camps in Germany. Once our troops arrived and all the camps were liberated, the press was allowed in. Our newspapers were emblazoned with headlines of the atrocities at Belsen, Auschwitz, and elsewhere, and the photographs were unbearable. The state of the surviving prisoners was appalling beyond words, some so emaciated they couldn't move. I saw pictures of mass graves, bodies dumped one on top of the other, bones sticking out all over the place. The photos resembled the paintings of Hieronymus Bosch, only worse, and England—along with most of the world—was horrified.

Even in those days, young as I was, I wondered: "How could we *not* have known about the atrocities?" I suppose the government knew, but why was the public so unaware of the inhumanity of it all?

War was still being waged in Japan, and the atomic bomb was dropped on Hiroshima, and on Nagasaki three days later.

On August 14, 1945, VJ—Victory in Japan—was declared, and World War II finally, mercifully ended.

I TRAVELED OCCASIONALLY with my parents to one town or another while they were performing, and it was around this time that I saw their act for the very first time. I remember being awed by the glamour of the theater: the velvet curtains, the bright lights, the creaminess of my mother's skin as she sat at the piano, and how beautiful she looked in her satin crinoline gown.

I sat in the first row of the balcony to watch their act and was simply mesmerized. Afterward, I was taken backstage and was surprised by the cavernous size—and the surprising shabbiness—of it all; how tall the flies were, how huge and wide the flats! And the *smells*—of the yellow and pink gels on all the lamps, of paint and makeup, and grease and sweat, and most of all, of warm dust from the great drapes and the painted drops and the grubby, pockmarked stage. To this day, that smell is a turn-on.

Mum and Pop's act always started with a theme song. The audience would hear Pop's voice singing a refrain of the ballad "I Bring a Love Song." As he reached the final notes, the curtains would part, and there they would be—my mother sitting at the grand piano, the skirt of her dress draped prettily around her, and Pop in a dinner jacket at the microphone.

They began with classical arias, like Pagliacci's tenor aria "Vesti la Giubba," or Rodolfo's first aria from *La Bohème*, "Che Gelida Manina." Pop sang them in English. They would then perform a few ballads, after which Pop would introduce Mum and she'd play a solo. Finally Pop would come back with his guitar and together they'd finish up with the popular songs of the day. There was a certain amount of class about their act; it was well thought out, and they performed for about thirty minutes.

Mum really came into her own with her solos, and her flourish of double octaves at the end always went down well. Pop was fairly good at orchestration, having studied just enough to do the necessary arrangements for the pit orchestras that played when they toured, which generally consisted of ten to twelve people.

When I traveled with them, I would watch the show every night. Once they were bathed in the lights from the front of the house, it seemed very glamorous. Mum and Pop were never "top of the bill," but they were generally "second top," which was fairly prestigious in music hall. My mother used to say that it was much better to have second billing, because top had all the responsibility of making the show a success. Second top usually closed the first act. Comedians, always the big draw, were the most important and were saved for the end of the show.

Performances were twice nightly, and I remember my mother talking about "first house" and "second house." Before I actually saw them perform, I would say, "What's that, Mummy? Do you go out to different people's houses?" She laughingly explained that the audience in a theater was always called "the house" and that with two shows a night, the first audience was the first house and the next was the second.

One day Pop and I traveled up north a day ahead of Mum. I don't exactly know why or what it was she was doing, but she was due to join us later. It was the first time I had ever been alone with my stepfather. We checked into our digs—one room with twin beds. Pop took one and I settled into the other. It was uncomfortably quiet, and suddenly Pop said, "Come into bed with me and I'll keep you warm."

I replied, "I'm fine . . . I'm a bit sleepy."

"No, no, come on, come on," he pressed. "Let's have a cuddle."

Very reluctantly I climbed into bed and lay with my back to him.

"I'll show you how I cuddle with Mummy," he said. "Give me your feet." He placed them between his legs, and I was acutely aware of his heaviness on my tiny limbs. I felt trapped and claustrophobic.

Eventually, summoning my courage, I claimed that I was too hot and that I was going back to my own bed. To my relief and surprise, he let me go. Something about it didn't feel right to me at all, and I was very grateful when my mother arrived the following day.

JUST BEFORE MY tenth birthday, Mum said to me, "Pop's going to invite you to sing on the stage with us tonight." Apparently, my parents had asked permission from the front-of-house manager, and he had nervously agreed.

When the moment arrived, Pop said to the audience, "We have a little surprise for you. Our daughter is with us this week and we'd like to invite her onstage to sing a duet with me." A beer crate was placed beside Pop, which I stood upon in order to reach the single microphone. No orchestration, of course—just Mum accompanying us in a song called "Come to the Fair."

It went down well. I knew no fear at that time, and I didn't let the side down. My stepfather's voice ringing in my ear was a little irritating, and my mother urged us along with rather heavy piano playing, but the audience seemed entertained. I was a novelty. Little by little I began to join their act more often—not every night, but when it was convenient, and gradually I became aware of what it felt like to be behind the footlights looking out into the black auditorium with the spotlights on me. I rather enjoyed it.

I BEGAN AT Woodbrook in the fall as planned. It was a fine girls' school run by two genteel ladies, Miss Meade and Miss Evans, who were probably partners in every sense. It was my first formal academic experience, and I liked it very much. There followed a period of stability during which I actually made some friends my own age. I was cast in the school plays and loved them. I remember playing Robin Hood in a swashbuckling way, a lot of manly (so I thought) thigh-slapping and posturing, legs akimbo, hands on hips, as I called out, "Follow me, men!"

At morning congregation, the students gathered in the main hall for roll call and to sing hymns. This was a joy, because the seniors would sing the descants, and suddenly my head was filled with their wonderful counter-melodies. I seldom had the chance to sing choral work with others.

At Woodbrook, I was treated like a regular kid. I was encouraged to play sports—at which I was hopeless—and to join the Brownies. The problem was, I had trouble finding my niche. Every week, the Brownie pack would meet after school. There would be tests: knot tying (I was reasonably good), lighting a fire with two sticks only (hopeless), and other things at which I was simply awful. I had hopes that I might cut it in the sartorial department, and I entered the competition for the best-dressed, neatest Brownie. I went off to school, well prepared, convinced that I would pass with flying colors, but the Brownie pack leader discovered a splodge of yellow egg yolk on my tie. So much for that!

Most mortifying for me were sports. Everyone was so "jolly hockey sticks" and hearty; I was reed thin, with bandy legs. During netball, I was always placed as guard to some huge, strong opponent, and when I attempted to block these astonishingly healthy girls, they would leap in front of me, knock me sideways, steal the ball, and leave me staring after them, agape with wonder.

One day we were playing a very important match and my family came to watch. I was tearing about, trying to do *something* right, and I suddenly noticed that the kids were pointing at my ankles and laughing hilariously.

"Look at Julie's potatoes!"

My bare heels were showing through large holes in my socks. They kept coming up out of my shoes and, worse, I was getting blisters. The game for me became all about trying to hide my shame—and our team was trounced.

The annual sports days were a nightmare. The idea of having to compete in obstacle races and get down on my knees and crawl beneath a tarpaulin or climb over ropes and fall down and stumble in front of everybody was humiliating. I was always last. I was hopeless at the three-legged race, pulling my partner down with me. How could I be competent at dance, how could I sing so well, yet not be good at sports?

Miss Meade began to give me piano lessons at school, after classes. I enjoyed them, but they only lasted a short while. Mum had given me the basics of the piano, but I believe two things prevented her from teaching me further: she was busy raising kids, and she didn't have the patience for it. She always said she was not a good teacher. Though she accompanied me when I sang, she wanted me to get the rudiments of music from somebody else.

Whether it was because I didn't want to compete with my mother's brilliance, or the fact that I was a rank beginner, or perhaps because I *had* my mother to accompany me, I didn't have the will to continue with piano lessons. Perhaps I was simply taking on too much. Whatever the reason, my mother didn't push me, and to this day, I regret it.

*

I HAD A good bicycle and I cycled to school and back, sometimes even coming home for the lunch break. My bike had a basket on the front, and I would lay my satchel on top of it, weaving the straps through the handlebars. Using the two straps as reins, I pretended that my bike was my horse. Rides to school were great fun, as I cantered off down the road. In winter, I folded the tips of my knitted gloves over the holes in the fingers, for the frost was painful on my skin.

On Saturday mornings, our local cinema presented programs for children: cartoons, shorts, Westerns. The place was usually packed. Whenever possible, I simply loved to attend—for it was a moment of complete freedom for me when I lost myself in the magic of Hollywood. Oblivious to the chaos and noise around me, I focused on the adventures of the Lone Ranger, Roy Rogers, Gene Autry, Hopalong Cassidy, Mowgli, and Tarzan.

By now, Donald was a toddler and Mum hired a housemaid. Whenever my mother was away performing with my stepfather, this North Country girl would look after us. I didn't like her, and I baited her considerably. One day she got so upset that she hit me around the head— really walloped me. I told my mother, and the girl was quickly dismissed. I shouldn't have baited her, but I didn't like her taking care of me.

Mum then hired a rather formidable-looking lady, who had a son named Howard, with a substantial black mole on the very tip of his nose. He was a bit older than I was. After a while, we began sneaking into the cupboard under the stairs to practice kissing, which I'm sure I instigated. I would do my best to blot out the image of the mole on his nose. He was my first kiss, and I kept thinking, "I do hope I don't have to *marry* this boy." I didn't think there would ever be another man in my life. Luckily, the housekeeper and Howard didn't stay with us long, either.

ONE DAY AT Woodbrook, Miss Meade came to find me.

"Your mother has asked if I would send you home early today," she announced breathlessly.

I thought perhaps my mother was ill.

"Is everything all right?"

"Yes, yes. Your mother wants you home because you're going to sing in London tonight." I thought it a bit short notice, but I was glad to get out of school early.

Mum told me to bathe and dress quickly, and we set off for London, arriving at our theater in the city as dusk was falling. My stepfather was about to park the car, when a liveried doorman came over and said, "Sorry, sir, you can't park here. This spot is for the Queen's car."

Pop said, "Of course. We'll find another place."

As we drove away I said, "Did he say the *Queen's* car . . . ?"

My mother said, "No, no. I think he said the *Greens'* car. God knows who they are!" I didn't think any more about it.

We went into the theater and were held in a waiting room with other actors, until a man, a sort of equerry, came in. "Now, when Her Majesty comes backstage, here is the protocol," he said, and proceeded to explain. "You do not speak until spoken to. Always address her as 'Ma'am.' Also, remember, when you have finished your performance, you must curtsy or bow to the Queen *first*, before acknowledging the audience."

I discovered that we were at the Stage Door Canteen, and were about to perform for Queen Elizabeth, wife of King George VI.

The Stage Door Canteen was a wonderful place where the armed forces could get a square meal, attend dances, and find some entertainment. Probably because of my parents' connection with ENSA, they had been invited to perform that evening, and had decided to take me with them. I think they felt it would make their act more memorable, and that it would be an experience I would never forget. They were right.

My parents performed a couple of songs, then I sang an aria and my duet with Pop. Afterward, Her Majesty, in an exquisite beaded dress and sparkling tiara, came backstage to meet the performers, who were assembled in a receiving line. She had a sweetly pretty face and her manner was charming and friendly. After I curtsied to her, she said to me, "You sang beautifully tonight," and moved on to speak to my mother and stepfather.

At school the next day, Miss Meade, Miss Evans, and the students were agog. I was amazed at how impressed they all were, especially the girls. It was my first taste of celebrity—the school klutz was suddenly the center of attention. Everyone became aware that my parents were in "showbiz," and I relished being accepted at last.

MY PARENTS GOT fed up with forever living in digs when they traveled, so they bought a little trailer—a caravan—which was hitched to our Packard car. Pop always bought good secondhand cars. My mother would name them as if they were beloved friends—sometimes the letters on the license plate made a funny name—but this Packard was called "The Pack." It was navy blue, big and roomy, with a pointed front, whitewall tires, wonderful hubs, and a tow bar at the back.

The trailer was maybe twenty feet long. I slept on the little banquette by the dining table and my parents had the double bed at the back. When we arrived in the town where we were performing, we would pull into some local farm, or perhaps a parking lot beside a pub, and Pop would ask if he could hitch up to their water supply and pay rent. My parents loved the pub parking best, because after the theater they could have a good meal and a drink. Sometimes Mum would cook on the little stove in the trailer. There was a small loo and shower, but only a tiny water tank, which was always rather smelly and mildewed, so we mostly bathed in the theaters, farmhouses, or pubs.

I loved feeling the wind buffeting our little home at night, or hearing the rain teeming down on the roof. Being snug inside, bunked in with the family, was an adventure.

Driving up to these venues, or coming home from them, was often fun. Mum and Pop would make me a bed in the back of the car, and I would snuggle into an eiderdown and read on the long journeys up to the north of England. As soon as Saturday night second house was over, we'd head back home as quickly as we could, often driving through the night.

Sometimes Mum and I still had our theatrical makeup on. Pop flung everything into the car as quickly as possible in order to get out of the theater and the town and get a head start on the journey. At about one-thirty in the morning, we would stop at a transport café on one of the long highways that run through England. We'd pull into a scruffy pit stop, its parking lot filled with huge trucks and semis.

The cafés often had a big potbellied stove inside and there would be a warm fug of smoke hanging in the room. With the smell of cooking and the fire glowing, it was a cozy place to be in the middle of a damp night. The truckers were friendly, it was busy and lively with conversation, and we would have bacon-and-egg sandwiches and steaming hot mugs of tea before journeying on.

We drove through rain and snow often and the windshield wipers would swish back and forth, their sound very soothing to me. The fogs in those days were awful—"pea soupers," they were called; fog thickened by coal smoke. On such nights, my mother would take the wheel and Pop would get out and walk in front of the car with a flashlight. I would wake up and lean over the front seat, peering ahead, helping to spot any danger.

My mother took great delight in the north of England. She would point out the coal-mining towns and tell me a little of their history. She showed me the collieries with the huge wheels on towers, and shafts and lifts that went way down into the mines beneath. There were slag heaps—huge, cone-shaped mountains of coal refuse.

Sheffield was famous for its steel. I remember the hilly streets, and line upon line of identical houses with not a tree in sight. To me it seemed awfully depressing and simply black with soot. But every doorstep was whitewashed and every window had white curtains. People who lived in the North took great pride in washing down their pavements and doorsteps and keeping their homes as immaculate as possible.

At that time, I couldn't see anything redeeming about the North Country; it just seemed industrial and sad. But my mother had memories from her youth, and she very much wanted to share them with me. Over the years, I grew to appreciate that part of England: the moors, the heather and gorse, the thin-steepled churches, the low stone walls, and tiny cottages huddling into the hills and vales to protect them from the biting winds.

NINE

W IN HAD GIVEN birth to a baby girl in September of 1945—my half sister, named Celia. I have no recollection of the day she was born, though I knew Win was expecting a baby. At first I was not happy that there was another little girl in my dad's life. As she grew older, Celia may have felt the same way about me. We've subsequently become very close indeed, but with roughly ten years' age difference between us, initially it was difficult.

MUM, POP, AND I went to entertain the American troops at one of their army bases. Although the war was over, there were still many American personnel stationed in England. The evening was fascinating. We gave our little concert and received a mild response. I suspect a drawing-room musical performance was not the most stimulating act the young men could have seen, and they seemed vaguely restless—perhaps puzzled by the young girl singing her coloratura aria. Not your average, everyday troop entertainment. Afterward, we were given a bang-up dinner in a vast cafeteria: a huge T-bone steak for each of us, French fries, veggies, salads, and pie à la mode. I'd never had such a meal.

DAD TOOK JOHNNY and me for a picnic on the river one day. Our boat was moored to a willow, and we were lazing around having crisps and sandwiches. Four or five noisy teenage lads came down to the water's edge, much to Johnny's and my annoyance, since they were interrupting our idyllic time with Dad.

The boys decided they would swim out to a barge anchored in the middle of the stream—all except for one lad who declined. The others teased him so unmercifully that he felt compelled to join them. My father became suddenly alert. The boy—who obviously could barely swim—began to flounder, and he went under, surfaced, then went under again. My dad said, "Oh my God. You two stay on the boat. Do *not* move." He dived overboard fully clothed and rescued the lad, bringing him back to the riverbank and tending to him. Then he really laced into the others and advised them to get the boy home immediately.

During this last process, Dad was without his pants; he had kicked them off in the river since they were weighing him down, so he had to travel home on the bus with a towel around his middle, which was as embarrassing for him as it was for us. But still we thought him a god, because he'd saved the boy's life.

Another day, Dad took us all—Johnny, me, and Celia—down to Eastbourne. We arrived at the beach, and Dad disappeared to change behind a rock. He then waded into the sea, Johnny and little Celia close behind. Not wanting to hurt or disappoint him, I bravely waded in too. It was blowing and bitterly cold, but when I came out of the water, teeth chattering, I smiled and said, "Oh, Dad, this is the stuff of life!" I don't know why I said it—maybe because I knew it would please him, maybe because it was a healthy dose of reality or there was triumph in having overcome the freezing, piercing quality of the wind. But Dad never forgot it. He quoted me often and took it to mean that I really loved those kinds of activities—and I guess I did. But I was always a bit of a softie.

ON MAY 12, 1946, my mother gave birth to my youngest brother, Christopher Stuart Andrews. Once again, Mum went to Rodney House, the maternity hospital in Walton.

This time I stayed with family friends in the village, Madge and Arthur Waters. Arthur was our local bank manager. His wife, Madge, a strong, stout woman, was a member of the local Red Cross. They had two daughters, Virginia (Ginny) and Patricia (Trisha), the girl I danced with in Auntie's production of "Wynken, Blynken, and Nod," and who remains my good friend to this day.

The happy news was that I was now old enough to visit Mum in the maternity hospital. The first time I did so, Chris was placed in my lap and promptly peed in it . . . a bonding of sorts.

When Mum and baby finally came home, it became obvious that the Beckenham house was no longer big enough.

Mum and Pop started making regular visits back to Walton-on-Thames to scout for a new home. Mum's love for Walton had never gone away—it represented safety, roots, everything she yearned for. Besides, their vaudeville act was doing well, and they were presumably ready to take a chance and step up in the world.

On these trips, they would always stop to have lunch or tea with friends, then go off to look at houses in the area. I was left to play with Trisha Waters at her house, or at the home of Gladys and William Barker.

Gladys was my mum's closest friend. Smart and genuine, she had married William, who came from a long line of farmers and who had a wonderful market gardening establishment called Rivernook Farm. They were people of the land and as real and good as they come. Uncle Bill was bombastic, larger than life but generous to a fault, and relied on his wife completely.

They had a daughter a year younger than me named Susan, and a son, John. The Barkers loved kids, and they had a dress-up box—a huge trunk full of old clothes and trinkets, fake jewelry, paper hats, and Christmas crowns—and best of all, they had a summerhouse in their garden, a tiny place with a very small verandah jutting out under the roof. It made a perfect little theater.

Thus began a period of creativity for us girls—Trisha, Susan, and me. We put on plays for our families, and all their relatives, plus whoever happened to be around, including the farmhands.

Being totally bossy, I always wrote, directed, and starred in the plays, which featured lots of swashbuckling, gypsies, and princesses. I would write furiously for the first hour or so of my visit, then time would run out on us, at which point Sue, Trish, and I would make up the rest of the play as we went along. Our audience was asked to sit on garden chairs on the lawn. We'd put on makeup and costumes from the trunk and act our heads off, hamming it up for all we were worth. Our efforts were rewarded by generous, hearty applause. We'd charge a penny a ticket, thinking we'd donate the proceeds to a nearby camp for German prisoners of war, so that they could buy socks—but we never made enough money to buy even one pair.

The Barkers' farm was situated between the river and one of the main roads to London, and whenever we passed by, it was a joy to see the orderly fields of fat cabbages, or row upon row of pale green lettuce. One section was always planted with flowers—sometimes nothing but tulips—and they blazed across the fields. Another time it would be a great swath of daffodils, or narcissi.

William had big green vans with "Wm. Barker & Son" printed in gold on the side. They would be carefully packed with boxes of vegetables and flowers, then driven up to London in the middle of the night in order to sell the goods at Covent Garden by five or six A.M. Poor Bill didn't get much sleep in those days, but the idea of getting up in the middle of the night, loading up, and going in a convoy to London seemed like fun to me.

One day, Mum said with great excitement, "We've purchased a new house, and you are going to love it. It has two acres of ground and there's even an owl in the garden." The thought of an owl hooting in the middle of the night was a scary one, but Mum's excitement about the place was palpable. The house was to become what I now think of as the real home of my childhood.

TEN

"THE OLD MEUSE," as the house was called, was at No. 1 West Grove, situated right on the border between Walton and Hersham. The street had a row of run-down, Dickensian-looking almshouses on one side—but about halfway up the other was a long driveway to our house. Next door to us was the Belgrave Recovery Home, a convalescent residence that was once a fine manor. The Old Meuse had been the servants' quarters to that manor, and the great joy for my mother was that her mother, Granny Julia, had worked as a below-stairs maid there.

It was obvious that this was the house of Mum's dreams. It was certainly bigger than anything we had occupied before, and was considered very upmarket at the time. I believe it cost all of £11,000 (about $22,000 at today's exchange rate, although property values have so escalated since then that the value would now be in the millions). For my mother and stepfather, the price was absolutely prohibitive. They had a huge mortgage, and I soon became aware that they were overreaching in getting the place.

The house sat in the middle of the property, which comprised about 2.2 acres. Because it had been the servants' quarters, the back garden consisted of a vegetable garden, an orchard, a run-down tennis court, a little plot of woodland, and several outbuildings.

On the left of the house was a porte cochere, which led to an inner courtyard at the back with three fairly substantial garages: one single, one triple with a small loft area in it for storage, and next to that, another single. The courtyard also had a potting shed set in a stone wall and a side gate leading to the back garden.

Fir trees and large rhododendrons lined the drive; lilacs divided the front garden from the back. A pretty silver birch tree stood by the house, and indeed the owl did come most nights to sit in it. At first, I would lie in bed with the covers drawn tight, feeling a little spooked by its call, but I eventually came to love it and felt comforted knowing it was there—a guardian of the night.

The house had four bedrooms: one for Mum and Pop, one which the two boys shared, one for guests, and one for me. We had no furniture to speak of, so my stepfather turned his hand to carpentry: he built a trestle dining table with coffee table to match, some window seats with storage below, bookcases, and coat racks. My mother purchased a monk's bench, which remains in our family to this day. We didn't have closets or wardrobes, so Mum ran up some curtains on her old Singer sewing machine and hung them on string across the corners of the bedrooms. My stepfather added poles behind them, so that we could hang our clothes.

All the bedrooms had sinks with the exception of mine, which was right opposite the bathroom. There was a separate toilet upstairs and one downstairs with a wash-basin, plus one outside by the garage area. Almost every room had a small fireplace, which was the only source of heating.

The main living room was big, with a bay window—a long room, which we used mostly for parties and for housing Mum's piano. The room we occupied most was a second, slightly smaller lounge, on the other side of the entrance hall. My stepfather built a bar there, complete with foot rail. The kitchen was large and square, with an old gas cooker, an ancient sink, and a small breakfast room next to it. Most of the windows were leaded in traditional, latticework style, and there were wood floors throughout.

Mum and Pop freshened up the whole house with emulsion paint. They stuccoed the long, rather dark living room in white, then stippled onto it a rose maroon color, and applied a high gloss over the lot. It was probably the fashionable thing to do, but the walls looked waxy, and with the warmth of a crowd or if the fire was lit, they would run with condensation.

My mother found a terrific bed for me—essentially a mattress on a strong wooden box with two big doors that opened for storage underneath. My little bedroom had a window seat and a fireplace, with a mantelpiece above for all my knickknacks. Pop created a dressing table by putting up a mirror and a shelf against the wall, and Mum covered the lower half with chintz fabric and added a stool.

They purchased a prefab bungalow for the garden, inviting Uncle Hadge and his wife, Kit, to come and live there and be our gardener/caretakers.

Hadge said that if he was really going to develop the garden, he would need a greenhouse, so a glass lean-to was added to the wall by the back door in the courtyard. A heater was installed, and to watch Hadge's cuttings and plants flourish in their bedding boxes and to smell that delicious, earthy smell before entering the kitchen was to be hit with sudden, sensual delight. To this day I know of no more heady perfume than the smell of warm, damp earth.

For a few brief shining months, Hadge revealed the magic that was in his fingertips. He pared back the roses on the arbor. He weeded the overgrown tennis court, mowed it, rolled it, marked out the tennis lines, and put up a net. He pruned the trees and the orchard began to bloom. There were canes of raspberries, black currants, cherry trees, apple trees—Cox's Orange Pippins—and a plum tree. He grew beautiful sweet peas, lines and lines of them, and runner beans. Everything about the garden began to fall into shape, and it became my joy, my realm, my fantasyland. Life suddenly seemed a lot better and we finally had a place we could truly call home.

I found a secret hiding place, down by the small copse beyond the tennis court—a little freak of nature where the forsythia had grown into a complete natural arch. I would lie on the ground looking up into the yellow sprigs and dream the day away. I began to wonder what I would do when I got older. I didn't really feel that I was good at anything, and I certainly didn't recognize the value of my voice at that time. I made a resolve to myself that whatever I did, I would do it to the best of my ability and make myself useful. If I was to be someone's secretary, I'd be the best secretary in the world; if I was a florist, I'd be the best florist in the world. I would apply myself, and work hard to become valuable and needed.

HADGE AND KIT, sadly, did not stay with us very long. When he was good, he was very, very good—but when he was bad, he'd disappear for days and get horribly drunk. Mum and Pop had to let them go. This was difficult for my mother, since she had spent a great deal of her young life in Hadge's company.

Not long after they moved out, the idea arose of my aunt taking over the garages at the back of the house for her dancing school. She and Uncle Bill moved into the bungalow—or "the bung," as we fondly called it. Auntie christened it "Twigs," and Uncle fashioned the name from branches found in the garden and put it up over the door. The little place didn't even have a foundation, being just a two-room pre-fab with a Calor gas stove for cooking. A mirror and ballet barre were installed in the big three-car garage. One single garage was converted into a waiting room, and the outside toilet serviced Auntie's students. Auntie began her classes.

She also made the little bungalow come to life, and planted flowerbeds along the outside walls. There were prettily arranged flowers inside, too, and she filled vases for our house as well. When Mum and Pop were away, Auntie and Uncle Bill kept an eye on me and Donald and Chris. Best of all, there was music and dance around The Meuse all day long.

For a while, my mother played the piano for the dance school, and the music would echo across the garden, accompanied by the sounds of Auntie teaching, her hands clapping, keeping time. From our upstairs bathroom window, I would look down into the courtyard and see heads bobbing in the studio and listen to Auntie's trilling laugh, or hear her chattering with the mothers as she sorted change for their payments. Though a good deal of merriment floated up from outside, often the main house inside would be quiet, empty, and dark.

Auntie offered everything from children's classes to character and ballroom dancing, and she was a good teacher, evidenced by the endless parade of cars, bicycles, and people walking up and down the driveway.

I especially loved watching the toddlers, skipping around pretending to be fairies, running and flying. Aunt was so gentle with them, helping to strengthen and shape their little bodies and feet. If I wasn't studying or working, I would go across to the studio and either join in the older children's classes, or watch. Aunt would give me private ballet lessons whenever she could. She had some terrific ballroom students who were eight to ten years older than I, and they eventually became what we called "the gang." Special friends included Keith Oldham, a handsome fellow who had a glass eye. He had a sweet girlfriend, Margaret, whom he eventually married. There was Ted Owen—a skinny fellow nicknamed "Tappets," because he was always having trouble with the tappets on his motorbike.

When the evening classes were over, they often headed for Auntie's bungalow. The little potbellied fire would be stoked. There'd be some ale or cups of tea and biscuits, and everybody would smoke and play canasta. It was a pleasure to cross from our big empty house to the toasty little bungalow and to just sit and enjoy the company. Eventually I learned the card games, too, and got to be pretty good at them.

Uncle Bill came into his own at these times. By day, he was a civil servant, working at the Milk Marketing Board, but in the evenings he loved to socialize. He also loved to gamble, and was especially fond of the horse races. From time to time he would take me with him to local Sandown Park, and this I simply adored. Uncle Bill taught me how to spot a good-looking horse and which one might just win. He'd go to the tote booth and lay down bets for us both. We always sat in the cheapest seats or stood at the rails, and it was thrilling to see the horses come thundering round the bend, heading for the finish line. I became familiar with all the jockeys' names and eventually became rather good at picking a winner.

I had seen the film *My Friend Flicka*, the story of a boy and a beautiful horse, at our local cinema, and had fallen madly in love with the film's star, Roddy McDowall. The character he played in the story, Ken McLaughlin, lived on the huge Goose Bar Ranch. I was so obsessed with the film that I fantasized I was married to Ken and that we owned many properties, many horses. After a day at the races with Uncle Bill, I would keep the race card and laboriously copy into a ledger all the horses' names, their dams, sires, and pedigree details. My "Goose Bar Ranch" was very real to me, and I thought of little else for a while. I made property deeds, sealed them with wax, and tied them with red string. They would state "This is to certify that Mr. and Mrs. Ken McLaughlin own the [name of ranch] and other parts of the United States and Canada." I even kept a "stable" of Hadge's old beanpoles in the garden. I'd attach a string at one end for reins and gallop the length of the property. In my imagination, these were the shiniest, healthiest horses in the world.

My mother seemed to be experiencing a new feeling of well-being: she'd settled into her dream house, she'd had the two sons that Pop wanted, their vaudeville act was doing reasonably well. Pop had become a member of one of the local golf clubs, where he did a lot of networking and socializing. He was a left-handed scratch player, and very good—my mother often said that she was a golfing widow. I think my stepfather's greatest dream was to win the British Amateur Golfing Championship. Sadly, he never did.

For the first time in my memory, Mum began to practice the piano again, the way she used to when she was a young classical pianist.

I remember being awed by the lovely music that emanated from our big living room. I would creep in to sit in a dark corner and watch my mother at the other end of the room, bent over the piano keys, completely absorbed in her scales or beautiful pieces of Chopin or Rachmaninoff or de Falla. She would lean into the instrument, or rock back with her face toward the ceiling, her eyes closed. This was clearly a source of great joy for her, and I rejoiced, too.

That first year at The Meuse felt like we'd really stepped up in the world. So many sweet things come to mind. Little Chris, cycling around on his tricycle, trying so hard to learn to whistle. He couldn't say the words "Uncle Bill," and referred to him as "Dingle Bell"—a name we all adopted, eventually shortening it to "Dingle" and then "Ding."

Great-Aunt Mina came to work for Mummy, helping to clean the house and keep us all tidy. She was a wonderful character, large and ruddy-faced. She would climb the stepladder to wipe an overhead lamp and declare "*Bar*-bur-a! The dust on this lamp is *ow-dacious!*" Or, answering the phone for my mother, she would clutch it in one hand and yell up the stairs, "*Bar*-bur-a! Missus So-and-So's on the phone for you . . . You're not in? Right, I'll tell her!"

Dad would come over to The Meuse some weekends, bicycling all the way from Chessington. I would accompany him back, riding my own bike. Pedaling my way up Esher Hill, my legs would ache horribly. Dad would give me a great shove, his hand in the small of my back, and I would shoot ahead of him, only to stall a few rotations later as the ascent got the better of me. We would always stop at a pub along the way for lemonade and crisps. I do not know how Dad managed his travels without a car.

Our local cinema showed Astaire-Rogers movies from time to time. Whenever one was playing, Aunt would arrange for us to see it together. I think she lived vicariously through the famous couple. We would have such fun—Aunt rhapsodizing aloud throughout the movie at Ginger's loveliness and her gowns, and Fred's brilliant work. I was equally impressed, though more silent, munching on my Mars bars. Aunt would note down every dance step she could, trying them out by cavorting on the sidewalk all the way home, and incorporating them into her own choreographic works as quickly as possible.

Through sheer hard work and all of us pulling together, it seemed that life was finally going to be okay. The divorce had been painful, Mum's guilt had been tremendous, and the poverty had been oppressive, but, gradually, she and Pop were building a better name and a better life for themselves. In retrospect, it was actually the pinnacle of Mum's and Pop's success and happiness. Alas, everything went downhill from there.

ELEVEN

J UST BEFORE MOVING to The Old Meuse, I did my first radio
broadcast for the BBC, at a place called the Aeolian Hall in Bond
Street, in London. My parents were performing on the show. I do not
know why I was asked to perform as well, but I sang the "Polonaise"
from Ambroise Thomas's opera *Mignon*. In rehearsal, the engineers
kept asking me to back off from the microphone because my voice was
blasting their sound system, but the broadcast went well, and may have
contributed to what happened next.

Not long after, my stepfather brought home a famous producer, the
managing director of the Moss Empires circuit, named Val Parnell. Pop
had met him at the golf club, and being the good salesman that he was,
he'd persuaded Mr. Parnell to come and hear his "extraordinary little
stepdaughter with the phenomenal voice." I remember being sum-
moned in from the garden and asked to sing for this impressive gentleman. My mother accompanied me on the piano.

The next thing I knew, I was invited to take part in Mr. Parnell's new
musical revue in London called *Starlight Roof*. The production was to be
staged at the London Hippodrome, which was at the corner of Leicester
Square and Charing Cross Road. I was given a contract for one year,
pending the show's success.

Mum and Pop had been professionally represented by the agency of
Lew and Leslie Grade (Lew later became Sir Lew, and then Lord Grade,
of television and film production fame). But at this time, an American
by the name of Charles L. Tucker became their agent, and subsequently

mine. Charles was from Hartford, Connecticut. He was a comfortably large, elegantly dressed man with a cheerful, moon-shaped face, gray, curly hair, and a wonderful chuckle. He had been a vaudeville violinist in the States, but had moved to London and become a talent agent, and he represented some fairly high-end clients.

AS THE NAME suggests, *Starlight Roof* was glamorous—a series of assorted theatrical entertainments strung together: sketches, songs, dance, comedy. The show was a perfect night out. It was light, witty, elegant to look at, and featured several big production numbers. There were two performances a night—one at 6:00 and one at 8:35.

The all-star cast included Vic Oliver, a stylish musician and comedian who played the violin and conducted the orchestra occasionally; Pat Kirkwood, one of the reigning glamour ladies of the day; the comedians Fred Emney and Wally Boag; a beautiful ballerina by the name of Marilyn Hightower; and a young newcomer, Michael Bentine. The show was staged by Robert Nesbitt, a dignified gentleman with dark, brilliantined hair. He had a fine reputation for bringing class and distinction to his productions, and his mere presence commanded everyone's attention.

During rehearsals, I would sit in the theater and watch the lighting being designed and the numbers being rehearsed. I saw truly talented people doing their stuff, and it was a big learning curve for me. It was my first taste of real glamour—of the art and magic of professional stagecraft.

Originally, I was to sing Weber's "The Skater's Waltz," a fairly innocuous song, not particularly difficult. I appeared in the show as if I were a member of the audience.

Wally Boag was a loose-limbed, adorable American who told stories and did silly dances, flinging his amazingly double-jointed legs out to the side and twisting them in all directions while at the same time making extraordinary balloon animals. By the end of his act, he'd created a giraffe, an elephant, and several dogs and make-believe creatures. Vic Oliver would come onstage and suggest that Wally give them away to the patrons in the theater.

Wally asked, "Who'd like one of these?" and as people came forward, I would run down from the back of the stalls, having been waiting behind an exit curtain, saying, "*I'd* like one, please!"

My costume was a pale blue, pleated smock made of silk, with a line of white rickrack at my bosom, such as it was. Over it was a simple blue coat with patch pockets on the front. On my feet I wore socks with ballet slippers—odd things to be wearing, considering I was supposed to be a member of the public.

Wally and Vic Oliver deliberately left me until last. As I was given my balloon, Mr. Oliver would say, "How old are you?"

"I'm twelve," I'd reply. "How old are you?"

"I think *I'd* better ask the questions!" he'd respond, after the chuckles subsided. "Apart from going to school, what do you do?"

"I sing!"

"Would you care to sing for us tonight?"

"Oh, yes!"

"What would you like to sing?"

"I'd like to sing 'The Skater's Waltz.'"

"Oh, lovely!" he'd say with a twinkle. "Just the kind of junk I like!" And he'd conduct the orchestra for me.

There was a fair-sized orchestra in the pit, but there was also another onstage called George Melachrino's Starlight Orchestra. This consisted of mostly stringed instruments, and the musicians were very good and elegantly dressed in white dinner jackets. Vic Oliver loved to conduct; in fact, after *Starlight Roof* ended, he traveled around England conducting with various symphony orchestras.

Literally the day before our opening night, the producers decided that I appeared too innocent, too young to be in a sophisticated revue. My being in the show was coming across as unnecessary and perhaps even inappropriate. I was to be let go. Mum, Pop, and Charles Tucker descended upon poor Val Parnell and his assistant Cissy Williams. I remember hanging back and waiting while they had a long, heated conference.

"You cannot do this to a young child!" they protested. "First of all, it's her big break; secondly, she'll be heartbroken. Third, we can make what she does even better."

Mum and Pop asked me to sing the "Polonaise" from *Mignon,* which I did. The "Polonaise" is a hundred times more difficult than "The Skater's Waltz"—it's a real coloratura tour de force, finishing with a high F above top C. Originally written in French, the English translation is silly beyond belief, but I belted it out, leaping octaves and ripping off cadenzas and changes of key with bravura and dash. When I finished, there was a momentary pause—then, to everyone's delight, I was reinstated in the show.

OPENING NIGHT WAS October 23, 1947. Mum escorted me up to London on the train. As we walked from the station to the theater, we saw an English flower seller tucked into a convenient corner of Leicester Square, with her baskets and flowers spread around her.

"I'll buy you some flowers for luck," said my mother.

"What does she need luck for, dearie?" the flower seller queried, in a strong Cockney accent.

"Well, do you see that name on the bottom of the poster there?" Mum pointed at it. "That's my daughter, and she's going to be opening tonight, singing in the show."

"Then you ain't buyin' these," said the lady, handing me a beautiful fresh bunch of violets. "I'm givin' them to 'er for good luck."

Later that evening, when my big moment came, I ran fearlessly down the theater aisle. I went up onstage, sang the "Polonaise" from *Mignon*, and at the end I hit that high F above top C. There was a hush—and then the audience went absolutely wild. People rose to their feet and would not stop clapping. My song literally stopped the show. The aria was so difficult, and I was barely twelve years old, a sprite of a thing, really, with this freakish voice, and it caused a sensation. It was the first of three major stepping-stones in my career.

The press followed us home that night. They took photographs of me posed on the bed with my teddy bear, and bombarded me with questions.

The next morning, *Starlight Roof* received very good notices, and I was treated exceedingly well. "Prodigy with Pigtails!" and "Pocket-money Star Stops the Show!" the reviews said.

Needless to say, the flower seller's gift was indeed a lucky one, and violets took on a new meaning for me in the years that followed.

TWELVE

W<small>E PLAYED TWO</small> performances every night but Sunday, with no matinees, for a total of twelve shows a week. It quickly became obvious that I could not attend school regularly, so a tutor was hired for me. The London County Council, which protected children in the theater up to the age of fifteen, insisted that I have a chaperone to and from the theater, as well as a private dressing room. I was also not allowed to take a final curtain call with the company, since the law stated I could not appear on stage after 10 P.M. Historically, children in the theater had been treated appallingly—so the government had strict rules under the Child Labor Law.

My first tutor was a young, pretty, ineffectual woman, whose name I don't recall. I walked all over her, claiming that I was far too busy to do homework. Within two months she was gone, and a new tutor, much older, by the name of Miss Gladys Knight was hired—and she brooked no excuses. She was a disciplinarian, a darling, and a good teacher. We worked together for four hours every day, and I finally began to get the education I should have had all along.

It became increasingly difficult for Mum to travel up to London with me every evening, so sometimes Uncle Bill came with me, sometimes Aunt Joan, and then eventually, as the year continued, a lady called Mickey Smith was engaged to become my chaperone.

"Auntie Mickey," as I called her, was a genteel spinster. Her sister was nanny to Lord and Lady Rupert Nevill's children, which Mickey flaunted, albeit discreetly. She was a plain woman, who had a large gap between her teeth, and blinked a lot behind her thick spectacles—but she knew a great deal about being appropriate.

She said, "Julie, your nails are appalling. I shall give you a manicure, but I want you to scrub them completely clean before I start to file them." I returned to the sink several times before she was satisfied.

It seems I was belting out my aria twice nightly with dirt under my fingernails, holes in my socks, and looking scruffy beyond words. So between shows, after my homework was completed, she would push back my cuticles and polish my nails or give me a pedicure. My hair was brushed and braided, my outfit pressed and kept clean, and in general I looked a lot better. I was grateful for the attention.

Auntie Mickey lived in Surbiton, three stops before Walton on the railway line. At the end of each evening, we'd get on the train together in London and she would get off first at her station and I would go on alone to mine. My family would pick me up from there, or I would walk home.

I began to rate myself in terms of how well I sang each night. I kept a little book, writing "X" for excellent or "Fairly Good" or "TERRIBLE." Because I had to manage that F above top C twice a night, I developed an excruciating habit of testing and re-testing the high note to make sure it was always there. I must have driven everyone crazy, because eventually a complaint was made to the stage manager. But I needed to ensure that my voice was lodged and secure, particularly if I wasn't feeling very strong.

There were nights when my voice did *not* hold up, of course. It didn't happen often, but occasionally I swallowed or gargled my top note from either sheer fatigue or stress. Truthfully, I think that performing an aria twice a night for a year was more than any twelve-year-old should have been doing. I had the facility, but there were nights in the smoke-filled theater (and *everybody* smoked in those days) when my vocal cords dried up and the famous top F didn't come out as well as it should have. On other nights, it was as easy as could be.

I had at least two hours between my appearances, since I was in the first half of the show and then had to wait through the second half plus the interval between the shows. After I'd done my homework, my chaperone and I would sometimes go out into Leicester Square for a meal—usually to a chain restaurant such as Quality Inn or Forte's. Leicester

Square was gaudy, pungent with smells and bright with neon, but it was always a treat for me.

Uncle Bill—"Dingle"—was my favorite chaperone, because he would often take me to a movie between shows. There was a cinema in nearby Charing Cross Road that just showed cartoons, and I had the best time watching an hour of Mickey Mouse, Bugs Bunny, and all the great animated funnies from America. After this happy distraction, we'd go back to the theater, I'd sing my song again, and be taken home.

When my parents escorted me up to London, they would go to the Backstage Club between shows, a theatrical hangout where they could drink and socialize. Because I was underage, I wasn't allowed in the club, so I would have to stay in the hall—where I could smell and see the bar and hear the clink of glasses.

The Backstage Club had one of those wonderful cage elevators, which was operated by a lever. One had to anticipate exactly when the elevator would align with the floor of one's choice. The porter, an old man in a shabby uniform, befriended me and would let me try operating the lift, and I became pretty good at conveying customers up and down.

Driving home with my parents at night, I would notice elegant women standing in doorways or walking the streets of Mayfair. On foggy nights when London was blanketed by a pea souper, these mystery ladies would lurk on corners or stand near the curb.

"Those are prostitutes," Mum would explain.

When I grasped what they were all about, I asked, "But where do they go? Where do they live?"

"They probably have little apartments somewhere, or they get taken into the hotels," Mum replied. The area was pretty notorious—Shepherd's Market and Park Lane especially. The ladies struck me as being sad, somewhat mysterious, and no end intriguing.

DURING THE YEAR I was in the show, I developed the most intense crush on our headliner, Vic Oliver. In truth, he was probably older than he looked—with a balding patch in his hair—but he seemed totally suave, wore an immaculate white evening jacket, and to me, seemed the epitome of class and style. He was married to Winston Churchill's daughter, Sarah, and appeared to travel in upper-class circles—always going to supper after the show accompanied by a group of friends. I found myself fantasizing about him and became a terrible groupie, hanging around the stage door for the chance to say good night to him. I didn't know Pat Kirkwood very well, but I did get to know her understudy, Jeannie Carson. Jeannie was a member of the chorus, and was pretty and petite. She took over from Pat several times and was much loved by the company. I later worked with her again, and eventually she made quite a name for herself in English musical theater.

And there was Michael Bentine. Michael was attractive and brilliant, a young comedian with a shock of black hair and an enormous toothy smile. He had two appearances in the show, both times playing a frenetic, dedicated salesman. In the first segment, he attempted to convince the audience to purchase a toilet plunger by showing its many possible uses: a peg leg, a hat, or the electrical conduit from a tram to its wire. Later in the show he came back on with the upper half of a chair, extolling the many functions of its lattice woodwork.

While performing in *Starlight Roof,* Michael met and wooed a beautiful young ballerina in the chorus, Clementina, who was Marilyn Hightower's understudy. Later, Michael and Clementina married, and I became godmother to one of their sons, Richard. Michael went on to have a wonderful career uniting with Spike Milligan, Harry Secombe, and Peter Sellers as founding members of The Goons, brilliant performers who were the precursors of the Monty Python gang. Michael was eccentric, energetic, and enthusiastic. One could not help loving him, and he became a lifelong friend.

DURING THE EARLY part of our run, a recording company expressed some interest in me, and I made several 78 acetate discs. I did the "Polonaise," of course; the love song from *Romeo and Juliet;* another song called "The Wren"; and with Pop, I recorded "Come to the Fair." One song, based on the Theme and Variations by Mozart with the title *"Ah! Vous Dirai-je Maman,"* had the most incredibly difficult coloratura passages and long cadenzas.

I was also invited to do a screen test for Joe Pasternak, a big film producer from the U.S. who had made all the films starring Deanna Durbin. Deanna was a popular young soprano in Hollywood, and I was often compared to her.

The screen test took place at MGM Studios in Elstree. A lot of still photographs were taken, but it soon became apparent that they needed to gussy me up a bit because I was so exceedingly plain. The hair department curled my hair into ringlets and I ended up looking like a ghastly version of Shirley Temple. We pressed on.

For the screen test itself I sang a song, then I talked to Mr. Pasternak on camera, and finally I performed a little scene. The storyline was that I was being tucked into bed by my mother, and we discussed the fact that my father had disappeared and not been home for years and years. (This made me tear up, which was embarrassing.) As I was lying in the bed, almost asleep, the door opened, a man entered, and I sat up with arms outstretched and cried, "Daddy!"

Suffice it to say that the end result was so bad that had it ever emerged, I might never have worked again. The final determination was "She's not photogenic enough for film," and that was the end of that.

SUBSEQUENT TO THE screen test fiasco, my mother decided I had better get some acting lessons, and for a while the local drama teacher came over to The Meuse to tutor me. I remember working on the death scene from Shakespeare's *Romeo and Juliet*.

"Nurse? What should she do here?" I'd emote. "My dismal scene I needs must act alone. *Come*, vial!"

I was absolutely *awful*—nothing was thought out, there was nothing behind my eyes. I could actually see this poor lady gritting her teeth at the amateur theatricality of it all. Not that she was much help; she gave me no technique to work it through, simply, "Move here, do this, now say it for real." It seemed another hopeless enterprise.

Mum also signed me up for piano lessons again, this time with an ex-pupil of hers who lived in the village.

Although the lady was adept at teaching the scales—the sharps, the flats, the fingering—the ironic problem was that I had such a good ear. I would pick up every piano piece too quickly and then not follow through on the actual reading of the music. I raced ahead of myself, learning everything by heart. I'm ashamed to say that to this day I do not read music well.

I must have played well enough, since I was entered for an early grade exam. I was certain I would fail because of my inability to read music, but I performed my Clementi pieces with great flourish, and the examiner seemed fairly impressed. To my total surprise, I won the top grade for that exam in the whole of Surrey. I was astounded—somehow I got a "highly commended," and I received a book based on the life of Schubert as a prize from the county.

Of course my mother was pleased, but I remember ruefully thinking, "I *still* can't read music."

THIRTEEN

URING THE RUN of *Starlight Roof*, Aunt Joan became pregnant. Being a dancer, she had always had a lovely slim figure. Throughout her pregnancy, she remained trim, dressed prettily, and looked adorable.

I sensed that she wasn't thrilled about being pregnant; but she may just have been extremely nervous. She continued to teach throughout her term.

Geoffrey Wilby was born on April 21, 1948. It was a traumatic and difficult delivery, and tragically, the little boy's head was badly damaged by forceps. He died eight days later.

Our household went very quiet for a while. Auntie came home, distraught. My mother took care of her, and my brothers and I kept a respectful distance. Aunt went into a real decline, and it certainly didn't help her marriage to Uncle Bill. I don't believe Auntie ever tried to become pregnant again, and I know that many years later she still mourned the loss of her son.

My mother made a callous remark to me at one point, which was indicative of the love-hate relationship between the two sisters.

"Joan should never have had a child anyway," she said. "She doesn't have the hips for it."

BECAUSE OF THE County Council laws, I was only allowed to perform in *Starlight Roof* for one year, and that year flew by. On the day of my last performance, I was so choked with sadness, I could barely sing.

The company gathered at the side of the stage and applauded and cheered, and as I made my way back through the audience and went round backstage, they called words of encouragement.

"Well done, Julie!"

"We'll miss you!"

I remember rushing past them in floods of tears and sobbing my heart out in my dressing room. I honestly thought that was the end of my career, the end of all the fun, and that I would never work again. I recognized, quite sensibly, that I might just be a flash in the pan. I'd sung the great song that I could sing; I'd done what I was asked to do. What on earth would there be out there for me ever again? I really thought, "That's it. Now I have to get on with life and be just an ordinary girl."

MY MOTHER FORBADE me to open any of my fan mail. While I was in the show, the stage doorman would give me a package of whatever letters came for me, and I would take them home to her. Mum worried that disturbed people might write to me and say inappropriate things. She also wouldn't ever let me talk about my salary, saying, "One does not talk about how much money one earns, nor does one *ever* ask other people." I was simply told that money was being put into an account for me, though I'm pretty sure that it was also being used to help with the family expenses. I got a weekly allowance of two shillings and sixpence, and once I really started working continuously, it was raised to one pound.

A week or two after the show ended, I said to my mother, "Oh, Mum, here's some mail that I forgot to give you—and a telegram."

My mother opened it. "Oh my God!" she said, and clutched her chest.

It was an invitation—a command—to appear at the Royal Variety Show that year. It had been in my pocket for two weeks, and the deadline for answering was literally the next day.

This "Royal Command Performance" (as it is formally known) is a one-night, annual show that draws on the best talent in Britain and raises huge sums for charity. The Royal Family always attends, and it is a grand and glorious evening for all concerned, including the Royals. Danny Kaye was to top the bill, since he was performing at the London Palladium that year. I was to sing the "Polonaise," with Melachrino's

Starlight Orchestra, and to my delight, I was asked to lead the entire company in "God Save the King" at the finale.

FOR THE REHEARSAL the day before, the only outfit I had that was clean and halfway decent was a blouse, jacket, and my riding jodhpurs.

I was asked to sit on Danny Kaye's lap for publicity pictures. There I was in this odd attire, and while the flashbulbs popped, Danny Kaye said, "What are you going to be singing?"

"Oh, I don't suppose you'd know it," I replied modestly. "It's an aria, the 'Polonaise' from *Mignon*."

"Oh, you mean the one that goes like this?" He hummed it perfectly.

His Majesty, King George VI, was ill at the time of this command performance, so Queen Elizabeth attended without him. The young Princess Elizabeth and her soon-to-be husband, Prince Philip, were also in the royal box.

I treasure a photograph of that night, taken from the side of the theater. I am standing on the stage and the Queen, Princess Elizabeth, and Prince Philip are watching along with the audience. A sign to the right of the proscenium shows that I was ninth on the program. A press photographer sent it to me, and for years, it was stashed away, forgotten and creased. When I rediscovered it, I had a new appreciation for its significance, and had it repaired. It now hangs in my office.

MY MOTHER LOVED to throw a good party. At least twice a year, Mum and Pop threw a huge bash at The Meuse, and throughout my teens these parties were undoubtedly the best in our little village.

The evenings began with Mum or Pop hosting at the bar. Once the guests had imbibed enough, the party moved into the big living room. The moment we all waited for was when Mum came in to play the piano. The carpet would have been rolled back, and she would gradually begin whipping up the intensity. I can still picture her, leaning into the piano, singing as well sometimes, her elbows wide for extra strength of sound, her skirt pulled above her knees. Her energy alone made the party shift gear and come alive. Those crimson stuccoed walls became sweaty, the dampness running down the stippled shiny paint. I remember the brown baseboards, the dark floors, the bright floral curtains at the leaded bay window, the dim light, the candles.

Auntie helped, too, pulling some of her pupils into the dance. We mostly wanted to jitterbug of course. Tappets was the best dancer, and as he got into the action, drops of perspiration would fly off him in all directions. Sue Barker and her parents attended, as did Trisha Waters, and anybody who was current in my parents' life theatrically. Uncle Bill was always gallant and would ask me for a dance.

Pop would eventually sing. Guests would sit on the floor around the room, and he would stand by the piano with Mum accompanying him. Sometimes he sang wonderfully, other times he'd been drinking—and since he didn't practice much, he was short of breath. Even then I'd think to myself, "What a waste of a good voice."

I was always asked to sing as well, though I never liked to do so. I didn't mind an audience in the theater, a distance away, behind spotlights, but with my friends being so close and looking into my face, I always felt shy and uncomfortable. I did it mostly for Gladys Barker, who was genuinely appreciative. I think she knew that it cost me a lot to do it with good grace.

Once the party settled in, and the diffident few had left, the fun really began. There were quiet lulls for eating, usually things like baked potatoes, maybe some stew. I remember pink blancmange and cups of tea. Mum would have a drink, usually scotch. People would chat and smoke, then it would start all over again.

Suddenly in the midst of it all, Mum, still playing the piano, would call out, "Julia! Go to bed!" as if she'd been remiss and I'd been naughty to take advantage by staying up so late. I would hang around as long as I could, and I doubt she really minded, but perhaps she thought it sounded appropriate to others.

The parties lasted well into the night. People crashed on couches, and later in the morning, amid the smell of beer and alcohol and cigarettes, there'd be bacon and eggs for the stragglers. The kitchen would be a complete mess, and the cleanup took forever.

My mother decided that my thirteenth birthday was a good excuse for a party. She was adept at running up simple dresses for me on her trusty sewing machine, usually strips of gathered material, hemmed in tiers for the skirt. They always looked pretty and were cheap to make. For this party, she made me an evening gown out of pink cotton, shirred at the bodice. She finished it the night before the party.

We had recently acquired a dog, a little corgi. His pedigree name was "Whisper of Whey," but Auntie, with her flair for naming everything, said, "Let's call him 'Hush.'" Unfortunately, Hush was teased a lot by my brothers, who were too young to know any better, and as a result he was rather manic and snapped at people.

The morning of the big party, Hush saw the dress hanging on the kitchen door, jumped up, grabbed the hem, and shredded it. I was devastated, but Mum, bless her, went back to her sewing machine and managed to fix it just in time.

"These things are sent to test us," she said, an expression she often used when life's little problems threatened to overwhelm.

Came the evening and my mother was tearing around downstairs making sure that everything was ready, and I was sitting at the dressing table in my room, carefully applying a little makeup, with my dress laid out on the bed.

I clearly remember thinking to myself, "At this moment, I am as free as I am ever going to be."

I knew somehow that I was still innocent, unfettered in any way. I was young enough that my parents were managing my career; I had no taxes to pay, no big responsibilities. I could see my mother's problems, I could see my stepfather's problems, I wasn't yet cluttered by the obligations of being a grown-up. I knew that boys and all the mess of being adult would soon attack me, and I felt quite distinctly that this was probably the last moment in my life that would be relatively unpressured.

Mum had dressed my hair, pulling it straight back with a ribbon in a ponytail—and I thought it looked a bit severe.

But as I came down the stairs, my mother glanced up and stopped whatever she was doing to stare at me for a moment.

"Well, Julia," she said. "You just might turn out to be quite pretty one day."

I said to her, "I feel that I'm wiser now than I ever will be when I'm older."

"And *that* is a very smart remark," she replied.

FOURTEEN

A FEW WEEKS after I finished performing in *Starlight Roof*, my parents received an offer for me to be in the pantomime of *Humpty Dumpty* at a theater called the London Casino, and to play the egg itself. Miracle of miracles—another job!

English pantomimes are seasonal Christmas extravaganzas—mostly for children, though adults join in the fun—and they are nearly always based on the great fairy tales: "Cinderella," "Red Riding Hood," "Aladdin," "Jack and the Beanstalk," "Mother Goose," "Dick Whittington." If a story is produced in London one year, it goes out to the provinces the next, probably with the same sets, which have been whittled down to accommodate the new venue.

Humpty Dumpty was written, produced, and directed by Emile Littler. Emile and Prince Littler were impresario brothers who became the most powerful figures in the West End and the provinces, with a virtual monopoly on producing musicals and pantomimes throughout the country. Prince was by far the better known, having become chairman of Moss Empires in 1947, which encompassed the biggest theater circuit in England. If one booked a Moss Empires tour, it was considered an "A" tour.

Pantomimes are not mimed shows, as the word might imply. Far from it. In my youth, pantomimes did not have songs written especially for them as they do now, although they were musical in content. Popular songs of the day were incorporated into the old stories, so the scripts often sounded quite ridiculous. The Prince might say to the Princess, for example, "Oh, dear Princess, I love you so much that . . . (key note on the piano) . . . I want to take you on a *slow boat to Chi-na* . . ."

The tradition of pantomime is that there is always a principal girl and a principal boy to play the serious leads. In those days, the principal boy was always played by a woman, and his/her costumes were always designed to show off his/her best features. In the case of *Humpty Dumpty*, our principal boy was Pat Kirkwood, who had great legs, and she played the role of "Prince Rupert, of Truly Rural."

The men had all the comedic roles. The mother, or the postmistress, for example, was played by a man in drag. There was always a comedy slapstick scene, usually a kitchen scene, with hilarious misunderstandings and pies flying in all directions, or a laundry washroom scene with suds everywhere. With plenty of glamorous production, there was usually a glorious ballet to close the first half, and of course a wedding or a happily ever after scene at the end.

Every comedian who worked in a "panto," whether playing a henchman or a silly farmer or whatever, would contribute his usual shtick to the show. Depending on what his forte was, his material was simply inserted into the script, so the whole story would come to a halt for a sketch or something as ridiculous as an army drill that was all messed up. Somehow the result was a wonderful, odd conglomeration: a hodgepodge of popular songs, comedy, craziness, and fun.

Vic Oliver played "King Yolk of Eggville" in *Humpty Dumpty*, and a wonderful comedian called Richard Hearne, popularly known as "Mr. Pastry"—an adorable, bumbling television character beloved by children—played "Agatha Applepip, the Postmistress of Moth-Hole Village."

REHEARSALS BEGAN AT the London Casino itself. At lunch break that first day, Charlie Tucker took my mother and me to an upscale restaurant called Isolabella, not far from the theater. It was a restaurant he often visited, and as a result we received the most immaculate service.

On subsequent days, however, I was not escorted. I traveled to London and went through the rehearsal process alone. I had been given pocket money to get something to eat for myself, so on the second or third day I brightly decided to go back to the Isolabella, which seemed safe.

When I asked for a table, the maitre d' looked me and up and down and said, "Are you alone?"

"Well, yes, I am. I was here the other day . . ."

He seated me reluctantly. I looked at the menu and suddenly realized how much everything cost. I ordered a very simple salad and sat there feeling painfully embarrassed. From then on I sat in the lobby of the theater at the lunch hour, eating sandwiches I brought from home.

Compared to the relative elegance of *Starlight Roof* (and even other pantomimes), *Humpty Dumpty* was an oddity. The cast included characters named Tiddley-Winks, Penelope the Horse, and . . . the Wuffempoof! The latter was a long, blue, feathered piece of material. Pantomimes feature a great deal of audience participation, and in this case the patrons were told that if they ever saw the Wuffem-poof, they should shout a warning. The Wuffem-poof would show up in any scene, working its way across the set or appearing over the proscenium on the wall behind someone's head. The audience, especially the children, would go crazy—yelling, "Look out, it's *behind* you!" (Most pantos feature similar games, and "It's behind you!" is a stock phrase associated with the genre to this day.)

My first entrance in the show was accompanied by great flashes of lightning and a blackout. The big, prop egg on the wall toppled backward and I, lying on my back in a second, cracked egg backstage, would be thrust upright and through a hidden door in the wall during the blackout to be revealed, sitting cross-legged and surprised, at the foot of it.

I was dressed as a boy, with shorts, suspenders, and a jacket. I don't remember much about my role, but at some point in the show I sang an obligatory song, "I Heard a Robin Singing," which had nothing whatsoever to do with the story. Fortunately, once again, I received a lovely ovation from the audience on opening night, and the following morning the headlines of one review stated: "Young Julie Andrews as usual stole the show."

I spent a good deal of time traveling back and forth to the theater. Oddly, I do not recall the presence of a regular chaperone, though there must have been one. I do remember sitting on the train all by myself, frequently with orange pancake makeup all over my legs. They were normally pale and skinny, and you could have bowled a hoop through them. My self-description at the time was "boss-eyed, buck-toothed, and bandy." It had been suggested that I paint my legs to give a healthier effect for the show. I would apply the color in the evening, and be so tired when I got home that I wouldn't bother to wash it off. If we had a matinee the next day, which we often did, it really didn't seem worth taking a bath to remove it, since it would be going on again so soon—so I'd go back up on the train with the makeup, rather streaky now, still on my legs! God knows what the state of my sheets was in those days, but I do remember getting some odd looks on the train.

At one point during the run of the show, I came down with the mumps. I kept telling my mother that my glands felt a bit swollen, but by the time I had been diagnosed, I was already past the infectious stage. Mum said, "Don't you dare tell *anyone* about this!"

CHRISTMAS THAT YEAR was memorable. Donald received a toy trumpet from Santa in his stocking. The blasts of sound began at about 5:30 A.M., and continued until breakfast, by which time the family was ready to throttle him. Mid-morning, after the main presents had been given, I innocently said, "I don't know why, but it just *doesn't* seem like Christmas this year." My mother gave me such a glare that I quickly shut up.

She had a tradition at Christmas that I continue to this day. Having two young sons who barely looked at one gift before pouncing on another, she wisely saved one small gift each for the evening. She called them "tree gifts," and each member of the family was given a little parcel which had been hidden in the branches of our Christmas tree. It was a great way to extend the festivities and to gather the family one last time. If we were lucky, there was a pleasant sense of unity. We had hot drinks and snacks by the fire, and were then bundled off to our respective beds, happy and content.

ONE EVENING, DURING a performance of *Humpty Dumpty*, I happened to notice three extremely rowdy teenage boys in the front row.

They were restless, nudging each other and roaring with laughter, having a terrific night out.

I remember thinking, "Ugh, *boys!*"

Later, as I was traveling home, the same lads suddenly appeared at the door of my train compartment.

"We just saw you in *Humpty Dumpty!*" one of them said.

I recognized them instantly.

"Oh, yes. I remember you sitting in the front row," I said, somewhat pointedly.

They were still giggling and being silly, and I couldn't wait to get rid of them—but to my surprise, they, too, got off at Walton-on-Thames station. As we clattered down the iron staircase, one of the boys said, "You live in Walton, too? Where do you live?"

Doing some quick thinking, I sagely replied, "Oh, the other side of the bridge," and left it at that. I dashed to Mum, waiting in the car, and thought, "Well, I've got rid of *them!*"

The next morning there was a knock at the door of The Meuse.

"There are two boys here. They want to talk to you," Mum said, intrigued.

Apparently the great adventure for the fellows had been to find all the Andrews families in the phone book that lived "on the other side of the bridge," and they'd worked out which house might be mine and then come to supposedly ask for my autograph.

They turned out to be a pair of robust, good-natured brothers, by the name of Tony and Richard Walton. Richard was the youngest; Tony was a year older than I.

My mother, who had been hovering, asked where they went to school.

Tony said, "I go to Radley College," which was a boarding school in Abingdon, Oxfordshire. Richard was preparing to enter Pangbourne Naval Academy. Both boys were home for the Christmas holidays.

A week later, my mother said to me, "You've received a charming letter from that boy who came to the door." It was eight pages, on very small note paper.

"*I am one of the boys who came and visited you last Sunday. (The fattest one, who was 14),*" Tony wrote. "*. . . It was grand fun coming to your house and talking to you, and I hope we did not keep you too long. I got your record on Monday, and I think it is 'jolly dee!' . . . I am trying to write a sort of children's book, it is all about a rabbit called Wiggin. I am doing it because I like drawing and painting . . .*" He included five or six pen-and-ink drawings of characters from the book, which were charming, and signed it "*Yours very thankfully, (i.e. Love from) Tony Walton,*" followed by a sweet caricature of Humpty Dumpty.

"This is enchanting," my mother said. "He's gone to so much trouble, I want you to answer it."

"Oh gosh, Mummy!" I replied, somewhat aghast. "He's just a *boy*. I don't want to answer that. I don't want to write to him. I don't *like* him . . ."

My mother insisted. "Julie, you *will* answer this. You should, and it'll be nice to have a friend."

I wasn't so sure, but with her help, I composed a reply and thus began a correspondence, which to my surprise quickly switched from being a chore to being a pleasure.

The next time Tony came home on holiday, he appeared at our front door again—and we began an easy and pleasant relationship. I could never have guessed the effect this young schoolboy was to have on my life.

"Would you like to come to tea at my house?" Tony asked one day. I was still painfully shy and somewhat loath to go, but I went.

Tony's mother and father were enchanting people. Dr. Lance Walton and his wife, Dawn, and family lived in a big residence called "Nethercliffe," a black and white, half-timbered Tudor-style house, with French windows at the back leading to a generous garden.

I met Tony's fun-loving older sister, Jennifer, who seemed really friendly, and his adorable younger sister, Carol. His dashing younger brother, Richard, whom I had already met, was also there. Mrs. Walton was exceedingly pretty and vivacious. She was a terrific hostess, the epitome of how you would imagine a doctor's wife to be. Dr. Walton was a craggy, handsome man, an orthopedic surgeon who worked extremely hard dividing his time between a Harley Street office in London and a private practice at his house.

They instantly welcomed me into the family. Everything about their home was gracious, warm, and lovely. There were fresh-cut flowers and bowls piled high with fruit. Candles and magazines were comfortably placed around the house; a cozy fire was in the grate. The best silver was laid out. A trolley was wheeled into the living room at tea-time, full of tempting goodies. Everything was soothing, pleasant, and spoke of a real home—quite a contrast to my own rather sad and disorganized one.

My mother, realizing that Tony was now a friend and a decent boy, encouraged me to go for walks with him. Tony would come up the drive promptly as my lessons with Miss Knight were ending for the day, pushing or riding his bike, and I would either take my own bike and join him, or we would walk together. Our route was always the same—the road up to the station, then across and down toward the Half-Way House (a local pub on our village green) and back up West Grove. These walks gave Tony and me wonderful opportunities to talk.

We chatted endlessly about what we both liked, how it was for him at school, what he did there. He was incredibly creative, designing school theater projects, and making and operating puppets for a production of *The Magic Flute,* which he also directed. I told him that I enjoyed writing stories in my spare time, and I came up with ideas for two tales about an orchestra—"Conceited Mister Concerto" and "Peter Piccolo's Great Idea." Tony offered to illustrate them. Letters went back and forth while he was at boarding school, with "Peter Piccolo" or "Mister Concerto" drawings arriving regularly in the post.

There came a day when Tony's parents asked if I would like to go with them to visit Tony at his college for the summer picnic, a special yearly event called "Gaudy." With some trepidation, I went. I wasn't sure how I should behave or whether I would seem appropriate.

My mother had some American friends, a pilot and his wife, who were stationed in England just after the war. Clothing and supplies were still extremely limited for us, so occasionally this husband and wife would give us secondhand items sent over from America, and we were always very grateful.

This particular year, they sent me three dresses, but they barely fit. I was beginning to grow in all directions, so they were rather tight. I chose to wear one, a taffeta plaid dress, with a little high collar, for the Radley picnic.

We took a tour of the school, which was magnificent, then sat on the lawn under a tree with Mum Walton presiding over our meal. There were delicious cucumber sandwiches, hard-boiled eggs, and the freshest tomatoes I'd ever tasted, plus cookies, cakes, and bananas. With the sun shining and a gentle breeze, that meal seemed like the best I'd ever had.

Everything was perfect, except for my taffeta dress. It was so tight under the armpits that it rubbed me raw, and I began to sweat. Being a hand-me-down, it was a little spoiled anyway, and by the end of the day, I smelled positively rank. Everyone else was relaxed and easy, having a great time. I was horribly aware of my state and acutely embarrassed all afternoon.

MY MOTHER WAS impressed by the Waltons. She envied Dawn, I believe. She once said how fortunate Dawn was to be placed on such a wonderful pedestal by her husband. Mum didn't begrudge Dawn anything, but she longed for that style of living. I suppose we both felt ourselves on a lower social level than this lovely family.

Occasionally, Dr. and Mrs. Walton took business trips to America, where Dawn could also take the sun for her arthritis. One year, they became aware that young Carol was really unhappy they were going away, so they simply packed her up and took her with them.

Each summer the entire family went for a wonderful vacation at a hotel just outside Bournemouth, on the South Coast. There was always an empty feeling while they were away and when I didn't see Tony.

At Christmastime, their house was decorated marvelously, and mistletoe was hung over the front door. I knew that Tony hoped to kiss me there, but I was too shy, and wanted nothing to do with it. I think he won out with a peck on my cheek.

AFTER THE WAR ended, it was a surprise for many when Winston Churchill, who had done so much to lead the country throughout World War II, was not reelected. The Labor Party gained power, and Clement Attlee became prime minister.

The National Health Service was created, and suddenly Dr. Walton had to change his life radically. From being a private doctor and surgeon, he was now obliged to donate half his time performing operations and giving consultations to those who couldn't afford private medicine.

Although he still had private patients, these new regulations probably halved Dr. Walton's income. He was very respected, both in Walton and in the London community of surgeons, and received a good salary for his private work.

Now expenses in the Walton household suddenly had to be reduced, and I sensed there was enormous panic on Dawn's part. I remember her cancelling all the magazine and newspaper subscriptions, saying, "We've got to cut down in every possible way we can."

A polio epidemic had been creeping steadily across both America and England. Dr. Walton was much impressed by the work of a nurse called Sister Kenny, who was a pioneer in the treatment of infantile paralysis, cerebral palsy, and polio in the United States. He became passionate about using her methods in England, reinvigorating tissue with fascia massage and heat, which helped bring circulation back to seemingly dead areas. I helped christen and open the home for polio patients that Dr. Walton founded, called "Silverwood." He really was a man ahead of his time.

FIFTEEN

Mᵁᴹ, ᴾᴼᴾ, ᴬᴺᴰ I spent the summer of 1949 working in Black-pool, the most popular resort on the northwest coast of England.

It wasn't a pretty town, but it boasted three long, fairly attractive piers—the South, Central, and North—and they each had a theater, which, during the season, was in full swing. There was a fair amount of rivalry between them, each vying with the others as to who could put on the best show. Their productions were equal to those in London in terms of scale, and to play a summer show at Blackpool was to be guaranteed a full three months of work.

Blackpool seemed to me an aptly named town. Trams ran all around the city. The beaches were packed with people. I remember being amazed by the men, workers and miners who would go down to the beach in their dark suits, to sit in deckchairs. Some would even keep their bowler hats on. Some rolled up their shirtsleeves and trousers and placed newspapers over their faces to protect them from the sun. Very few wore bathing trunks. The beaches were literally black with men in suits.

Blackpool was also famous for its "illuminations." North Country people referred to them as "the lights." These were enormous displays of lightbulb art, vast superstructures all along the seafront. Sometimes the bulbs would wink or appear to chase each other; other times they'd just be set pieces. There was also a huge Ferris wheel. It was all a part of the attraction of the holiday season, and people thronged into the town. There were bed-and-breakfast accommodations in every house along every side street.

Blackpool was a riot of neon—yet to me, it seemed a dark and disturbing place. The stench of fish and chips and ale and toilets along the beachfront, the seething mass of humanity that went from pier to pier, the trams that constantly rattled past provided a rather sordid setting for the events that followed.

MUM AND POP were second top of the bill in what promised to be a good show, starring the comedian Frankie Howerd on the Central Pier.

Frankie was a kind man who kept very much to himself. He seemed shy and, I thought, rather lonely. Onstage, though, he was outgoing and extremely funny. Untidily toupeed, tall, lumpily shaped, and shabby, he was full of bluster and spittle, his eyebrows raised in mock surprise and outrage as he related the trials and tribulations of his life. He would lower his voice conspiratorially to share some appalling confidence. Indicating his humorless female accompanist, he would say, "No, don't laugh. Poor dear, she's had everything removed." He sang "The Three Little Fishes," with explosive sounds, contorted facial expressions, and body movements each time he arrived at the refrain, "*Swim, swam, dittem, dat-tem, what-tem, CHU!*"

I was working in the center of Blackpool theater, at the Hippodrome, in a variety show much like *Starlight Roof,* called *Coconut Grove.* A comedy team, Jewel and Warriss, topped the bill, with Jeannie Carson (Pat Kirkwood's understudy from *Starlight Roof,* who had since come into her own) and Wally Boag. I was billed as "Julie Andrews—Melody of Youth." Once again, I came out of the audience to receive a balloon toy from Wally, and once again I sang an aria, twice nightly.

My parents rented a small row house in St. Anne's, which was a decent little suburb outside of town. Miss Knight came with us for the first few weeks, until the summer holidays began.

I didn't see much of my own show, because once I'd done my turn, a taxi would take me to the Central Pier, where my parents were performing. For the next hour or so I would either walk the pier with Donald and play the slot machines like the tourists, or watch Mum and Pop's show. The taxi would then take me back to the Hippodrome in time for my second appearance, after which it would take me home.

Mum and Pop's show ended much later than mine, so I would come home to a quiet house save for Miss Knight, who would usually have set out a salad for me to eat.

One night, just before she left, Miss Knight said, "Let's have scrambled eggs."

"I can't cook," I said. "I don't know how."

"When I'm gone, you'll need to know how to make yourself something," she replied. "I'll show you how to make a scrambled egg."

Every night from then on, I would come home and make myself a scrambled egg before putting myself to bed.

There were some nights when I went directly to the pier and waited for my parents and we'd all come home together, but Mum was fairly strict about my getting to bed early.

It was at this point that I really began to notice how much my stepfather was drinking.

As the summer progressed, it became increasingly difficult for me to watch their act, because by the second show Pop was very obviously drunk. I would sit in the audience agonizing as he began slurring and forgetting lyrics. My mother would try to push him through the songs with her accompaniment, and she would keep up a good face, but I was acutely embarrassed for them both. I couldn't believe Pop would behave like that onstage. I don't recall my stepfather drinking a great deal before Blackpool, but I may have been too busy to pick up on it.

He and my mother began to fight. I would hear them come home and soon there would be raised voices, then scuffles and thumps, followed by my stepfather slamming out of their bedroom and into the guest room.

I lay in bed, listening, worried about what might happen—what Pop might do to my mother. It seemed that she often baited him. She was no doubt angry at his being drunk onstage, but I sensed something else as well. Perhaps having had a father who beat her, there was a compulsion to recreate that. It seemed to me that it was almost a thrill for her to whip him up to the point where he might become violent. I got the impression that she would physically press herself on him and he would fling her off, and she would cry, "No, Ted, *NO!*" It appeared to be almost ritualistic.

Occasionally I would come out of my room to try and stop them—my room was next door to theirs on the same floor—and once in a while it worked, but a lot of the time I was too timid. I slept in only a vest and underpants and didn't have a dressing gown, so I felt insufficiently clad, cold with fear, and embarrassed to show myself in front of Pop. Don and Chris slept on the floor above ours. Once, Donald came downstairs because of the noise, but I scooped him up to block his view and took him away.

One particular night, there was a big fight and I heard my mother weeping. An enormous scuffle followed, then a terrible thud, and I knew she had fallen. My stepfather slammed into the guest bedroom, and I simply had to go and see if she was all right.

My mother was a basket case. I couldn't console her, and I didn't know what to do.

"I think you'd better call Auntie Joan," she said between sobs. "Ask her if she could get up here."

"I don't know Auntie's number," I stammered.

"Here it is." She scribbled on a piece of paper. "Go down to the phone in the front hall and dial."

Wearing only my undergarments, I crept down the four flights of stairs in the dark and groped my way along the hall to the lamp and the old-fashioned dial phone. When my aunt picked up the receiver, I burst into tears.

"Auntie! Mummy says can you come?"

While we were talking, I heard a door open. I became aware that someone had come out onto the upstairs landing and was listening to my conversation. To this day, it remains a mystery to me as to which of my parents it was. Pop would probably have been too drunk, and of course he could not have known that my mother had asked me to make the call. But it seemed odd that my distraught mother would come out and listen to what I was saying downstairs. If she was able to do so, why hadn't she made the call herself?

Auntie came as quickly as she could. I'm not sure if she came mostly for us children or for my mother, but the feeling of having someone else in the house created a degree of safety for me. It took the weight off somehow—I didn't feel quite as responsible for the boys, for the house, or for my mother's well-being.

Auntie stayed for the rest of the summer. Pop made some effort to pull himself together, and with Aunt in the house he did seem to calm down for a bit. I know he wasn't happy that she came, as she was always a thorn in his side. Whatever the case, the improvement was short-lived.

There was a publicity photo taken during this period of the family walking together along the front at Blackpool, looking very happy. These days, my brothers and I marvel at how far removed that photograph was from the reality of what was actually going on.

POP CONTINUED HIS descent into alcoholism fairly rapidly, going on ever-worsening benders. He would be filled with remorse afterward, and occasionally go away and "take the cure"—I never knew where. It was always a tremendous relief when he wasn't around. Then he would come home, and life would resume as before—tense and unpleasant. Sometimes he would be sober for six months or a year, but being a true alcoholic, he would eventually fall off the wagon again.

Mum would issue a warning that Pop was on a new rampage. There followed an agonizing wait for him to come home from the pub.

There was always this feeling of "When is he coming? When is he coming?" and "What will the damage be this time?"

Finally, he would stagger up the long drive and immediately go into the downstairs toilet to vomit. We could not use the toilet for the rest of the day, the stench was so overwhelming. Then he'd pass out and sleep it off.

At the beginning, Mum didn't go much to the pub, but eventually, I think because she couldn't stop him, she joined him. Ultimately, she, too, became an alcoholic. I always thought, in that somewhat clear way that children have, that she did it out of helpless rage. In retrospect, she probably always had a tendency to drink, inherited from her own father. Between the two of them, things got very difficult.

They continued to fight with each other, but he never threw her around again the way he did in Blackpool. What I sensed more than anything else was an estrangement; they ended up having separate rooms. Pop slept at one end of the house and Mum slept in the room next to me. Occasionally, Mum would follow Pop and bait him, and sometimes I would hear Pop going into Mum's room very late at night—so there was obviously some physical life between them once in a while—but mostly they were apart, which probably lessened the incidences of fighting.

I suspect the music hall booking agents became aware of Pop's drinking, because it wasn't long thereafter that he stopped being hired. He couldn't get work in the theater, so he became a cash register salesman.

DEPENDING ON MY schedule, Mum sometimes sent me off to visit Dad for a weekend. Chris was now three, and I had been looking after him since he was a baby, changing his nappies and tending to him. Even then I didn't feel he was getting the care he needed. But now I was caring for Donald as well, giving them both lunch, doing their ironing. More and more, it seemed, my mother wasn't around, and I was always anxious about leaving them.

(Later, I even ironed Pop's shirts for him. My mother gave up or was punishing him, I suppose. When he didn't have a shirt ready to wear for his job, he would ask me if I would be kind enough to press one for him. It was always painful for me. In spite of how I felt about him, it seemed sad that he had to ask the stepdaughter who he must have known had no respect for him to do his laundry.)

Often the boys ended up accompanying me to my dad's. When he came to pick me up, these two sad little fellows would be waving goodbye to us, and my father couldn't bear it. "Daddy Wells," as the boys called him, would say to my mother, "Can I take the boys as well?" This was always received with mixed emotions on my part, since I looked forward to having Dad all to myself.

The more Pop drank, the more abusive he became. Donald received his first caning when he was just six. Apparently a less-than-stellar report card from school was the cause, and Pop stepped in and had at him with a walking stick. After that, poor Donald seemed always to be in trouble, and was caned about three or four times a year. His transgressions became such that my mother despaired, and Pop would lead him away to the cold front living room with the awful pink stucco.

I would stand in the dark hallway and listen to the thwack of the stick or the strap, and the muffled sobs coming from the other side of the door. I would be rooted with terror, awed by the enormity of the sin being visited on a young, defenseless soul, wondering how he could bear it.

In later years, Donald confessed that it gave him a sort of fierce pleasure to have "got the old bugger so worked up." But the statement was belied by the pinch of his face, the guarded eyes, and above all, by his trembling lower lip.

I did nothing to stop the beatings, which lasted so long that I suspected Pop enjoyed it, or could not stop himself. When the door finally opened, Donald would emerge with red, swollen, tearstained cheeks, seemingly mortified that the family knew of his degradation, his spirit beaten into submission. Still I did nothing, for fear of taking sides, for fear that if I reached out, I might be the next recipient. My brain would turn on a dime and I would think, "Well, he *had* been naughty."

For a while Donald would really behave, until the rage in him built up once more and it happened all over again. His relationship with Pop grew progressively more explosive. He would accompany his father to the golf range to retrieve golf balls, and he claimed Pop would actually aim them in his direction, forcing the boy to dodge them and retrieve them at the same time. He finally lobbed all the golf balls over the garden wall into the greenhouse of the Belgrave Recovery Home, which resulted in yet another caning.

Donald later told me that at age sixteen, just before he departed from The Meuse to go into the Merchant Navy for two years, he went into Pop's bedroom, took out the canes that were kept in an overhead closet, and in front of his father, methodically broke every single one. Good for him!

Another dreadful day, little Chris accidentally soiled the toilet seat. Being only a toddler, he hadn't thought to clean it, and when Pop discovered it he rubbed Chris's nose in it to teach him a lesson.

Mum was appalled, but attempted to soften the impact by saying,

"You know, at times Pop can be a very kind man. He does have a tender side."

At the age of five or six, Don was enrolled in St. Martin's boarding school in Walton-on-Thames, not far from our house. It was difficult for him. The other children at school would say, "But you live just around the corner. Why are you *boarding*?" The justification was that our parents were away so much of the time, traveling and performing.

Chris started boarding school a year or two later, when he was just four. He was terribly homesick, and there was a lot of bed-wetting. It was heartbreaking. I don't know whose idea the boarding school was, or how Mum felt about sending Don and Chris away—whether or not she felt any guilt. Maybe she felt the boys would be safer. I vowed never to do that to my own children, and worried that I, too, might be sent off.

Auntie was busy teaching in her studio, making a living, so she was unable to help with the boys. "Dingle" had developed tuberculosis as a result of his incarceration during the war, and he was thin and weak. But Aunt did cook a roast or a stew for us all occasionally, which was wonderful. We would go over to the Bung and enjoy it, or she would bring it into our house. But, like the rest of us, she was scared of Pop, and disliked him intensely. She didn't really venture into Mum and Pop's life after that summer in Blackpool, although she was ever-present in mine, and in many ways a second mother to me.

I began to menstruate, and it happened at a time when Mum and Pop were away. I vaguely knew what was happening to me, and I went across to Aunt and said, "I may be wrong, but . . ."

"Oh, Julie!" she said. "You've become a woman."

I didn't feel much like a woman. Here I was, singing my big arias and pretending to be "the little girl with the phenomenal voice." To my shame, I still had to wear the smock dresses that kept my developing chest flat, and ankle socks with Mary Janes. There was not much grace to my growing up.

SIXTEEN

D AD AND WIN moved to a village on the Sussex/Surrey border called Ockley. Dad said Ockley had the ideal distribution of education: one school, two churches, and four pubs.

He and Win bought a semidetached cottage in a row of five, which had once been the gardeners' quarters of a huge estate. Although very modest, "Leith Vale" had a lovely view across the fields to the manor house.

Whenever Dad came to pick me up, he would say, "Shall we go home directly, or shall we take the pretty way?" If time permitted, we would drive together through the countryside, choosing all the little roads rather than the main one. We would pass through exquisite villages, and Dad would bring to my attention some feature of the land or explain its historic significance. He taught me to appreciate real English country hedges, and told me what trees and bushes they were made of. We would admire the lilac or mimosa, and the great clumps of rhododendrons.

One of our delights was to drive over Leith Hill, a beautiful spot below which Ockley lies. Tiny hamlets cling to the side of the hill and the trees on the crown grow in great arches over the narrow lanes. From the top, one can see the South Downs, and my father would point out Chanctonbury Ring—a perfect circle of trees on another hill in the distance, possibly once a Druid site. Dad showed me traces of the old Roman road running through the countryside, now mostly hidden. A tower had been built by an eccentric on top of Leith Hill, in order to bring the elevation up to exactly one thousand feet. To this day, Leith Hill becomes a sea of bluebells in the late spring, a shimmering haze in every direction.

If time allowed, we would stop for a pub lunch, probably a "ploughman's"—cheese and pickles and good bread—or a piece of pork pie and a glass of lemonade. Driving with Dad provided wonderful quality time for us both.

I remember my first stay in Ockley. I have never seen so many daffodils in my life—they were everywhere, in riotous display. Ockley was a hundred times more rural than Beckenham or Walton. There was a small, ancient church named Okewood, which was in a sylvan setting of exquisite beauty. On the way there, primroses were dotted in clumps beneath birch trees. Baby rabbits scampered and played. The church had been built as a token of gratitude by a man who had survived the attack of a wild boar. It stood on a slight rise; a tiny gate opening onto a pebble path led through the moss-covered headstones to the main porch. Dad loved to visit it, especially at Easter, for then the little chapel was filled with fresh flowers.

Leith Vale was surrounded by farms. Standon Farm, across the lane, had a bull, and Johnny made me weak with laughter when he bellowed from his bedroom window like a cow and received an answering call from the bull. He and I took a leisurely walk one late afternoon and were just turning for home when we spotted a large bird with a bullet head and an enormous wing span, flying very low along the lane toward us. It was the local barn owl. It did not see us until it was very close, at which point it veered off into a nearby tree. Johnny and I stood utterly still in silence, wondering what the owl would do next. After turning its head several times from side to side, it suddenly dropped from the tree in a straight dive. Its huge wings beat on the grass and it lifted off a moment later and flew right past us again, a tiny rodent in its beak. We rushed home to tell Dad about our wonderful adventure.

Wherever he lived, Dad's first priority was his garden, and I remember him sweating it out in Ockley, planting stands of runner beans and rows of potatoes, which were essential to the family. Dad would go out to the nearby ditches with a wheelbarrow and dig up huge, heavy clumps of leaf mold. He worked it into the garden soil, providing it with all the necessary nutrients.

Win would serve up great meals: fresh beans, potatoes, tomatoes, and peas, all from their little plot. My relationship with her in those days was a little strained. I suspect that it was a chore for her when I visited, but like any good stepparent, she understood and accepted the slight hostility coming from me. She knew that the most important thing for me was to spend time with my father.

One memorable night, Dad said, "There's something I want to share with you."

He had collected me from the theater and it was close to midnight as we drove up the moonlit lanes of Leith Hill. We came to an open patch with a five-barred gate and Dad parked the car and we got out.

"Now," he said. "Be *very* quiet."

I kept still and listened.

I became aware that all around us, in every direction, the nightingales were in full voice. Their singing echoed across the downs.

"Isn't that *lovely*, Chick?" he said.

It was an intimate moment between us, and I realized he was trying to give me an antidote to whatever else was going on in my life, to the dramas happening at Walton. As always, it was hard to return home after one of those visits.

MUM AND I didn't tour much with Pop after that fateful summer in Blackpool. From their original billing as "Ted and Barbara Andrews—with Julie (in small letters underneath)," it had now become "Julie Andrews—with Ted and Barbara." It must have rankled my stepfather and made him feel emasculated. In spite of his having originally been the one who encouraged me to sing, I suspect it hurt him to be displaced by a fourteen-year-old stepdaughter.

Mum and Pop had apparently bought The Meuse with every penny they had, and they were now in well over their heads. My mother's conversations about it were quite open, and in the back of my mind there was a constant anxiety that, unless I kept working, we would lose our home. In truth, we probably would have. It mattered desperately to me that we hold onto it—the thought of returning to some place like Mornington Crescent was unbearable. So when gigs came along, and Pop wasn't asked, Mum and I took whatever we could. In between, I continued my studies with Miss Knight.

The more Mum and I performed alone together, the more my act developed. With my mother accompanying, I would sing a few arias, then a ballad, then she would play a piano solo, and finally I would come back and do a big medley, followed by a farewell song. It was similar in structure to the show that she and Pop had performed for years.

Wherever we went, I was still made to do my singing practice every day. The grand piano would have been pushed to the bare back wall of the theater, tucked away in a corner of the stage, and my mother would insist that I sit at it and do my scales.

The big safety curtain was usually raised, exposing the empty auditorium, and there were always a few stagehands and ushers milling about. I was acutely conscious of them stopping to listen to me. I would pick out the notes, doing my five-nine-thirteen's, and feel embarrassed at having to do warm-ups in front of them.

We mostly traveled by train. I would stock up with every book or magazine I could get my hands on—*Girls' Crystal* and *The Girls' Own Paper*, books by Enid Blyton. Reading was my favorite pastime, but I was always amazed that for those several hours of travel, my mother would just sit and stare out of the window. She never read a newspaper or bought a book; she never amused herself in any way. I couldn't understand it. It wasn't until many years later that I realized she must have been using the journey to put her world in order again. She was so stressed, and with so much to think over and deal with, simply sitting and staring must have been a form of therapy for her. I doubt she even noticed the countryside.

A memorable journey was a trip to Aberdeen, Scotland, for a week. Mum and Pop had been rowing dreadfully, and she wept all the way north. I think she was suffering a mini-breakdown. She was worried about finances, the boys, her marriage. I remember trying to infuse her with my energy. I hugged her, tried to comfort her, and told her we were going to have a great week of peace and quiet.

". . . and I will help make it right and continue working," I said. "We *will* get through this."

Then and there, I committed myself wholeheartedly to assuming responsibility for the entire family. It seemed solely up to me now to hold us together, for there was no one else to do it.

There are, of course, funny memories, too, particularly of the characters we met and the acts that performed on the same bill with us. One was a North Country comedian called Albert Modley. He never played in the south of England, but was very popular in the north. He was a little fellow, deliciously cheeky and childlike. He would pretend to be a naughty schoolboy, and part of his act was to play with a set of drums. He simply toyed with them occasionally, absently thumping the bass drum or banging a cymbal. He would pretend to be a tram driver and whirl the cymbal arm, and the cymbal itself, round and round, pretending it was the lever that operated the tram.

Albert would jog along, commenting on the various people he pretended were aboard his vehicle. At one point, he would say with an impish smile, "We're going to *Duplicate!*"

"Duplicate" was the name written on the backup tram in places like Blackpool that picked up the leftover tourists who didn't make it onto the first tram. "We're going to Duplicate!" became a stock phrase in our house.

Once, we were on the bill with Albert, along with a bear act. Word went round that when the bears were performing, no one was to cross behind the backdrop, because the bears always turned and attacked whomever they sensed was behind them.

One night, after making me promise to stay safely in our dressing room, my mother headed off for her usual drink at the bar. She locked the door behind her, since the bears traveled along our corridor on their way to the stage. Suddenly I heard the doorknob rattling, and moaning coming from the other side. I was rigid with fear, until I realized it was just Albert teasing me and enjoying himself hugely.

Mum often came back from these trips to the bar fairly tipsy, and consequently the second performance never went as well as the first. She would dominate with her accompaniment, thumping away at the piano and pushing me on if I tried to do a beautiful rallentando or express myself in some way. I would introduce her solo in a gracious manner, and she would play something like "The Dream of Olwen"—a very corny piece with her famous double octaves added at the end, all of which she now fluffed dreadfully.

As I stood in the wings, waiting to return to the stage, I wished fervently that she would be more respectful of her craft and get back to being the beautiful pianist that she had once been, and could still be. She hardly practiced at all anymore. She must have been so overwhelmed and preoccupied. But I longed for her to be as disciplined as I was trying to be. I felt the act could have been so much better if only she had cared to try.

SEVENTEEN

I CONTINUED TO work with Madame Stiles-Allen. Early in my relationship with her, she decided to stop teaching in London and remain in Yorkshire, where her home was. Once she moved north permanently, it became obvious that if my voice was to continue to improve and I was to take my lessons seriously, the only thing I could do was to go up there to study with her. Sometimes it would be for a long weekend, sometimes a full week at a time.

She lived in a rambling, half-timbered farmhouse in a village called Headingly, just outside Leeds. "The Old Farm" had a giant kitchen that doubled as a dining room, with an Aga cooker and a large fireplace. The furniture was old but comfortable, with loose floral-patterned slipcovers on the sofas and chairs. There was an authentic spinning wheel in the big, main hallway, and its spools and treadle, evoking another era, fired my imagination. The halls were lit with gas lamps, their flames sputtering above the tiny gas jets.

A vast, upstairs music room contained bookcases piled high with books and files, her big, grand piano, and an old, hand-cranked phonograph on which we would listen to 78-rpm records of Caruso, Gigli, Galli-Curci, and Adelina Patti. The room wasn't used much, the main reason being the cost of heating in the bitterly cold, damp winters. There was a smaller teaching room right next to it, with an upright piano and an electric fire, and this was where Madame primarily worked with her students.

My mother would put me on the train, and Madame's husband, Sidney George Jeffries-Harris, simply known as Jeff, would pick me up at

Leeds and drive me out to Headingly. A dapper, retired army ma
a small military mustache, Jeff was as diminutive as Madame was la
Though he had served in India and had a sparkling but sardonic sense
of humor, one got the feeling that Madame undoubtedly ruled the
household. They had a teenage son, Michael, who was a few years older
than I.

Madame had a live-in housekeeper, a friend for many years, called
Jessie. Although slightly younger than Madame, she was equally large
and very robust, with a great sense of humor and a jolly spirit.

Lunch was the main event of the day. Michael would come home
from school, and we would all sit around the big square table in the old-
fashioned farmhouse kitchen and eat our fill. Jessie cooked enormous
meals: mutton stews with large boiled potatoes and peas and carrots.

Jeff brewed his own homemade ginger beer, which Madame adored.
It was potent, gaseous stuff, and whenever a bottle was opened, the cork
simply exploded out of it. Madame would drain her ginger beer from a
tall glass; then, taking the large damask napkin from her lap and putting
the corner of it up to her face, she would belch hugely—an enormous
"trombone slide" with an actual bass tone to it. She would flutter her
long eyelashes and smile sweetly.

"Ex*cuse* me!" she'd say demurely.

Sometimes I would sit in on other pupils' lessons. Madame thought
this important, and I did pick up a great deal, just watching and listening. Simply talking with Madame, I would discover that my voice had a
better pitch to it. Madame's voice was so warm and melodious—so
exquisitely placed—that I would find my own lifting in imitation.

She once described the joy of singing with a full orchestra: "As if one
is being carried aloft in the most wonderfully comfortable arm-chair." I
knew exactly what she meant.

During those lessons, Madame gave me a valuable piece of advice,
which has stayed with me over the years.

"Julie," she said. "Remember: the amateur works until he can get it
right. The professional works until he cannot go wrong."

In the evenings, we'd retire to her small study where there was a fire.
She would sit in an armchair on one side of it and Jeff would occupy the

chair on the other side, puffing on his pipe and reading. Sometimes Jessie would come in and join us. Madame did exquisite embroidery, which she said helped her to relax. She bought me silk threads and an embroidery frame, put some handkerchief material over it, and taught me to do some basic stitches, which I truly enjoyed. As we embroidered together, we would all listen to the radio or sit and talk.

Quite often, during those evenings, she would counsel me, "When you get older, darling, buy property. You will never lose on property. You can always trade up, and it will always be something to fall back on. It's a wonderful investment for your money." I have tried to follow her advice.

When the embers of the fire burned low, Madame and Jeff would go to their bedroom at one end of the house and I would head to mine, going down a long, drafty, gas-lit corridor, to a freezing cold room with a chamber pot under the bed. Once between the sheets, I never dared get out—not merely because of the icy temperature, but because I was convinced that the place was haunted. I would burrow down, hiding, almost suffocating myself. I didn't sleep much.

I WENT UP to Leeds fairly consistently during my teens. I would return home with my voice fresher and stronger, and my mother would immediately ask me to sing for her so that she could hear if I had improved.

Occasionally Madame would still come down to London, and I'd be able to pick up a quick lesson with her. Once, she stayed with us in Walton. She and my mother indulged in long discussions about spiritualism and particularly reincarnation. Madame believed in it wholeheartedly, and in fact, she felt sure that I was the reincarnation of the famous soprano Adelina Patti. My mother, who was superstitious, liked the thrill of believing reincarnation possible. I was completely spooked by their eerie conversations, and eventually chose not to listen to them, for my nights after that became fraught with the fear that ghosts were coming out of my closet or that someone who had "passed on" might be wishing to get in touch with me.

While she was with us, Madame attended a radio broadcast that I was doing. I sang the aria from *La Traviata* with the recitative *"Ah, fors'è lui,"* which leads to the very difficult *"Sempre Libera."* There is an à cappella cadenza before the main aria begins. My pitch was usually flawless, but because Madame was in the audience, I tried too hard to sing correctly for her, and I began listening to my own sound. The result was that when I finished the cadenza, I landed a halftone high. As the orchestra picked up the melody, I realized that I was sharp. My mother, who was also in the audience, berated me for making the mistake. I'm sure she wanted me to shine for Madame as much as I did. I was mortified that I had goofed, especially as this had been a live radio broadcast. I was as much my own critic as anyone else.

Madame rose to my defense.

"Be gentle with her, Barbara, she sang beautifully. She was trying so hard; you have to be a little kinder. She's only a young girl."

Later, Madame said to me, "Your mother was inappropriate with you. I thought you sang well."

I had never sung sharp before, but I learned to watch my pitch even more closely from then on. I was forever grateful to Madame for her kind words.

EIGHTEEN

SOMETIME THAT AUTUMN, my mother announced that she and I were going to a party at a friend's house in a town nearby. On the way there, in the car, she said, "Julie, I want you to do me a favor. If I ask you to sing, will you do it?" I remember being miffed, because my singing was always something my mother used, in a way. I reluctantly agreed.

The party was at a pleasant house, set on a hill in an upper-middle-class residential area. I sang one song, with Mum at the piano, and was relieved when it was over. Afterward, the owner of the house approached me. He was tall and fleshily handsome. I recognized him as a man who had come round to visit at The Meuse once or twice, in earlier years.

This evening he came and sat on the couch beside me and seemed genuinely interested, asking questions almost piercingly. In retrospect, I remember feeling an electricity between us that I couldn't explain.

As the party continued, my mother proceeded to get extremely drunk. When it came time to leave, she was clearly unable to drive. Though I was not yet licensed to operate a vehicle, I had been practicing with my dad in preparation for the test I would be eligible for the following year. After some confusion, my mother said, "*You* drive. I'll show you the way."

It was dark and foggy. We said good-bye to our hosts and I drove off, carefully concentrating with every fiber of my being on the road in front of me. I prayed that we wouldn't be stopped by the police.

"Did you like that family?" Mum asked after a while.

"Yes," I replied. "They seemed very nice."

"Did you wonder why I wanted you to sing?"

"No, it didn't cross my mind."

There was a pause. Then she said, "What did you think of the husband?"

"He . . . seemed pleasant," I answered, trying not to lose focus on the task at hand.

"Did you wonder why I took you there tonight?"

Suddenly I had the impression that something akin to a freight train was about to come at me. I had no idea what it was, but I had the distinct feeling that it was going to be unpleasant.

"Would you like me to tell you?" Mum's eyes were a little moist.

"It doesn't really matter, Mum, it's fine."

"Well, I'll tell you why," she said. "Because that man is your father."

My brain slammed into defense mode. My very first thought was of the man I had supposed was my father all these years. Words rushed to my mind's eye: "IT DOESN'T MATTER. IT DOESN'T MAKE ANY DIFFERENCE." Whether the man this evening was my actual father did not alter the fact that the man who had raised me was the man I *loved*. I would always consider him my father.

I tried to react carefully. Keeping my eyes on the road, I said something banal like "Oh, that's interesting. How do you know?"

"I *know*," she replied. "Can you imagine how long I've been waiting to tell you? Fourteen years . . ."

She explained that she had a one-time liaison with the man by a beautiful lake not far from Walton. She went on to say that it had been very hard to keep this secret for so long, and that she had no wish to hurt me, but the affair had been the result of an overwhelming attraction that she couldn't deny.

It seemed to matter very much that I stayed quiet and calm, because she had become tearful, overwhelmed perhaps at getting this out of her system.

As I pulled the car to a halt on the gravel in front of The Meuse, there was an empty silence between us. She seemed embarrassed now that she had told me, and went quickly up to her room, leaving me to think about it as I prepared for bed.

For the next couple of days, she kept her distance from me. She didn't say anything about the incident, and neither did I. I think I was afraid to. Eventually, however, I simply had to gain some clarity or go crazy.

"Mum?" I stood tentatively beside her at the kitchen stove. "You mentioned something in the car the other evening about that man at the party . . . Is it true what you said?"

"Yes," she replied.

"How do you *know*," I pressed, "since you were married to Dad at the time?" The question had been burning in my brain.

"Because Daddy and I weren't being romantic in those days," she said, after a moment.

I didn't know what to ask next. It may sound odd, but it was almost as if I had asked one question and that was enough—I didn't know where to go from there. I didn't think to ask her, "Does Daddy know?"

Finally I said, "Are you *sure*?"

"Yes," she answered. "Very sure."

And we left it at that.

SOMEHOW, I WAS able to push it away to a dark corner of my mind. Since I didn't know whether or not Dad knew, I assumed she must have slept with him afterward in order to say "I'm pregnant." I went into denial. I told myself that my mother had been drunk when she chose to tell the story. Maybe it wasn't even true.

Nearly forty years later, some time after my mother's death in the 1980s when I was making the film *Victor/Victoria*, I was chatting with Aunt Joan about the past, and suddenly the opportunity to broach the subject presented itself.

I asked if she remembered the certain gentleman who had come to visit once or twice in my youth.

"Why do you ask?" my aunt said, very sharply.

"Well . . . because Mum hinted a couple of times that *perhaps* he was my father."

There was a long silence. Aunt seemed to be weighing something in her mind. Then she murmured, "Yes. He was."

"But Auntie, how do you know?" I asked.

"Because I was around at the time," she replied, "and Mum spoke to me about it."

"What about Daddy?" I asked. "Did he know?"

"Yes. He did," she said.

And that simply knocked me sideways.

ACCORDING TO AUNTIE, my father was so in love with my mother, he decided it shouldn't make any difference. Two years later, Johnny was born—his legitimate son. Several years after that, my mother had the affair with Pop and became pregnant with Donald. The fact that Dad had offered to take me, and later Donald, under his wing to keep the marriage intact is extraordinary. If he knew about my heritage, he certainly never treated me any differently. I believe he loved me dearly. And because I did not know then that he knew, I didn't have the heart to ask him about it before he died. I thought I was protecting him from some deep hurt.

I also never asked Win, my stepmother. And I never mentioned it to any of my siblings. Until the day I spoke with Auntie, I just wasn't sure of my facts, so I thought I shouldn't rock the boat. When I began to write this book, I felt they should hear the truth from me before my story was published. I was not happy being the bearer of such news, but it seemed right to set the record straight. It was a painful time for us all.

The important thing is that my love for the man I thought of as my father—Ted Wells—did not change in any way. I was fierce about it, and after that I wanted nothing to do with the other man. I wasn't curious; I had no desire to start a relationship. I disliked the specter that he was. I didn't see him again until some nine years later.

THINGS BETWEEN MUM and Pop further deteriorated. My mother seemed to fall deeper into depression, finances were growing increasingly difficult, and we were having trouble with house payments. The Meuse itself was becoming unkempt. There was a mouse in my bedroom, and at one point it ran over my hair, which scared the hell out of me. I began to hear voices in my head at night, a crazy chatter, and I worried that I might go mad, like Betty, my father's sister.

A source of comfort for me was the late-night train that rattled through the nearby railway station. As it approached, coming up from the coast to London, I'd hear the wheels of the steam engine clattering over the railroad ties, the puffs of the chimney and shrieks of the whistle. Lying in the dark, the sounds were always reassuring. They implied that there was life out there . . . the world was going about its business, and that made me feel more sane.

Not long after the revelation from my mother, I was gazing out of my bedroom window one day, feeling a little sorry for myself. I stared at the garden, watching the birds swoop down and around the rosebushes.

Uncle Hadge had long since moved up to London with Auntie Kit, and the bitter truth was that all the magic he had made in that garden had fallen apart. It mattered deeply to me that it not sink back into disarray, but it had. The tennis court was overgrown, the roses had become wild, the gladioli were spindly, and everything was generally a mess. It seemed symbolic of the condition of our family.

It was a hot summer afternoon, still and perfect. It began to rain, lightly at first, but quickly becoming fat, heavy drops. I thought, "Someone send me a sign that there is something better in the world, something beautiful and worthwhile, something more to life than this."

I was gazing at a particularly large, full-blown rose, when all of a sudden one extra raindrop was just too much for it. All its petals cascaded to the ground at once. It was startling, and oddly comforting.

I subsequently wrote a poem about it:

> *A rose lay open in full bloom*
> *and, looking from my garden room,*
> *I watched the sun-baked flower fill with rain.*
> *It seemed so fragile, resting there,*
> *and such a silence filled the air,*
> *the beauty of the moment caused me pain.*
> *"What more?" I thought. "There must be more."*
> *As if in answer then, I saw*

one weighty drop that caused my rose to fall.
It trembled, then cascaded down
to earth just staining gentle brown
and, since then, I've felt different.
That's all.

NINETEEN

IN JUNE OF 1950, I began work as a resident singer on a weekly BBC radio show called *Educating Archie*. Created as an unlikely showcase for the popular ventriloquist Peter Brough and his dummy, "Archie Andrews," the show was originally slated for a six-week run as filler, but ended up running for thirty consecutive weeks without a break and playing to a regular audience of about twelve million listeners.

Although Peter Brough was not especially impressive at throwing his voice (one could always see his lips moving), he was charming, sartorially elegant, and came from a family of ventriloquists. Archie, the manic-eyed dummy dressed in a broad striped blazer, played the character of a bratty kid. Peter was his tolerant father who either argued with or placated him. The other cast members included Robert Moreton as Archie's tutor, Max Bygraves (a budding comedian at the time) as an odd-jobsman, and as the neighbor Agatha Dinglebody, the comedienne Hattie Jacques, who, a few years later, would show me a kindness that changed the course of my life.

I was supposedly the little girl next door. If I was lucky, I got a few lines with the dummy; if not, I just sang. Working closely with Mum and Madame, I learned many new songs and arias, like "The Shadow Song" from *Dinorah;* "The Wren"; the waltz songs from *Romeo and Juliet* and *Tom Jones;* "Invitation to the Dance"; "The Blue Danube"; "Caro Nome" from *Rigoletto;* and "Lo, Hear the Gentle Lark."

Pop, in one of his sober periods, used the opportunity to make some money by doing my orchestrations. I was thrilled to have the opportunity to sing with a big orchestra on a regular basis.

Though not broadcast live, the program was recorded in front of a live audience, and I was able to sit in on many of the read-throughs and the show itself. I would rehearse my one aria, then watch these brilliant comedians and actors perform for radio. Many wonderful artists appeared on the show, all of whom became big headliners, like Tony Hancock, Harry Secombe, and Alfred Marks. Eric Sykes wrote many of the scripts, but later also became a well-known comedian.

The first broadcast of *Educating Archie* aired on June 6, 1950. As we only recorded one day a week and I was not in every episode, I was able to continue touring with Mum from time to time.

An impresario, Harold Fielding, promoted a series of elegant concert evenings, usually in the summer, called *Music for the Millions*. His venues were the concert halls along the South Coast of England, towns such as Eastbourne, Margate, Bournemouth. The shows were purely musical presentations, and quite classy. I was invited to do several of these shows in the late summer.

Mr. Fielding was a diminutive, exquisitely neat gentleman, very kind and enthusiastic, and always in good humor. He seemed to have a soft spot for me, and I loved working for him. His concerts felt to me like a step up in the world, and I appeared on the bill with wonderful performers: The Western Brothers, who did satirical monologues to music; Elsie and Doris Waters, who chatted about inconsequential things; Rawicz and Landauer, a piano duo; Anne Ziegler and Webster Booth, the Jeanette MacDonald and Nelson Eddy of the British stage; Larry Adler, harmonica player, and Joyce Grenfell, a gentle comedienne and singer who many years later played the role of my mother in the film *The Americanization of Emily*.

One particular Bank Holiday, Mum and I were contracted to appear in Eastbourne. I had said to my mother that I was old enough now to pack my theatrical gear myself, and I did just that. We drove to the south coast in a terrible downpour. It seemed like the wettest Bank Holiday on record.

We waded through the puddles to the stage door of the Winter Garden and shivered through a damp rehearsal. Setting out my clothes for the evening, I discovered to my horror that, though I had packed my frilly party dress, I had omitted my ballet shoes. I had traveled to Eastbourne in a pair of heavy brogues, which were totally unsuited to my outfit. Since it was a Bank Holiday, not a single shop was open, and there were no dancers on the program who could, perhaps, have lent me a pair of appropriate shoes.

My mother despaired. Rummaging through my theatrical kit, she found the white liquid paint that we used to freshen up my ballet slippers.

"There's only one thing to be done," said Mum. "I'll *paint* a ballet shoe on your socks."

Alas, my socks were not only mud-spattered, but also full of holes. My mother designed a white shoe on the grayish material and filled in the holes by daubing my bare skin beneath. My socks—and feet—didn't dry in time for the show, and I made my entrance onto the stage leaving a trail of white footprints in my wake.

There were no footlights in the Winter Garden, and the audience couldn't be sure that they were seeing what they thought they were seeing. Heads craned and a buzz of whispered comments continued throughout my performance. I tried hiding one foot behind the other, then reversing them, all to no avail. Mum thumped away in a spirited fashion at the piano, I sang my songs faster than usual—and was never so happy to leave the stage. I was mortified; no extra bows for me that night.

On October 1, I turned fifteen and was officially freed from the London County Council's child performer restrictions. My mother decided that Miss Knight, my tutor, was now no longer necessary—and thus ended my formal education.

"Aren't I going to get any schooling at all?" I asked. I had the good sense to know I would be missing out on something important.

"You'll get a greater education from life, Julie, than from going to school," she replied. And because I was busy, and school was an extra burden, I didn't argue.

To celebrate my "liberation," Mum threw one of her great parties. There must have been about sixty people in the house. Everybody danced and jitterbugged and had a fine old time. Don and Chris, having been sent to bed, crept out to watch the party through the banister railings.

At some point, we took a break to have something to eat, and Pop made a very inappropriate remark about me and my friends, Susan Barker and Patricia Waters. I don't recall what he said, but Gladdy Barker had been getting more and more irritated by his drunken behavior. There was a large dish of blancmange—a milky, jelly-like English pudding—sitting on the table nearby, and she suddenly picked it up and hurled it at him. Pop ducked in the nick of time and it hit the wall behind him. There was utter silence in the room as everyone watched the wobbly pink goop slide slowly down the wall and into the bookcase. Then everyone began talking at once. The goop was cleaned up, and the party continued on into the night.

TOWARD THE END of the year, I began to perform occasionally without my mother. She had the two boys and Pop to look after and simply couldn't be with me all the time. I went on the road with a gentleman pianist who was good, but he didn't know my idiosyncrasies or have the fine musical instincts my mother had.

In November of that year, I landed the title role in *Red Riding Hood*, the Christmas pantomime at the Theatre Royal in Nottingham, a historic town in the British Midlands, famous for its lace, Sherwood Forest, and Robin Hood lore.

Mum and Auntie came up to help me settle in. We took our trailer and parked it next to the wall of a big cinema, and lived there during rehearsals. After they returned home, I moved into a hotel.

Since I was only fifteen, I still needed a chaperone, and I believe that the leading lady, Cherry Lind, who played Prince Valiant, was asked to keep an eye on me. Happily, she was also in the same hotel.

I was a gauche Red Riding Hood. Tony Heaton was Mother Hubbard (my mother); Tony Hancock, the comedian, was Jolly Jenkins, a bumbling, well-meaning Baron's page; and the variety artist brothers Albert and Les Ward were the Baron's Henchmen. They played guitars, bicycle pumps, washboards, and practically anything that would provide accompaniment to their country-and-western-style songs. Kirby's Flying Ballet were the fairies and woodland creatures. In true panto tradition, the comedians brought their own shtick to the show—and, as always, the songs had nothing to do with the story. I contributed a highly technical coloratura aria called "The Gypsy and the Bird," which I sang in the forest on the way to Grandma's house. (So I, too, brought my own shtick, so to speak.)

One matinee, I was performing this aria and I became aware of giggles coming from the audience. I thought, "Oh Lord! My petticoat's probably falling!" What I didn't know until I finished the song was that one of the Flying Ballet wires had broken loose from its moorings. The wires were weighted with sandbags and tied off at the side of the stage, and one large sandbag had broken free and was swinging on its wire the entire width of the proscenium, missing me by inches while I was trilling away. I was told later that had I stepped back a mere inch or two, I would have been clobbered.

Being a teenager and much on my own, I became rather unprofessional and would arrive at the theater as late as I possibly could. Sometimes, I washed my hair before the performance, and it would still be dripping wet when I went onstage. Nobody ever said anything; nobody cared.

Mum didn't visit much, and I was horribly homesick. When she and Auntie came up for a weekend, they found me in tears and quite depressed. They hadn't the heart to return home right away, so they stayed a few more days and gave me some much-needed cheer.

Fortunately, I was an avid reader, so that took up some of my time. I had a fairly big break between scenes, and I would often read in my dressing room. One day I was so engrossed in my book that I missed my cue. I heard thunderous footsteps as the assistant stage manager came running down the corridor to pound my dressing room door, and the loudspeaker clicked on backstage.

"Julie? Get down here! You're on!"

I flew down the stairs, and by the time I made my entrance, the audience was chatting loudly, wondering what was supposed to happen next.

The inmates of the local asylum came to a matinee, and following their visit, I received an explicit letter from a patient suggesting that if I cut an orange in half and rubbed it on certain private parts of my anatomy, I would be "purified." My mother was appalled.

"All the more reason to *never* open your own mail!" she admonished.

An audience member gushed to me once, "It must be *so* exciting performing in the theater! Tell me, do you all meet onstage between shows and have picnics together?"

To the contrary, the hotel dining room was always closed by the time we returned after the evening's performance. The kitchen would leave out a salad and some cold chicken, and Cherry Lind and her mother and I, and sometimes Cherry's boyfriend, would sit and eat in the empty dining room, which was eerily quiet with only a few lights left glowing in the darkened hotel. I remember Cherry showing me how to make a vinaigrette salad dressing, a recipe I have used ever since. Sometimes I simply ate alone.

Occasionally the cast would get together after the show. Tony Hancock and his wife often entertained at their digs. Since he had performed in *Educating Archie*, I knew him a little and liked him, although we hadn't had much connection on the radio show. He was heavyset, with a woebegone clown's face and large, sad eyes. In his hilarious sketches, life was always tough, and he would stand, gazing out at the audience with thick-fingered, "wet fish" hands at his side, trying to understand the trials and tribulations that befell him. In real life, he was a depressed man, an alcoholic who eventually committed suicide. But he became quite famous long before that sad moment.

Red Riding Hood ended in March of 1951, and I was extremely relieved to go home.

TWENTY

Aᶠᵗᵉʳ *RED RIDING HOOD* closed, I went out on the road again. Mum and I made a memorable trip to the Isle of Wight off the South Coast of England for a Sunday evening appearance at the Shanklin Theatre.

Royal Navy ships were moored in the harbor, and the theatrical performers received an invitation to go aboard their frigate after the show. We trooped down to the pier and climbed into one of the tenders. Mum was wearing high heels, which kept slipping through the holes in the wrought iron steps of the jetty. We were ferried over to the main ship and shown into the officers' mess, where everyone was plied with drinks.

Mum was very much the life and soul of the party that night, and she got completely "plotzed" from the size of the Navy rations and the fact that there was no curfew on board. It must have been one o'clock in the morning before we left the ship. We settled Mum into the tender, but getting her out of the little boat, which was rocking in the swell, was not easy, and I had to push her up the same iron steps.

When we got back to our digs, she said, "I'm going to the loo," which was at the end of a long hallway. After some time had passed and she hadn't returned, I tiptoed down, very nervous of waking the landlady and causing a fuss. I tried the bathroom door. It was locked.

"Mum?" I whispered. No reply. "*Mum!*"

I heard a grunt from the other side.

"Open up. You've locked the door."

She had fallen asleep on the john, and it took a while to awaken her and to encourage her to come back to our room. I managed to get her clothes off and put her on the bed, and she lay there, not wishing to turn the lights out. With some humor despite her condition, she groaned, "Oh, *God*. Over the bed, under the bed, anywhere but *on* the bed!"

The following day, I woke her and helped her dress for our trip home on the ferry. The ocean was rough, and her hangover was monumental. She was dreadfully seasick.

ONCE OR TWICE a year, Auntie held exams for her entire student body. She hired an examiner from the Royal Academy of Dance to come and test her ballet students, and another examiner came to judge her ballroom pupils. I was fairly good at ballroom dancing, because every chance I had, I would be in the studio joining the classes. I was excited about trying for my bronze medal, and with Tappets, who was a whiz, as my partner, I knew the exam would be a lead pipe cinch.

Mum, Pop, and I were booked for a rare appearance together in Morecambe, Lancashire, that evening, and I hoped to take the long-anticipated exam before we commenced the journey north. But Pop was anxious to get on the road.

"Julie's got her exam this morning," Aunt reasoned with him. "I'll put her in first . . ."

Sadly, the examiner ran late. Pop kept saying, "We've got to go, we've *got* to go, we'll never make it in time!" Right down to the wire, my mother was torn between letting me take this exam and getting me into the car. Eventually, Pop said, "We *cannot* wait any longer." The pleasure of doing the exam was snatched from under my nose by minutes, and all the way to Morecambe I wept and sulked about it.

It wasn't anybody's fault, except perhaps the examiner's, but it was a sad moment for me because passing the exam would have been so good for my ego. It was only a bronze medal, but I never had another chance to take the test.

ALL OUR ENGAGEMENTS were booked by Charlie Tucker, who had managed both my parents' act and mine ever since *Starlight Roof*. He had an attractive top-floor office in Regent Street. Much like a good "dog robber," his desk drawers were stocked with perfumes, nylon stockings, pens, and cuff links from the U.S., which he handed out as favors to his clients. When my mother came to visit, Charlie would give her a bottle of perfume or some nylons to take home with her. Once or twice he gave me a bottle of Carnet de Bal by Revillon, which is a fine perfume, warm and luxurious, and occasionally, he would slip me a big, English £5 note. He would also take us both to lunch, at elegant places like the Caprice, or the Savoy. I remember walking beside him in London, and it felt like we were standing on top of the world; no poverty, no unpleasantness. Lunch was special, with clinking china and silverware, soft lights, pink tablecloths, and attentive waiters—a glimpse of a world otherwise beyond reach.

Miss Teresa Finnesey was Charlie's secretary. Everyone referred to her as "Finney," and she was the classic sweet battle-axe straight out of Central Casting. She was a good Catholic woman who loved Charlie dearly, even though he drove her to distraction. She kept his office running smoothly and was always kind to me, but if she was in a bad mood or if she and Charlie were rowing . . . look out!

Sometimes Charlie would berate my mother if he saw that my socks had holes or weren't especially clean.

"Barbara!" he would rant. "For God's sake, how could you let her walk around like that!"

Charlie was responsible for sending me to a good American dentist working in London. I had a gap between my two front teeth and, alas, a crooked canine. I was fitted with a night retainer.

Because he went back to the States a couple of times a year, Charlie always kept me abreast of the latest shows on Broadway. He told me about *The King and I*, starring Gertrude Lawrence, saying what a phenomenal success she was. Then he said, "One of these days, Julie, you'll be doing something like that, too." I never believed him, of course.

When we saw a woman in a fur coat, he said, "You'll have one of those before long."

"A *fur coat*?" I replied, amazed. "I'll never be able to afford that!"

"Julie, I promise you, by the time you're in your late teens, you'll have your first fur." There was something about his blind faith in me that made me feel that it might actually be possible.

I complained to him once about my mother, and he admonished me.

"Yes, she is a difficult woman," he said. "But she is your mother, and you must always show respect."

"But she's out at night drinking, she leaves us alone . . . ," I protested.

"Yes, but she is your *mother,* and you must never, ever bad-mouth her," he repeated firmly. It stopped me in my tracks.

During those early years, Charlie was very good to me. I was a young, silly girl, and he groomed me in many ways. Were it not for him, I would never have been who I am today, and I thank him with all my heart for the things he did for me.

TWENTY-ONE

IN LATE OCTOBER of that year, Pop managed to procure three seats for a preview of Rodgers and Hammerstein's *South Pacific*, starring Mary Martin and Wilbur Evans, and as yet relatively unknown actors Larry Hagman (who was Mary Martin's son and played Yeoman Herbert Quale) and Sean Connery (a mere chorus boy at the time). It all happened quite suddenly. Pop said, "We've got tickets—we're going," and Mum, Pop, and I set off for a night on the town, which was a rare occasion in itself.

The show was wonderful. What a difference between the tackiness of vaudeville and a legitimate American musical at the famous Theatre Royal, Drury Lane. Mary Martin was enchanting as Ensign Nellie Forbush—washing "that man right out of her hair," onstage, no less!

Wilbur Evans, a lovely baritone, played opposite her as Emile de Becque, and sang the glorious ballads "Some Enchanted Evening" and "This Nearly Was Mine." The male chorus performed "There Is Nothing Like a Dame" and brought the house down. There was a big orchestra, and the musical arrangements by Robert Russell Bennett were superb.

I will never forget the feeling of sitting in the packed theater watching that preview. I was in awe of it. Envious, too. I also felt a little hopeless. I thought I had neither the talent nor the experience to join that world. When the show opened, a week later, it captivated London.

ALTHOUGH I WAS very busy in 1951, I was somehow able to keep up a semblance of a social life. I was still seeing a great deal of Tony and the

Waltons, and occasionally, when I went home for weekends, Mum would take us out for a summer drink to some lovely spot—a club, or a pub, on the river.

We sometimes visited a place called the Gay Adventure. Its lawns swept down to the River Mole, and though it was a bit of a white elephant, students from Auntie's dancing class as well as Auntie, Uncle Bill, Tony, his brother and sister, and I enjoyed going there.

Early one beautiful summer evening, when everyone else was drinking indoors, Tony and I walked down to the river. We lay on the grass under a tree and chatted. At one point, Tony said, "Look at the pattern of lace the leaves make against the sky."

I looked at the canopy above us, and suddenly saw what he saw. My perspective completely shifted. I realized I didn't have his "eyes"—though once he pointed it out, it became obvious. It made me think, "My God, I never *look* enough," and in the years since, I've tried very hard to look—and look again.

WHEREVER I WAS working, I would do everything I could to get home between gigs, even for twelve hours. I had horrible separation anxiety while I was away, always worrying and wondering. Would my mother be all right? How were the boys holding up? I would travel all the way down from the north of England to spend just one day with the family, returning the next day for another week's work. Whenever I made it home, Mum would do whatever she could to make it special. There'd be a big Sunday lunch, and Dingle and Auntie would be there. They'd try to stoke me up with love and attention.

Around this time, Mum had a hysterectomy. It was a miserable time for her, and she was away for a few days. Pop was drinking again. Not on a binge, but certainly drinking. I felt I had to be alert, careful.

I was in my bedroom one evening, just about to climb into bed, when he came in, ostensibly to check on me because my mother was away.

"Everything okay?" he asked.

I noticed that he smelled of alcohol and was breathing heavily. He stood in the center of the room, said good night, and moved to kiss me on the cheek. Suddenly, he said, "I really must teach you how to kiss properly," and kissed me full on the lips. It was a deep, moist kiss—a very unpleasant experience.

Somehow I got him out of the room, pushed him maybe, saying, "Good night, Pop," minimizing the assault. I closed the door and climbed into bed.

Ten minutes later, he came back in. I was burrowed beneath the covers, facing the wall. He leaned over me and tried to kiss me again. I rolled nearer the wall and mumbled, "I'm *really* sleepy. Good night, now!"

Whatever decency was left in that befuddled brain of his made him leave. I prayed he wouldn't come back and, mercifully, he didn't.

The next day, I mentioned the incident to Aunt Joan. She didn't make a great fuss about it, but her lips pursed and she said, "I see. Well . . . I'll speak to Uncle Bill about it and we'll come up with something."

She was obviously very concerned, because by that evening Dingle had put a bolt on my door.

Pop did try to visit again that night, but obviously couldn't get in. He was puzzled as to why the lock had been installed. I don't know what I said, except perhaps that I needed my privacy. I do know that the lock made me feel a little safer, though he could easily have broken it.

My mother returned, horribly beat up from her operation. Her muscles were so weak, and I helped her try to climb the stairs so that she could rest in her bedroom. Her legs just wouldn't support her, and she was alarmingly fatigued. She sat on the stairs, overcome with depression, and simply wept. I rushed to get her a cup of tea and she sat awhile, drinking it slowly, then, still seated, she carefully eased herself backward up the remaining steps. My heart ached for her.

Aunt must have told her about the incident with Pop. Mum never discussed it with me, but all hell let loose between her and my stepfather. There was a strained feeling in the house, an icy coldness between my parents.

My relationship with Pop after that was more distant than ever. He never tried anything with me again, and I did my best never to be alone with him.

*

MY MOTHER SELDOM talked to me about sex, but one day we were chatting about Tony Walton and she suddenly said, "You know he's such a nice boy. I suspect he'll make a great lover one day."

"EEEEUW Mum!" I protested. "I'm not interested in that. He's just a *friend*."

But I was aware that my body was changing: my breasts were budding, my waist was tiny, my legs long (albeit still bandy!). I remember being suspicious and careful with men when they were near me. Dingle gave me a big hug—he often did—but it suddenly didn't feel right anymore. Charlie Tucker gave me a fond squeeze when I was in his office, and I shrugged him away. Maybe the encounter with Pop had left its mark.

Fortunately I also became aware that I had a sense of humor, and I realized with some delight that I could make the family laugh. I don't know how I discovered I could do it; maybe I'd been exposed so often to the humor in vaudeville. My antics and impersonations would make everyone smile and giggle. It made my brothers feel better, the whole family seemed to enjoy it, and it gave me a new sense of control over my environment.

TWENTY-TWO

THAT CHRISTMAS OF 1951, I was invited to play the role of
Princess Balroulbadour—the principal girl—in Emile Littler's holiday pantomime *Aladdin* back at the London Casino. Jean Carson was to
play the title role.

Aladdin was an elaborate production. The Genie's cave at the end of
the first act was dazzling to behold, and there was a huge ballet, beautifully designed and executed, in the second act.

I wore exotic, sparkling headdresses, which I loved, and a lot of satin
kimono-style robes with long, draped arms. The setting was Middle-
Eastern, but I looked more Japanese than Persian. I also wore ballet
slippers, to keep my height down and make Jean Carson look taller
than me.

The cast included a Danish acrobatic troupe, the Olanders—five lads
who, clad in silk pantaloons and waistcoats, performed death-defying
gymnastics: springboards, leaps, balancing acts. Every time they were
onstage, I had to come down to watch—they were that good. A special
combination of bravura and muscular strength, with lean, beautiful bodies.

One of the acrobats—the best—was a young man called Fred who
executed something like twelve amazing butterfly leaps around the
stage. He was attractive, fit (obviously), and very gentle and dear.

My mother knew that I was fond of him, and she said, wisely, "Bring
him down to The Meuse for a weekend." Later she joked that he never
stopped swinging from our chandeliers (we didn't have any).

My mother was ever-present. Fred and I would sit on the couch, bodies pressed together, and there was a lot of hugging and kissing. Mum plied her sewing machine across the room, her back to us but rigidly alert.

I was heartbroken when the run of the show ended. Fred went off with the Olanders as they continued to tour around England and Europe. Later in the year, I went with Auntie Gladdy to see their act at a theater outside London and was able to say hello to him backstage. My heart broke all over again because I thought this would be the last time I'd ever see him.

Walking along the station platform to board our train home, I was miserable. I said something dramatic to Auntie Gladdy, like, "How will life *ever* be the same?" I must have been a complete bore all evening, because she simply exploded.

"Oh for God's sake, Julie! You've got your whole life in front of you. You don't think there'll be *other* lovely young men?"

She said it so clearly that life just fell back into perspective, thank goodness. Fred occasionally wrote to me from Denmark, but eventually our friendship just petered out.

DURING THE RUN of *Aladdin*, I traveled to London, as always, on the train. I would then either take a taxi or go on the Underground to the theater, do my two performances, then travel home late at night. If my mother or Dingle didn't pick me up from the station, I would walk home. There was an outside light by The Meuse's front door, but my mother would often forget to turn it on. The long driveway with the towering rhododendron bushes on either side was dark as could be, and I would whistle cheerfully in order to confound the molester I imagined was waiting to pounce on me.

I complained about the front door light and expressed my fear to Mum.

"Who on earth would be interested in you?" she said. "Why would anyone want to attack *you*?"

That did the trick!

*

ON FEBRUARY 6, 1952, King George VI died. He had been our monarch for sixteen years—almost my entire life—since reluctantly being crowned after the unexpected abdication of his brother, Edward, in 1936.

He had been in failing health for some time. The war had taken its toll, and his heavy smoking had led to the development of lung cancer. Princess Elizabeth had assumed more and more of her father's royal duties as his health deteriorated. She received the news of his passing during the first stage of a Commonwealth tour to Kenya, Australia, and New Zealand. Having left Britain a princess, she returned as Queen at the age of twenty-five.

FOLLOWING *ALADDIN*, I spent the spring touring the provinces in a revue produced by Charlie Tucker called *Look In*. Charlie had many clients, and he decided to put several of them together in one show, presumably to guarantee them work. I believe it was his first attempt at a production, and it was tacky beyond words.

Among the many venues, we played at the Theatre Royal—Portsmouth, the Birmingham Hippodrome, the Nottingham Empire, the Palace in Blackpool, the Finsbury Park Empire in London (which I liked, as it meant I could stay at home and travel up to the show each day), the Bristol Hippodrome, and theaters in Swindon, Cardiff, Swansea, and Northampton.

The show starred a comedian, Alfred Marks, with whom I had briefly worked on the radio show *Educating Archie*, but I didn't know him very well. He seemed a little hedonistic, a man with large appetites. His girlfriend, Paddie O'Neil, was also in the show. She was bleach-blonde—a soubrette—and onstage she exuded a winning awareness of all things sexy. She and Alfred made a good team.

Both the show and the tour were done on a shoestring; the costumes were rented, which meant they had all been worn before. The sets were pieced together from other productions. The title of the show referred to the increasing importance of television in people's lives, *Look In* being a take on the more familiar "Listen In" catchphrase used by radio.

Because I was touring on my own, my mother and, I suspect, Charlie Tucker asked Alfred and Paddie if they would keep an eye on me and take me under their wing. Initially I slept in the same room as they did, on a rollaway cot. I would take myself to bed early and they would return to the hotel quite late. It was difficult for me, and must have been truly irritating for them. None of us was happy about the arrangement, and a separate room for me was soon provided.

Paddie behaved strangely toward me. On the one hand, she kindly showed me how to put on a basic stage makeup. In those days, one plastered greasy panstick on one's face, but it would cake around the hairline. "Once you've put it on and powdered, take a toothbrush and scrub the hairline to get the pancake and powder out and smooth the edge a little better," she told me. But another time, as she came offstage, I was in the wings and gushed, "That was great, Paddie. Oh, I *do* love you!" She brushed past me and said, "Well, I *hate* you."

I may have been foolish and sycophantic, but it was a difficult remark to weather. Paddie could be charming, but I learned not to trust her. My diary entries for this period are filled with notes like "Can't wait to go home."

ALTHOUGH I WAS soon to be seventeen, I was still being billed as "Britain's youngest singing star" and I was now performing in the penultimate spot of the show. I did several radio broadcasts at this time, and continued the weeks of vaudeville and individual concerts. Throughout the year I suffered from bouts of laryngitis—my tonsils were chronically infected—but I didn't worry about it much, and always tried my best to sing through it.

In early September, I had a small introduction not only to the world of animated film but also to the art of dubbing, which I found fascinating. *The Rose of Baghdad* was a Czechoslovakian film originally made in 1949. It was now to be distributed in the UK, and it told the tale of a beautiful singing princess, somewhat in the spirit of *Aladdin* or *Ali Baba and the Forty Thieves*. The role of Princess Zeila had been sung by a soprano with a high voice of great beauty. The producers wanted me to dub the songs into English, but record with the original orchestrations. I had a coloratura voice, but these songs were so freakishly high that, though I managed them, there were some words that I struggled with in the upper register.

I wasn't terribly satisfied with the result. I didn't think I had sung my best. But I remember seeing the film and thinking that the animation was beautiful. I'm pleased now that I did the work, for since then I don't recall ever tackling such high technical material.

TWENTY-THREE

T ONY WALTON AND I continued to see each other whenever we could. He had graduated from Radley College that spring, and was due to fulfill his National Service obligations at the end of the summer. I still visited his adorable family, feeling easy and relaxed in their company.

It was late summer, I believe, when Tony asked me out on our first real date. We traveled to London and saw the movie *The Greatest Show on Earth*, which we both enjoyed. Though I was nearing the age of seventeen, I was still pretty gauche, my experiments with Fred notwithstanding. I was innocent, shy, my social skills lagging considerably behind my ability to fool a large crowd such as an audience. In the cinema Tony held my hand, but I was stiff and withdrawn, for I felt that he was becoming interested in a deeper relationship, which I wasn't ready for. Fortunately, nothing impeded our friendship.

Just after my birthday, I was contracted to appear in yet another holiday pantomime. This time I played the role of Princess Bettina in the Coventry Hippodrome's production of *Jack and the Beanstalk*. It was another principal girl role. I was never asked to play the principal boy, as I was, of course, too young, and, in spite of all the dancing lessons, my legs were not good enough.

Coventry is virtually in the center of England. Its famous cathedral was bombed to smithereens during the war, and its empty shell, standing adjacent to the new cathedral, is a stark reminder of that event.

The Hippodrome was relatively new at the time, run by a truly decent impresario called Sam Newsome. He was proud of his theater, and took me on a tour of it when I first arrived. The dressing rooms were upscale; the principals' rooms had private bathrooms—mine even had a big bath in it. The backstage area was modern and clean, so different from the shabby theaters I had been working in up to this point.

I roomed with a young soubrette called Joan Mann, also a client of Charlie Tucker's. She was to play the role of Jack, the principal boy. Joan was dark-haired, had a great figure, and she was lively and fun.

We did some early rehearsals in London with the respected choreographer Pauline Grant. Charlie Tucker had asked Pauline to be a mentor to me—to help with my deportment, to give me some West End polish. We became good friends, and she was a big influence in my life. Petite and packed tight in her skin, Pauline had slightly bulging eyes and pouting lips that were prettily bowed. She looked a little like Leslie Caron. A former dancer, she had exquisite small hands and when she walked, her feet seemed placed "at a quarter to three" (my mother's description). She always wore very high heels, and she dressed in suits and silk blouses with bows at the neck to soften the tailored image. If she could afford it, she bought herself one haute-couture Hardy Amies outfit every year. She taught me the value of having a few elegant pieces in my wardrobe, rather than a lot of cheap ones.

She had a good sense of humor, and she and Sam Newsome hit it off. He began to ask her out to dinner, and eventually they married.

The show started to take shape. Pauline was a task master with the corps de ballet. She would demonstrate with a flourish of the hands.

"I need a 'pyum!' here and a 'pyum!' there!"

Norman Wisdom, the comedian, was the main attraction of the pantomime. He was a cheeky little chap, a brilliant humorist, much in the manner of Chaplin. He wore a black suit that appeared too small for him and the peak of his cap was pushed to the side of his head. He adopted a funny walk and played a kid very well. He was married, and during the years I knew him, his wife seemed always to be pregnant.

Norman and I had a friendship of sorts; we worked well together onstage, and on the Saturday nights that he would travel home (returning on Monday), he would sometimes give me a lift as far as Ealing, on the north side of London, where he lived. My mother or Dingle would come up from Walton and wait by a certain roundabout. Norman would drop me off, I would swap cars, and Mum or Dingle would drive me on home.

Pauline Grant stayed with us through the beginning of the run in Coventry, then came back from time to time—ostensibly to check up on us, but also to see Sam Newsome. He would pop around backstage at the oddest times, his friendly face appearing at my dressing room door, and it was always a pleasure to see him. He was consistently gracious, his manners exquisite.

One night, after we had opened, we were all invited to his house for a celebration party. Most of the company were chauffeured there in limos. He lived in a stone lodge at Warwick Castle, situated just inside the main gate to the castle grounds. It was a beautifully appointed home, and I remember being impressed by the quiet luxury of it.

Mum and Pop bought a secondhand car—a Hillman Minx, which I called "Bettina" after my character in the show. It was a grand little automobile and extremely useful. I didn't drive it myself, although it was officially "my car." It was really my mother's to use and enjoy, but I was very proud of the fact that my earnings had paid for it.

My mother explained there would be tax benefits if I purchased her half of The Meuse. Pop and I would own it together. Pop was not working and was looking for a job, so by assigning a portion of the mortgage to me, they were able to keep cash flow going. I'm fairly sure that Charlie Tucker helped them work out the details of the transaction; maybe he even suggested it.

A year or two later, I also bought out Pop's share, and the deed to The Meuse was transferred to my name. This furthered my sense of obligation to work, as it was now my total responsibility to keep up the payments. Without my contribution, we really would go under. I didn't object, for I knew how much the place meant to my mother, and I had promised long ago that I would look after her and all the family. I justified working so hard by knowing that I was helping to maintain the roof over our heads. My passion to hold onto every home I have ever had since was influenced by the unthinkable prospect of losing The Meuse.

Dad, Win, Johnny, Auntie Gladys, Keith, Tappets, and the gang from Auntie's dancing class came up for the last night of *Jack and the Beanstalk*, and they helped with the huge pack-up to go home. Bettina, the car, was brought up, and all my luggage, trunks, makeup, and such were loaded into her and one other car, until both were stuffed to overflowing.

Tony had been to see the show, his National Service having been delayed a few months due to his having contracted glandular fever. He had now just returned from a ski trip with his family in Arosa, Switzerland, where he had broken his leg. The poor fellow was in a cast and on crutches, and was really suffering. Nonetheless, he was scheduled to fly to Canada in a few days' time to begin his tour of duty in the Royal Air Force. He looked terrific in his RAF uniform, but he was very distraught.

My mother said to him, "Why don't you paint a picture that you and Julie can share as a bond between you." Tony did a small but exquisite rendering of a little island. Mum said, "You could call it *Ours*." It was the first real painting Tony ever gave me. It has a view looking through trees and bushes to an idyllic setting, rather dark and sad. He left for Canada on Christmas Eve, and though I wouldn't see him again for two years, he wrote constantly and faithfully during the time he was away.

For me, this was a period of turmoil and some guilt. I knew that Tony was very fond of me and wanted more than I was able to give at the time. While I felt great affection toward him, I wished to experience more of life before committing myself to anyone. It wasn't until much later that I realized how much he mattered to me.

Great-Granny Emily Ward—mother of Julia, Mina, Fen, Kath, Doll, and Hadge—with Great-Grandpa William, whom I never met.
Julie Andrews Family Collection

My maternal grandparents, Arthur and Julia Morris, with my mother, Barbara.
Julie Andrews Family Collection

My mother, looking for all the world like my granddaughter, Hope.
Julie Andrews Family Collection

One of the earliest photos of me.
Julie Andrews Family Collection

Johnny and me on a sled, probably made by
Dad. *Julie Andrews Family Collection*

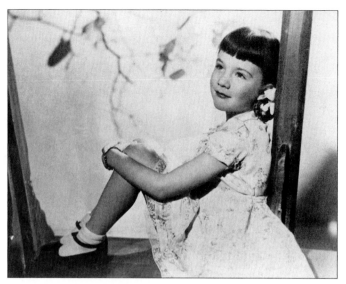

One of my first publicity photos. *Julie Andrews Family Collection*

Another promotional photograph, with the customary braids. *Julie Andrews Family Collection*

Ted and Barbara Andrews—Mum and Pop—in the photo they used to promote their act. *Julie Andrews Family Collection*

This is the photo Pop used for autograph requests—obviously taken at the same sitting. *Julie Andrews Family Collection*

With Mum, at the piano in Beckenham.
Copyright © Bettmann/CORBIS

An early photo of Pop and me onstage. I'm
probably standing on a beer crate.
Copyright © Hulton-Deutsch Collection/CORBIS

Meeting HM Queen Elizabeth (later the
Queen Mother) at the Stage Door Canteen
when I was ten years old.
Julie Andrews Family Collection

Appearing in the BBC-TV program *Radiolympia Showtime*. This is the blue and white dress I wore under my blue coat for *Starlight Roof*.

Julie Andrews Family Collection

With Vic Oliver from *Starlight Roof*.
Julie Andrews Family Collection

In my riding attire with Danny Kaye, at rehearsal for the Royal Command Performance, November 1948.
The Kobal Collection

The photograph I treasure, rediscovered and restored after so many years. Her Majesty, Queen Elizabeth, with Princess Elizabeth (later Queen Elizabeth II) and members of the Royal Family in the Royal Box, the George Melachrino Orchestra behind me onstage. *Julie Andrews Family Collection*

Appearing as Red Riding Hood in Nottingham, with Cherry Lind as Prince Valiant and Tony Heaton as Mother Hubbard. *Photofest*

The publicity photo of the family on the promenade at Blackpool,
June 1949. Left to right, Pop, Chris, Donald, me, and Mum.
Julie Andrews Family Collection

Cast members from the radio series *Educating
Archie*. Clockwise from top: Robert Moreton,
Hattie Jacques, Peter Brough, Max Bygraves,
our producer Roy Speer, Archie, and me.
Julie Andrews Family Collection

At The Old Meuse, not long after we moved in. *Julie Andrews Family Collection*

At Surbiton Lagoon with my siblings *(l. to r.)*: me, Johnny, Donald, Celia, Chris. *Julie Andrews Family Collection*

Publicity photo of Pop and me raking leaves at The Meuse—a very unlikely pastime for either of us. "The Pack" is behind me, my bedroom is the middle of the three windows above, and the trailer we toured with is on the right. *Julie Andrews Family Collection*

At my fifteenth birthday party, with
Auntie and Johnny.
Julie Andrews Family Collection

Me, Dad, Win, Johnny, and Celia in Ockley. *Julie Andrews Family Collection*

Johnny and me. *Julie Andrews Family Collection*

Aunt Joan with my miniature poodle, Shy.
Julie Andrews Family Collection

As Cinderella in the pantomime at the London Palladium.

Julie Andrews Family Collection

With Tony at the opening of Silverwood, Dad Walton's home for polio patients in Cobham, Surrey. *Julie Andrews Family Collection*

Dawn and Lance Walton, Tony's parents, outside Nethercliffe. *Julie Andrews Family Collection*

TWENTY-FOUR

A GIRL'S VOICE DOESN'T break like a boy's in the teens, but I
believe it undergoes some changes. I became aware that I was losing the top notes of my voice, and that it was beginning to mature. The
white, thin quality that had defined my coloratura was becoming
warmer, richer, and reaching the high notes was now more of a challenge. I may have just been fatigued, or perhaps there was an unconscious teenage rebellion at working so hard. I'm sure Madame would
have advised more technique, more practice. I began to worry, since the
"little girl with the high voice" image was still my gimmick.

That spring I had an important concert to do at the Winter Garden in
Bournemouth. I sang with the Bournemouth Symphony Orchestra led
by the conductor, Rudolf Schwarz. Nothing about my program particularly bothered me, with one exception—the high F above the top C in
the "Polonaise" from *Mignon*. I struggled with it during rehearsals.
Maestro Schwarz advised, "Don't take the top F, just hold onto the C,
then come down to the B flat. It's still appropriate." But I hated the idea.
I was known for those high notes—I felt I was cheating and that the end
of my song would seem flat and unexciting. To me, it smacked of failure.

I also sang "Caro Nome," the aria from *Rigoletto*. There is a small,
climbing passage in it that starts at the bottom of the scale. I was accustomed to my mother playing for me, and she always gave me a very strong
downbeat. I said to the Maestro, "Could you give me a slightly stronger
'plonk' just here, please?"

"Gentlemen," he said to the orchestra, with a slight smile, "Miss Andrews would like a stronger *plonk* on bar such-and-such." I got it, but I felt foolish.

We stayed for the weekend with a friend of my mother's named Sydney Miller. He and his partner, John, owned a health spa near Bournemouth. Sydney was a strange fellow, a healer, religious, almost bornagain—and wherever he went, his mother went, too. Needless to say, I was a basket case of nerves the entire time I was in Bournemouth, and Sydney understood that I needed to relax. There were many indigenous pine trees on his property, and he suggested that I go outside and sit beneath one with a lukewarm cup of tea, breathe the pine-scented air, and focus on my concert that evening. He intimated that if I did so, my voice would improve. He said he would pray for me.

I tried for my high note that night, and wished I hadn't. It sounded awful, and I was mortified.

A FEW WEEKS later I began work on another revue produced by Charlie Tucker, called *Cap and Belles*. Subtitled "The New Laugh, Song and Dance Show," the name was a play on the "cap and bells" worn by medieval court jesters. It starred the comedian Max Wall (billed as "The Queen's Jester"), who also wrote some of the music and lyrics. This time I was billed as "Britain's Youngest Prima Donna." I had two solo spots in the show, first performing a song called "My Heart Is Singing," and later "La Dansa," an Italian tarantella, which I sang, assisted by "Les Belles of the Ballet." Though I enjoyed its passionate flavor, I didn't understand a word of what I was singing. I wore a bilious green Spanish gown with a mass of red frills beneath a long train, and I carried a fan. I stamped my feet and swirled my skirt, kicking the red frills out of the way . . . a lot of Spanish attitude for an Italian song!

Max Wall was perhaps the most talented and cerebral of all the comedians I worked with. It wasn't just that he was good, there was a definite aura about him; I would rank him as one of a handful of great clowns.

He had the requisite tragic face, mournful but sweet. His eyes were sad and slanted downward, but when he was being naughty, they were full of mischief. He had rather horsey teeth and a deep speaking voice which he could make sound quite sepulchral. His body was a little twisted, almost as if he had a deformity. He had a large head and very thin legs. When he performed his famous character "Professor Wallofski," he dressed in black tights, a short jacket, and high-top leather shoes that looked too long for his feet. His backside stuck out, and with his hair pasted down either side of his face and his white pancake makeup, he looked grotesquely funny.

Offstage, he was a grave, dignified, and fairly absent man. One got the impression that he was moody and better left alone. I never saw him throw back his head with sudden laughter. I never saw him trade jokes. Onstage he was devastatingly cutting and funny, but one sensed a rage in him, which he channeled into humor.

Max was married at the time to a patient, pretty, and ever-present woman who seemed always to be knitting. My mother used to say that Max changed moods when there was a full moon, that he was slightly mad. He may have suffered from depression.

What I remember most is his extraordinary command of an audience. He needed only to appear in his odd costume with his strange chicken walk, and they would be in the palm of his hand.

A memorable part of his act was his attempt to sing "A Nightingale Sang in Berkeley Square." The orchestra would rush ahead of him and he would be stunned.

"Excuse me?" he would say. "*Excuse* me! Something is wrong here. Let's do it once more." They would start again, and at the identical spot the orchestra would race home. He'd then work himself up into a terrible tantrum.

"All right!" he'd say. "Let's have the manager! Bring the manager on, please! I want to report this conductor is *not* behaving himself!" As he was throwing his weight about, he would back up into the curtain behind him, then suddenly leap forward as if someone had goosed him.

"Did you see that?" he would say to the audience, outraged. "DID YOU SEE THAT? Right in the *middle* of my performance!"

*

OUR SCHEDULE OVER the summer and autumn of 1953 was nothing less than grueling. We played a week each in more than thirty towns across the UK.

My father once said to me, "No matter how far abroad you travel, it's important to know your own country first and foremost. Get to know it from top to bottom: the Pennines, the Lake District, the Broads, moors, rivers, history." I was receiving just such an education.

Joan Mann was also in *Cap and Belles,* and by now we had become good friends. We roomed in the same digs, and we would go down to the theater together in the evenings.

These were the dying days of vaudeville. The provincial theaters were shabby beyond compare, filthy, with terrible facilities and chipped, cracked paint everywhere. The wood on the dressing tables was splintered, the floors were sticky, lightbulbs dusty.

My mother purchased several brightly colored tablecloths for me. I would lay one over the dressing table and pin another around the edge with thumbtacks to make an island of cleanliness and cheer. I would set out my makeup, mirrors, and pictures of the family.

I had an old traveling wardrobe trunk, which stood on end when opened. It had drawers and hangers and functioned like a closet. My everyday clothes were packed in cases, but the trunk held all my theatrical gear and, along with everyone else's, it was collected by the stage management at the end of the week to be transported to the next venue.

On a Monday night in a new theater, before the first performance, I would go up to the wardrobe department and press my dresses, because there wasn't always a wardrobe mistress, and even if there was, she always had so many other costumes to attend to.

I had an ankle-length organza dress with a mass of fake green flowers across the bosom. They would become crushed, and I would rearrange them to look fresh and iron layers and layers of tulle. There was a lot to be done, what with traveling, moving into and out of digs, vocal exercises, and doing two shows a night.

The audiences were so rowdy in some towns that the management turned on the houselights in the balconies in order to see what was going on. During the second house, on a Saturday night in Glasgow, drunks would throw bottles at each other. Onstage, I trilled louder than usual, my hands clasped in front of me, belting out my arias over the shouting and the fighting.

It never occurred to me that I might be gaining certain skills: how to cope with an audience, how to manage if they were unruly, how to survive in a theater so filled with cigarette smoke that it spiraled down the great spotlights onto the stage. ("Do not *ever* let me hear you complain about smoke affecting your voice!" my mother once cautioned.) It also never occurred to me that I was learning valuable techniques, albeit unconsciously, from the great vaudevillians that I watched night after night. Much, much later I was to discover that all this early work stood me in good stead and prepared me for everything that was to follow.

THE CORONATION OF Queen Elizabeth II took place on June 2, 1953, and all the theaters were closed that day. London was especially decorated for the event; flags were flying everywhere, and floral garlands hung from the lampposts. It was the first time in history that a coronation ceremony was televised, and there was a thrilling commentary by Richard Dimbleby, a well-known reporter much beloved in England, who had a rich, deep voice: "Here comes Her Majesty now, walking with *immense* grace, carrying the sceptre and orb . . ."

My family and I watched the ceremony at home and were enthralled by it, most of all by the young queen bearing the weight of the heavy seven-pound jeweled crown, and sitting for hours in her voluminous white satin embroidered gown. The music was glorious and inspiring— a full orchestra, massed voices, fanfares. It was a spectacular affair. Her Majesty's speech to the nation was deeply moving; this lovely young woman, dedicating herself to the service of the British people. That night, all across Britain, just about every peak and hill had a bonfire burning atop it. Typically, my father went alone to the crown of Leith Hill, and privately pledged fidelity to his new queen.

WHENEVER MY MOTHER and I were in London, we would drive down The Mall toward Buckingham Palace and look to see if the Royal

Standard was flying over the roof. (I still do. If the flag is raised, that means Her Majesty is home.)

"She's *in*," my mother would say.

"Gosh, I wonder if I'll ever meet her," I'd muse. "Do you think she'll ever ask me to tea?"

"Well, maybe one day. If you try very hard."

There were many glamorous events and galas during the time of the coronation, and my mother and I were invited to perform one evening at a hotel on Park Lane. We set off in Bettina, our trusty car. There was a low bridge on the way to London, where the road took a huge dip. We were decked out in our best attire, and as happens so often in England, it was simply teeming with rain. Ahead of us, under the bridge, was a vast body of water.

"Oh, just plow through it," I advised Mum. "If we go fast enough, we'll come out the other side."

Mum gunned the engine, and Bettina came to a hissing stop right in the middle of the pool. Her motor had completely flooded. Dressed in our finery, we waded out of the deep water and stumbled to a garage to ask for the car to be towed to safety. We never did make the concert.

The beautiful and historic palace of Hampton Court on the river Thames was illuminated for the coronation and opened to the public. My mother, Pop, my brothers, and I went to view it. It was a balmy summer evening, with a strong scent of flowers in the air. The river nearby sparkled, reflecting the many lights. Strolling through the exquisite gardens under the stars, it was unbearably romantic. Everyone seemed to have a partner. I longed for someone I could share it with.

Tony was in Canada, and though he wrote practically every day, I think I missed him then more than I ever had before. The memory of that evening in Hampton Court is still seared on my brain today because it was so beautiful on that English summer night. I couldn't bear that someone of Tony's sensibility wasn't seeing and sharing it with me.

TWENTY-FIVE

Dduring the tour of *Cap and Belles*, I began to have serious doubts about my prospects for the future. I started to ask myself what I really had to offer, what I'd learned, what I hoped to achieve. I was now seventeen, still traveling endlessly, still singing the same songs night after night. My youthful "freak" voice seemed to be changing, and I worried what my appeal would be once I lost that gimmick.

My education had been pretty nonexistent, and I had learned no other craft. I was busy taking care of the family and bringing home the money, but I felt as if I was going around in circles. I had good instincts; I knew how to be decent and polite. But inside there was a locked-up individual, doing all the moves and trotting out the form like a hamster on a wheel.

Then, lo and behold, I was offered the title role in *Cinderella* at the London Palladium.

The theater has tremendous prestige and a great history. It was the jewel in the crown of the Moss Empires Corporation. Almost every American headliner has performed at the Palladium. It holds more than two thousand people, yet standing on the stage, one feels one can touch the entire audience. It is immaculate—nothing like the tacky vaudeville theaters I'd been playing in. It is also the best theater in London in which to see a pantomime.

Everything about that 1953/1954 production of *Cinderella* had a certain elegance. The show was glamorous and the costumes were fresh.

The staging was by Charles Henry, who had also been involved in *Starlight Roof*, and Pauline Grant was the choreographer.

Richard Hearne played Cinderella's put-upon father; Max Bygraves, the now-famous comedian whom I had first met on *Educating Archie*, played Buttons, who was enamored of Cinderella; Adele Dixon was Prince Charming; and Joan Mann played the Prince's Valet, Dandini.

Richard Hearne, that masterful clown, incorporated his Mr. Pastry character into his role, and he was totally endearing. The sketch he was famous for, and the audience waited for it, was "The Lancers"—an old-fashioned dance designed for a group of people, with a driving, jolly tune. Though Richard danced "The Lancers" solo, he performed it as if he were being pulled in every direction by a large and enthusiastic crowd.

Adele Dixon was married to a Cartier. The cast would show up in rehearsal clothes each day, and she would arrive wearing some exquisite suit made of wonderful fabric. Her trademark was a beautiful silk flower on her lapel—a chrysanthemum or a soft bunch of violets. She was perhaps a tad older than most people who played a principal boy, and she didn't have the great legs that Joan Mann did—but what she didn't have in pizzazz she made up for in style. She was an elegant, classy Prince Charming, and I was very admiring of her.

The production values on the show were terrific; there were revolving stages, and real white ponies pulling the spectacularly gilded coach. (The ponies were adorable, but had a phenomenal talent for taking a dump onstage whenever I had friends in the audience.) There was a glorious transformation scene when the Fairy Godmother worked her magic, enabling Cinderella to go to the ball. In the grand finale wedding sequence, my crinoline was so huge that I had to arrive backstage dressed in my bodice, sleeves, and petticoat, and walk into the crinoline skirt, which was braced on a stand because it was so bejeweled and cumbersome. The company, Prince Charming, and I were brought up from below stage on a hydraulic elevator, to be revealed in a sparkling white set and costumes for the final tableau.

Cinderella was very successful, and we received great reviews. After the opening night my mother said, "Julie, this is the perfect part for you

at the perfect age. It couldn't have come at a better time in your career."
I did two shows a day from December till March, and I loved it all.

Whoever plays the Palladium has a brass nameplate nailed to his or
her dressing room door. At the end of the show's run, the plaque is given
to the actor in acknowledgment of having played the great theater. My
dad took mine and set it on a wooden stand, and I have it to this day.

In spite of the success of *Cinderella*, I still didn't feel that I would
have an ongoing career. I could perform in radio, vaudeville, and pantomime—but I felt that with *Cinderella*, my career had peaked.

THERE WAS A very successful musical play running in London called
The Boy Friend, written and composed by Sandy Wilson. I hadn't been
able to see the show, because of my own performance schedule, but it
had been playing to enormous popularity and huge success—so much so
that two American producers, Cy Feuer and Ernest Martin, purchased
the rights for Broadway. They were renowned for such blockbuster hits
as *Guys and Dolls* and *Can-Can*. Since the London producers had no desire
to release any of their talented cast members, Feuer and Martin decided
to form an entirely new company for the Broadway production.

Charlie Tucker reported that a lady called Vida Hope, the director of
The Boy Friend, was coming to see an afternoon performance of *Cinderella*. Later, I learned that Hattie Jacques—the kind comedienne who
had been in *Educating Archie*—had suggested to Vida that she take a look
at the young lead at the Palladium. Sandy Wilson accompanied Vida to the
theater. The next thing I knew, I received a surprise offer of a two-year
contract to play the role of Polly Browne in *The Boy Friend* on Broadway.
I wonder if Hattie ever realized what a catalyst she was for me.

Given the fact that I was almost single-handedly holding the family
together, that Pop was drunk a great deal of the time, that my mother
was unhappy and my young brothers miserable, there was every reason
not to go. As I have mentioned, I always had terrible separation anxiety
about leaving home, and the prospect of being away from my family for
two years tore at my heart.

I wrestled with the decision at length. How could I abandon everyone? It sounds a little grandiose, but I thought everything would fall

apart if I left. How would they manage? How would I manage on my own in a new, strange country? It wasn't that I didn't have ambition. It was just that *The Boy Friend* seemed an impossibility for me. The anxiety was paralyzing.

I decided to talk to my father. He visited The Meuse and we walked in the garden together. I became tearful as I told him that I didn't know what to do about the offer to go to the United States—and for two whole years, for heaven's sake!

"Chick," he said gently, "I think you *should* go. It'll be the best thing in your life, and look, it could last a mere two *weeks* . . . two months. No one can say for sure that it's going to last two years. It'll open up your head, and you will see America. You should not miss that opportunity."

As always, he was the voice of reason.

Many years later, I asked him if it had been difficult to counsel me that way.

"I was dying inside," he replied. "I knew that I would not see you for a while, and that was so hard. But I also knew that it was the best thing that could happen to you."

I made my decision. With uncharacteristic stubbornness, I dug in my heels for the first time in my life and said to Charlie Tucker, "I *cannot* do it for two years, but I *will* do it for one." Charlie was simply horrified and told me I couldn't dictate to the American producers like that. But I was adamant, and with the hysterical feeling that comes from total panic, I said, "Look, I don't care! If they don't want me, that's all right."

I think I hoped that my insistence on a one-year contract instead of two would lead Messrs. Feuer and Martin to pass on their offer. To my great surprise, they agreed to my terms.

TWENTY-SIX

C*INDERELLA* ENDED ITS run in March, and I was not expected to leave for America until August. In the interim, Charlie Tucker told me that he had an offer for me to play an American girl from the South in a new "play with music" called *Mountain Fire*. I had always hoped to try legitimate theater, and here I was being asked to do a play. "Legit" at last!

I met the director, Peter Cotes, and his wife, Joan Miller, in their Kensington apartment. I think they hired me because I was the appropriate age and suitably nubile—it certainly wasn't for my Southern accent, which was, quite frankly, appalling.

The play, set in the mountains of Tennessee, was a dark, sad allegory based on the story of Sodom and Gomorrah. It was written by Bill Birney and Howard Richardson, who had also written the very successful *Dark of the Moon*.

I began to work on my role with Joan Miller. She tried to help me find the nuances that were needed for the part, but true to form—as with sad songs and the dreadful screen test—the emotions consumed me. The result was floods of tears, every day. I dreaded going to work.

Gillian Lynne, the now-famous choreographer of such triumphs as *Cats* and *The Phantom of the Opera*, played a young, wanton girl in the show. Jerry Wayne, who played the traveling salesman who seduced my character, Becky, was attractive, but at the time he was on a health kick, and he ate garlic until it was coming out of his ears. His clothing, breath, hair, everything reeked—and we had love scenes together. Someone told me that if you eat garlic in self-defense, you don't notice it on someone else, so I began to eat a lot of garlic myself. It didn't make the slightest difference, except to make other members of the company keep their distance from us both.

The music was by Stefan de Haan, a charming man, about fifteen years older than I, who also served as our musical director. He was European, erudite, shy, and fun. Our director couldn't decide whether he wanted the orchestra in the pit or offstage, or no orchestra at all. This was a play, after all, so he then thought maybe one instrument, a guitar, would be enough. We tried the show a different way every night.

Peter still wasn't satisfied. He thought maybe the musical introductions to the songs were impeding the flow of the story. Seeking to help, I made a suggestion.

"I've got perfect pitch. Perhaps I could just start my songs myself and the accompaniment could creep in later?"

Peter looked at me blankly. "But what about everybody else?"

"Ah! Well, I don't know about everybody else," I said, "but certainly in the duet with Jerry, for instance, I could hum his note quietly for him. He could pick it up from me and continue on."

We tried it that night. At the appropriate moment I hummed the note for Jerry, and he said, "What?"

"Hmmmm," I repeated, a little louder, hoping the audience wouldn't hear me. Needless to say, he never found the note, and it was a disaster.

The truth was, the play was not good, and although the company tried to make it work, we all sensed it was going to be a flop. I also knew beyond a shadow of a doubt that had the eminent London critic Kenneth Tynan seen my performance, it would have been the end of any career I hoped to have. Mercifully, *Mountain Fire* folded out of town.

The American producer of *The Boy Friend*, Cy Feuer, came to see the show before it closed, and when he visited me backstage, the only thing he managed to say to me about the play or my part in it was, "*You've* got perfect pitch!" He was a sparkling, jovial man with a freckled face and a sandy crew cut that made his head look like a bullet. I liked him immediately.

Speaking of perfect pitch, my mother had it, too. We would often play the game of "Guess That Note." Actually, only Mum's pitch was perfect—

mine is merely relative, meaning that I hear middle C in my head (having always begun my scales on that note), then I judge other notes by their distance from that. The interesting thing is that as the years went by, I regularly won the game, and Mum—who had been so right initially—was a whole tone flat. We would both stomp into the living room and hammer at the piano keys to prove our point. Ironically, these days my sense of pitch has also lowered. I guess everything drops with age!

WHILE WE WERE on the road with *Mountain Fire*, I began a friendship with a young Canadian actor in the play named Neil McCallum. He was very accomplished and had an endearing, asymmetrical face. Our relationship quickly blossomed into romance.

That July, after the show closed, Neil, Stefan, Aunt Joan, and I took a small vacation together. We rented a little riverboat and journeyed up the Thames. Auntie and Stefan got on very well, and she became an unspoken chaperone for Neil and me. We made a compatible foursome.

The boat was a little cabin cruiser, about thirty feet in length. We had a bunk each, and there was a small shower and head. Neil and Stefan were in charge of all things nautical. Auntie and I made beds, set out breakfast, put out the fenders and ropes, and generally made ourselves useful. In the evenings we moored on the towpath and went to a local pub for supper, or cooked aboard in the tiny galley.

For ten pleasant days we headed toward Oxford and then back. The sun shone occasionally, but mostly it poured with rain. We didn't care—it was an adventure.

Neil came down to The Meuse and was very kind to my brothers, even building Chris a swing in the garden. Shortly before I was due to leave for the United States, Neil had to return to Canada. I said to my mother, "Mum, I want to go down to Southampton to see him aboard his ship." She said, "I wish you wouldn't."

But my compulsion to be with him until the very last moment was too strong. Against her instincts and wishes, I said, "Mum, I *have* to do this. I'll be back in the morning once he's gone."

So I went. I knew my mother was concerned.

On the train down to Southampton, my time of the month suddenly and surprisingly commenced with a vengeance. I was mortified—and maybe a tad relieved. Neil and I spent the night together, but it was purely platonic. It must have been frustrating as hell for him. He promised that when I got to New York, he would come down to visit me. The next morning, he boarded his ship and I waved until he was out of sight ... then took the lonely train journey back to Walton-on-Thames.

When I arrived home, my mother was not there. She may have been annoyed at me, and decided not to be present when I returned. She may have just gone to the pub for a drink. Whatever, the house was depressingly empty, I felt miserable and sorry for myself, and I went to lie on my bed. Mum eventually showed up and came to find me. When I tearfully told her that Neil and I had not consummated our relationship, she wept also—with relief.

The grand pack-up for America began.

TWENTY-SEVEN

A FAREWELL PARTY had been planned for me: a last big bash at The Old Meuse. Everybody came: Auntie, Dingle, my brother John, all the dancing students, Auntie Gladdy and her husband Bill, Susan, Trisha Waters, friends from far and near.

Pop became horribly drunk that night. He had a terrible case of gout, and was limping around on a cane. Toward the end of the evening, when the party was in full swing and everyone was dancing, he walked into the big living room and looked up at the saucer-shaped porcelain light fixture on the ceiling.

"I never did like that thing!" he said loudly. He suddenly attacked it with his cane, smashing it to pieces.

The guests made a swift exodus. My brothers and I were hurried to our rooms, and Pop went on a colossal rampage. He stormed around the house ranting and raving. He wrapped a towel around his fist and went out to Auntie and Dingle's bungalow and punched out all the windows, saying, "I reckon that man owes me three hundred pounds!" He then punched Dingle, who somehow landed a punch of his own and gave Pop a bloody nose. My mother called the police, and Johnny called Dad, who came immediately and offered to take us all back to Ockley for the weekend.

I was due to leave for America in three days and had much packing to do, but I was hustled into Dad's car along with Donald, Chris, and Mum. Auntie was in a terrible state, but she was with Dingle. I don't know where they went that weekend.

Pop had been working himself up for days, his rage bubbling ever closer to the surface and threatening to explode. It may have been a coincidence that he acted out just as I was due to leave, but he must have seen that I was getting a great deal of attention. In contrast, Pop's career in vaudeville was nonexistent, and his work as a cash register salesman was not proving successful. Auntie and Dingle's presence on our premises seemed to drive him crazy; the dancing lessons taking place in the garden studio irked him, my mother's support of my aunt and neglect of him . . . he probably felt he didn't have a friend in the world or a place to call his own. And of course, he was an alcoholic. Later we discovered bottles of scotch and vodka stashed all over the house.

Mum found out that he'd put an ad in a "lonely hearts" magazine, seeking a dinner companion. When she asked how he could do such a thing, he replied that it wasn't for sex, it was for company. I don't know if that was true, but it was deeply sad and it rocked my mother's world for a while.

So I spent my last weekend with Dad, Win, and the two boys. Mum returned to The Meuse the following day to talk to the police, who took Pop away, but they released him forty-eight hours later. My mother obtained a restraining order to prevent him from coming near the house, at which point I was able to go back and finish packing for my departure.

The restraining order was for several weeks. Mum was distraught. Auntie was panicked and angry. I was in a dilemma; how could I leave my mother and the boys? Would she ever be safe? I begged her to file for a divorce. She said that she would.

Suffice it to say that my departure for America was a nightmare. Everyone urged me to get onto that airplane for the U.S. My mother, Dad, Aunt Joan, Dingle, Auntie Gladdy, Charlie Tucker, Johnny, Don, Chris—they all came to Northolt Airport to see me off. Saying goodbye was agony. Mum and Auntie were stoic, telling me everything would be fine and not to worry. Go!

I remember the plane's huge engines warming up on the tarmac. We had been grouped in a sort of army Nissen hut, which was the Northolt holding area for passengers. I walked across the concrete in the dark night and up the steps into the big four-engine Constellation, to take my first transatlantic voyage.

I had not yet met any of my fellow company members, who were traveling to America on the same flight. Everyone was bubbling with excitement, wondering what awaited us overseas. I tried to fit in, but I was very preoccupied. I sat next to Dilys Laye, the young girl who would be playing Dulcie in the show, and she seemed worldly and calm and not at all worried. She was a pleasant companion. We decided on the journey that we would try to room together. We spent a sleepless night traveling from London to New York, stopping to refuel at Gander, Newfoundland, on the way.

The trip took about eighteen hours, and I was wiped out and emotionally exhausted by the time we reached that amazing city. I couldn't stop thinking about the family. Would Mum hold out? Would she really go through with the divorce from Pop? What would happen to the house if she did? Where would she go? Would Don and Chris be all right? My *Boy Friend* salary was going to be small. I planned to send half of it home—but would that be enough for them, and would that leave enough for me to live on each week?

We arrived at Idlewild (now John F. Kennedy) Airport on August 24, 1954. We walked down the steps of the plane onto the boiling hot tarmac, to be met by a horde of press and photographers who asked us to pose on a baggage trolley.

The first thing they said to us was "Show us some cheesecake!"

I kept saying, "Excuse me?" but a couple of the girls knew what they wanted and hiked up their skirts. I felt embarrassed that the moment we got there, we had to show them our legs.

I was met at the airport by a diminutive man named Lou Wilson, a friend of Charlie Tucker's whom Charlie had arranged to be a sort of sub-agent/manager and keep an eye out for me. Lou was a small-time producer, entrepreneur, and a dreamer. He was sweet, kind, welcoming, and I warmed to him right away.

We were taken to the Piccadilly Hotel on Times Square and 45th Street (today it is the site of the Marriott Marquis Hotel). I was shown to a small room on the third floor, directly above the convention halls. It was noisy and hot.

I had a single bed, a tiny shower, toilet, and washbasin, and a tiny window that looked out over a large airshaft. I remember shutting the door behind me, feeling alone and somewhat dazed.

That first evening, there was a small dinner reception for us at Sardi's.

When Dilys and I returned to our hotel afterward, we piled into the elevator with a bunch of other people. A total stranger, a gregarious fellow, looked at us and said, "Y'all is mighty purty."

"I beg your pardon?" His thick Southern accent was unintelligible to me.

"Y'all is mighty purty," he repeated.

I grasped he was saying that I was pretty and I thanked him. He asked where I came from, so I politely told him, "Walton-on-Thames, Surrey," and received an empty look.

"Ah come from Georgia," he said.

"Oh, how nice," I replied.

When Dilys and I got out of the elevator, I asked, "Did you understand a word that man said?"

"Nope," she answered.

"Neither did I!"

But I did get the sense that Americans were very friendly.

Neil called from Canada, and I told him of the chaos surrounding my departure. He said, "I'll come down right away."

At sight of him, I really wept. I collapsed into his arms, and we tumbled into bed.

TWENTY-EIGHT

REHEARSALS FOR *The Boy Friend* were held at a theater on 46th Street, a block or so from the Piccadilly Hotel. Vida Hope, our director, was a loving den mother, theatrical and fun. She was a buxom woman and had a slight speech impediment. Our choreographer, John Heawood, was lively, very skinny, and very gay. Since they both had staged *The Boy Friend* in London, it wasn't so much a question of finding the nature of the show as it was putting it back together again.

Dilys Laye immediately found a wonderful character reading for her role as Dulcie. She knew just how to raise a shoulder, assume a stance, or bat her eyes. She had a husky voice, which she used to marvelous effect. Annie Wakefield was the young soubrette Madcap Maisie, Millicent Martin played Nancy, and Stella Claire played both Fay and Lolita, the voluptuous tango dancer. John Hewer played Tony Brockhurst, the boy friend.

There were perhaps nine English members of the company; the rest of the cast were American Equity performers. Everybody seemed to know exactly what they were doing. Everyone knew how to pose, how to be camp; everyone, that is, except me. I kept thinking "How do they *know*? I've never done anything like this; I've never lived in the twenties. How is it they grasp the style so easily?"

One morning, not long after rehearsals began, I was looking up the airshaft outside my hotel window, checking the weather, and I saw that it was raining. It made me feel much more at home and was certainly welcome, for New York had been unbearably hot and humid. I left for work, and as I walked down the street, I noticed that a lot of signs were swinging and canopies were straining at their bindings. The wind was certainly strong.

As I rounded the corner of Eighth Avenue and 45th Street, I had to hold onto a lamppost to keep my balance. I turned the next corner and a blast of rain lashed my face and drenched my clothing. I staggered up to the theater stage door, heaved it open, and stumbled inside. The place was empty, except for the doorman, who was in his cubicle.

"Where *is* everybody?" I asked him breathlessly.

"What do you mean?" he said.

"Well, aren't we rehearsing this morning?"

"Honey," he replied, "that's Hurricane Hazel out there!"

CY FEUER ATTENDED rehearsals almost every day. He had boundless energy and was the complete opposite of his business partner, Ernest Martin, who was dark-haired, very quiet, and a little dour.

I was still having difficulties with my character, Polly Browne, trying to discover who she was, and what I was supposed to be doing. I watched everybody else and tried to emulate them. I didn't know how to research a role, had no idea how to "break down" a script. Vida wasn't much help because she was so busy with the entire production. We were not going out of town for a tryout run, but were to open cold on Broadway since the show was already a known quantity. With so little time to prepare, every day, every moment of rehearsal mattered.

There were rumors that all was not well between Cy, Vida, and Sandy Wilson. Cy felt that although *The Boy Friend* had been a big hit in London, it now lacked the punch that was required for a Broadway audience. Sandy objected. He was the author, and felt that the style of the show had proven itself already. He was against any changes, and resented Cy's interference.

The day came when, to our dismay and horror, news flew around the company that Sandy and Vida had been dismissed and were actually barred from entering the theater. Cy was to take over the show. Something had obviously happened after hours, of which we were all unaware, and the company was anxious.

Cy came in like a drill sergeant. The first thing he did was to coach the girls. A lot of their dialogue was spoken in unison. When they cried, "Oh, *do* tell us about him, Polly!" for example, he energized it and made them say it with precision timing. Wherever the play was soft or vague, Cy tightened it, making it sharp and clean.

Truthfully, Cy's phenomenal energy was exactly what was needed. I don't think anybody, not even Vida or Sandy, had grasped the standard expected for a Broadway show. The English production had been a delicate piece of lace. Our production became crisp, full of liveliness and giddy fun.

We soon understood that this was not the first production Cy had taken over. But it seemed that whatever he touched, he turned to gold.

We moved into our own theater, the Royale, for dress rehearsals. We had a sizeable orchestra, bigger than the London production, with soprano saxes, a tuba, "wac-a-doo" trumpets, and a banjo. The orchestrations and the musicians were dynamite.

We played two weeks of previews, and I continued to feel that I was the only one who still needed to get my act together. Oddly, there were performances when I received wonderful laughs from the audience, and others when there was no reaction at all. I couldn't figure it out. I tried different things each night. In hindsight I was probably working so hard for a gag that it became the kiss of death; when I was just being real and innocent, people seemed to love it. But I didn't have the experience to grasp that.

The last preview of all was my worst performance, and I knew that I was drowning. The following morning, Cy Feuer collared me at rehearsals and said, "Come with me."

He took me out to the long, dark alley where the Golden, the Royale, and the Majestic stage doors converge. We sat on the fire escape steps.

The first thing he said to me was "You know you were terrible last night."

"*I know!*" I replied with equal candor. "I just don't understand what's wrong."

"Here's what you are going to do," Cy said. "I want you to play Polly Browne as *truthfully* as you possibly can. I want you to forget every funny, campy thing the others are doing and I want you to play her straight—right down the middle. When you lose your boy friend, I want your heart to break. Play the role sincerely; believe it with every fiber of your being. If you do as I say, you *may* stand a chance of being quite a success tonight."

I realized that Cy was giving me the answers I had been looking for, that he was throwing me the rope I needed. I grasped it with both hands, and with sudden clarity everything fell into place. Thank God for his guidance. That night I played Polly Browne as I believe she is meant to be played: an innocent, vulnerable little rich girl who wants nothing more than to be loved for herself.

It was September 30, 1954, the eve of my nineteenth birthday, and I will always remember that performance. The orchestra was superb, the company was superb, and every laugh I hoped to get came my way. The reception at the end was unbelievable. The audience rose to their feet as one, stomping and cheering. People danced the Charleston down the aisles as they exited the theater.

The crush backstage was tremendous, noisy, and enthusiastic. I tried to get through to my mum in England on the stage door telephone.

"Mum, it's over!" I shouted into the mouthpiece, a finger in my other ear. "We seem to be fine." But she could barely hear me.

Bill Birney, one of the authors of *Mountain Fire*, had asked to take me out for supper, and not knowing the traditions of a Broadway opening, I accepted. Everyone else repaired to Sardi's to await the reviews, and I went off with Bill to the Ambassador restaurant and had a staid and elegant meal. Eventually we headed for Sardi's, and the maître d' informed us that the company was gathered in an upstairs room. People were waving newspapers or poring over the reviews. Dilys received wonderful notices and, miraculously, so did I. *The Boy Friend* was a smash hit.

Ten days after we opened, I arrived at the theater and glanced up at the marquee. To my surprise it read: "The Boy Friend—with Julie Andrews."

TWENTY-NINE

O NCE THE SHOW opened, the really hard work began. We had to record the cast album immediately, so there was very little time to catch our breath. Every newspaper and important magazine wanted to shoot its own photo layout and center spreads. These were always done after the evening performance. In a way, it was like doing an extra show, and we often worked late into the night. With matinees as well, it was pretty exhausting.

Dilys and I pooled expenses and moved out of the Piccadilly Hotel and into a single-bedroom apartment at the Hotel Park Chambers, on West 58th Street. It had a living room, a closet-sized kitchen with a tiny fridge, hot plate, and sink, a bedroom with twin beds, and a bathroom.

It was a convenient location, and there was a good drugstore with a soda fountain across the street. Compared to the Piccadilly, it was heaven. We didn't have much room in our closets, or in our one bathroom, but we made it work.

I discovered that Dilys was wonderfully gregarious. Sometimes she would bring a boyfriend back to the apartment. They would occasionally become amorous, so I would retreat to the bedroom, but I couldn't help overhearing the mounting sexual exertions taking place on the couch in the next room.

Neil came down from Canada whenever he could. Most often Dilys let us take the bedroom, maybe because her friends could make their exit more easily from the living room.

*

I WAS LONELY at times, and extremely grateful for any connection with loved ones back home. I phoned my mother once a week, which in those days was a very expensive thing to do. In later years, Don and Chris both told me that they had always hovered by the phone, longing to say a few words, hoping for their own moment with me, but perhaps in Mum's enthusiasm to speak to me herself, she neglected to consider their feelings. Letters became my lifeline and I looked forward to the mail delivery each day. Tony continued to write occasionally, and I to him. I believe he was aware of my relationship with Neil, but he had the grace not to mention it.

My dad's letters were always exquisitely written in his fine hand, and full of news of the countryside; what blossom had just appeared, how the daffodils were showing their golden heads, how he had just built a garden gate for a neighbor . . . things that I relished and could identify with. I was still very concerned about my mother, and continued to beg her to separate from Pop. I wrote to both my father and Charlie Tucker asking them to intercede, and my dad wrote back. His typically eloquent letter is excerpted as follows:

Ockley, 24 November 1954

Darling Julie:
Following your letter of Tuesday 16th . . . I have phoned Mummy and as a result am now posting her the following:

> *"Dear Barbara:*
> *It was not my wish that last night's talk should become so bitter, and I do not want to cause you distress at a time of strain and difficult decision . . . When Julie left for U.S.A. she was happy in the knowledge that at last some positive action to break the impasse in your affairs had been initiated, and she asked me to do my utmost to help bring it to an effective conclusion. For her sake, and yours, I hoped it would be, but if now you decide otherwise, I hope your courage will be rewarded and that the doubts as to your future will be resolved. But, in that event, I*

*propose regularly to enquire into those aspects of the inevitable
negotiations that must take place that affect Julie . . . Please
believe that out of this I want only three things: Happiness for
Julie; the simple same for you and yours; and for myself the
satisfaction of having helped you both.*
Yours really sincerely, Ted."

*Now, my darling little girl . . . There is no need to get worried over
this; no need to lament your absence as a handicap to communication.
Just go on doing your job out there; leave it to us to get things right;
and, above all, far above all, look after yourself.*

*A thousand blessings,
Ever, Dad.*

I doubt if Dad's letter influenced Mum, as before long, she and Pop
were back together again. Auntie later wrote me that Pop was "*courting
Mum madly with phone calls, presents, dates for dinner.*"

EVERYTHING ABOUT NEW YORK at the beginning seemed like an
assault. The pace, the customs, the pressures of being in a wonderful hit
show, the exposure to so much that was exciting and new. There were
days when I was so overwhelmed that I literally found myself pausing in
shop doorways to gain my breath.

The press company for *The Boy Friend* set up numerous radio and
television interviews for me. I wore the same dress for every appoint-
ment, because funds were so short and I didn't have anything else.

My salary was $450 a week. Almost half of that was taken out for
taxes, and from the remaining money, I sent $150 home. It left me with
about $75 in total per week to help pay for the Park Chambers and food.
By the time Thursday came round, Dilys and I were usually completely
broke, with very little to eat in our tiny kitchen.

A lady by the name of Eleanor Lambert (who is considered the founder
of fashion PR, and who invented the "International Best Dressed List" in
1940) arranged for me to do a fashion layout for a magazine. I modeled

several dresses, which fitted me beautifully, and afterward she gave them to me. I protested, but she said, "No, no, you used them; please take them." I could not have been more grateful.

I was also asked to take part in a fashion show at the Waldorf-Astoria. Charlie Tucker had often talked about this great hotel, how grand and elegant it was—and he was right. I modeled a superb gown by the renowned designer Charles James. It was one of the most glamorous ball gowns I have ever worn. There was a communal dressing room backstage. A very pretty lady was putting on her makeup as I arrived to lay out my things. She said, "Hello. I think you're from England, aren't you? You're in *The Boy Friend*?"

"Yes," I said.

She extended her hand.

"My name's Grace Kelly."

THERE WAS ALWAYS someone well known coming to see the show. Truman Capote was there one evening and visited backstage. He was diminutive and dressed like Little Lord Fauntleroy, with an enormous, round, white shirt collar and a floppy bow at his neck. He spoke in an effeminate way, his voice that of a small boy, but one sensed the shining intellect behind the strange façade.

Another night we heard that Cary Grant was out front, and the company was hugely excited. We learned that he was coming backstage to see a friend in the show. Everyone dashed to the stage door to watch him pass by, but I had to remove my wig, take the wax beading off my eyelashes, and cleanse my face. By the time I was finished, he had gone.

I was just heading out of the stage door, looking rather greasy and disheveled, when Cary Grant suddenly reappeared, having left something behind. We very nearly bumped into each other. "Oh, hello," he said. "You don't know me but my name's Grant." I shook his extended hand and my knees turned to jelly. He said he loved the show, but I was so overwhelmed by his charm that I don't remember anything else we discussed.

Home

*

LOU WILSON WAS a regular visitor to the Park Chambers Hotel. If convenient, he would stop by after the show for a cup of tea and we'd just sit on the couch and talk. We chatted about his love of England, about Charlie Tucker, my parents, his divorce, his little daughter "Tuppence," whom he didn't see often. I think he, too, was lonely.

Lou loved to buy all the early morning newspapers as soon as they appeared on the stands, usually just after midnight. He would have read them cover to cover by dawn. He told me he didn't sleep much, and that he did his best thinking in the middle of the night. He kept a blank pad and pencil by his bed, and would scribble down a thought without even turning on the light. In the morning, his bedside would be littered with notes torn from the pad. He was compulsive, energetic, endearing, dapper, and unbelievably kind to Dilys and me.

She and I decided he had been so decent that we would cook him supper one night. We wondered what we could produce on our little two-burner stove. We certainly couldn't afford to take him to a restaurant. I went out and bought a can of Dinty Moore Beef Stew, and we dutifully heated it and served it up. He was very polite and ate every bite. But afterward, he tactfully inquired how much money we had, individually and together.

When we revealed our financial plight to him, he became quite concerned.

"I think perhaps I'd better become your manager in every sense," he said.

From then on, he took over many aspects of our day-to-day living. Most importantly, he recommended we move to a sublet apartment and not spend our precious money on the Park Chambers.

He found a fairly nice place for us on the top floor of a four-story brownstone on East 55th Street. Again, it had a single bedroom, a living room, a slightly bigger kitchen—and even a small balcony. Coming home the first night and turning on the lights, we were horrified to witness cockroaches scattering in all directions. We tried to get rid of them, without much success.

One day, Dilys came home with a puppy.

My heart sank. "Dilys! What have you *done*?"

"I couldn't resist, Julie, I just couldn't. I mean, look at her!" she said.

She'd seen this baby dachshund in the window of a pet shop. Perhaps by way of mollifying me, Dilys let me name it. My mother had always said that if ever she had another girl she would call her Melody, which I thought a ridiculous name. I was not too fond of the dog, so that's the name I gave her. Of course, somehow I ended up being the one who did all the feeding, the cleaning, the taking it out for walks. We called her Melly for short, and Melly came to the theater, and Melly pooped in the dressing room, and on the shag carpet in our living room, in the bedroom, in the kitchen, everywhere.

Since we were on the top floor of this walk-up, it soon became a real burden to take this puppy up and down the stairs all the time. I had a good idea. Knowing that manure is supposed to be very good for flowers, I folded some of it into the soil of the window boxes. The geraniums flourished, but the smell on the balcony was appalling!

When Neil was in Canada, we would have nightly phone conversations, and they grew longer and longer as time went by. Lou would admonish, "Julie, you've simply *got* to cut down on your long distance bill." But, as lovers do, we talked for an hour or more, and the minutes would just add up.

To my surprise, Neil became anxious and controlling, asking me to account for places I'd been and everything I was doing. Sometimes he didn't believe my answers and we would have heated discussions over the phone. I would say, "Neil, why do you doubt what I'm saying?" but still he would pump me. It was odd and eventually irritating. Sometimes I tried to make our conversations shorter, but that only served to make him more suspicious. I began to feel claustrophobic in the relationship.

One night on the phone, he asked me to marry him.

"Oh gosh," I stammered. "I've not actually gone so far as to think about marriage. Let me write home and see what my parents say."

Wimp that I was, I couldn't say, "I have the feeling this isn't going to work between us." I wrote to my mum, and she wrote back a very sensible letter, saying, *"I would prefer that you at least wait until your year is* over and let's talk about it when you get back. Marriage now, while you're in the throes of something so new, doesn't seem a very smart idea, and you'll be home soon enough."*

I was relieved, and showed the letter to Neil, saying, "I'm afraid we'll have to wait." He was not happy about it, and our relationship continued to deteriorate.

JOHN HEWER INVITED me and Dilys to stay for a summer weekend at the tiny house he'd rented on Fire Island. The Sunday was overcast, but very warm. We decided to go down to the beach, and I lay out on a towel without putting on any sunscreen. I fell asleep and woke up two hours later. The sun was blazing and I was already lobster red. I managed to do the show that night, but for the next two weeks, my skin literally hummed with fiery color.

I remember both Dilys and Millie Martin recommending, "Cold tea! You've got to lie in cold tea. The tannin helps." It was too painful for me to even bathe, so Dilys gently sponged my back and arms for me. I slathered chamomile lotion on myself, and for the show, I dabbed pancake makeup over that, but a purple glow still shone through. I'm surprised my skin wasn't permanently damaged.

Other silly moments occurred. There is a scene in the show where Tony and Polly are just about to kiss, but Hortense, the maid, interrupts them. One night, the actress playing Hortense missed her cue. Leaning in for the kiss, John Hewer and I paused and looked at each other. Not knowing what else to do, we leaned further, pecked discreetly, then pulled apart. Still no sign of Hortense. After a long moment, I said brightly, "Well, I have to go now!" and left poor John just standing there. He teased me about it for months afterward. As I walked away, I heard the thunderous sound of the actress's footsteps racing toward the stage.

LONDON'S SADLER'S WELLS ballet (later to become England's Royal Ballet) came to New York, and Dilys and I went to see a Sunday matinee of *Coppélia*. A young and extremely attractive dancer called David Blair was the male lead. His exhilarating leaps and spins and bravura performance took our breath away, and filled us with national pride.

After the performance, Dilys said, "Come on, we're going round to the stage door. We'll wait until he comes out and then congratulate him."

With reluctance I let her drag me round to the back entrance. Dilys thrust her way through the crowd of fans, and as David Blair appeared, she introduced herself. After all, we were British, and so was he!

He said, "Oh, you're the girls who are in *The Boy Friend*, right? Well, come on back to our hotel. We're going to have a drink."

Giddy with delight, we followed him and went up to a drab room where many dancers from the company were gathered. Drinks were handed out in paper cups. Sitting on the floor, midst the crush of people, was an exquisitely pretty lady doing what it seems every ballerina does—sewing her toe shoes, reinforcing them, attaching the tapes. I sat down beside her. Her name was Svetlana Beriosova. She was utterly delightful, and we chatted together for the remainder of the evening. She had been born in Lithuania, had lost her mother at an early age, and her father was ballet master for the Ballet Russe de Monte Carlo. Svetlana and I became instant, lifelong friends.

OUR LEASE ON the sublet was up, and Dilys and I moved to yet another apartment, which was a good deal nicer, with two bedrooms, on 57th Street, close to the East River. One night, along with some cast members of our company, Dilys arrived with Michael Kidd, the renowned choreographer of the film *Seven Brides for Seven Brothers*, and the Broadway productions of *Finian's Rainbow, Guys and Dolls*, and *Can-Can*. Everyone was enthralled to meet *the* Michael Kidd. He just sat in our midst, chatting amiably, seemingly unaware of his eminence. He was adorable—attractive, funny, and vital.

We didn't meet again until I went to Hollywood. Michael and I worked together several times in the years since. He was a beloved mentor—many times I turned to him for advice—and he and his lovely wife Shelah and their family became tender and understanding friends to my present husband, Blake, and me. But that is a story for another time.

DILYS'S MOTHER CAME to live with us. To my surprise, she was as gregarious as Dilys, and even competed with her daughter for the attention of Dilys' friends. Dilys would rail at her mother one minute, yet defend her the next, and was often reduced to tears. My heart went out to Dilys, for she was, to put it mildly, one difficult lady. I began to feel miserable. The woman was in our apartment, in my life, in my face, and making things awful for all of us. I considered moving to a place of my own, but couldn't manage it financially.

Miraculously, Dilys and her mother eventually decided to leave, and Millie Martin moved in with me instead. Dilys and I share a bond of friendship to this day, but Millie and I were easy and compatible house-mates and became great chums.

THIRTY

THE BOY FRIEND was a tremendous learning curve for me. Working for a year on one role, I was able to test myself again and again, night after night. I learned how to cement the humorous moments in the show, and the value of being real when playing comedy.

Madame Stiles-Allen had taught me how to work on a problematic note in a song by strengthening the note before it. I was amazed and humbled to discover that this technique can be applied to many aspects of theater: drama, comedy, song, or dance. It seems to me that if a moment in one's performance feels lost, it pays to take a look at the moment before it—to help set up and strengthen the troubling area. That year on Broadway was one of the best lessons in my life.

As my contract neared completion, I began to grow very excited about returning to London. Any problems that might be awaiting me at home were overshadowed by the thrill of seeing my family again after so long.

I received a phone call from a man called Dick Lamar. He told me that he represented the theatrical team of Alan Jay Lerner and Frederick Loewe, and explained that they were working on a musical version of George Bernard Shaw's classic play *Pygmalion*. I knew that these two gentlemen had written lovely musicals such as *Brigadoon* and *Paint Your Wagon* and, indeed, had seen both in London.

Mr. Lamar said, "I wonder if you could tell me how long a contract you have with *The Boy Friend*?"

"Oh, I'll be heading home by October 1st," I happily replied.

There was a slight intake of breath on the other end of the phone.

"My God!" Mr. Lamar exclaimed. "We assumed you had a two-year contract, like everyone else, and that you would not be available. I told Alan and Fritz that I'd make a phone call and find out for sure. It would only cost a dime."

My God indeed! If I had agreed to that two-year contract originally offered me for *The Boy Friend*—if I had not remained adamant about doing it for just one year . . . Was it chance? Luck? Karma? So many times in my life, I seem to have been blessed with inexplicable good fortune.

It was arranged that I would meet with the author and lyricist, Alan Jay Lerner, and read for him. I do not remember where the reading took place or which scenes from the play I worked on. But I remember that Mr. Lerner was extremely charismatic and that his manners were exquisite.

I thought my reading was appalling. I was surprised when Mr. Lerner asked for a second meeting, and I believe I read some scenes from other plays with his assistant, Bud Widney. I remember becoming emotionally undone by some particularly moving passage and dissolving into tears as usual.

A few days later, I was invited to meet Frederick (Fritz) Loewe, the composer. Whereas Mr. Lerner seemed a complicated man and difficult to fathom, Mr. Loewe was the complete opposite. He was the older of the two and was all Viennese charm. He greeted me with a welcoming smile and gallantly kissed my hand.

He and Lerner sang and played for me some of the songs they had already composed for the show, including "Just You Wait" and "Wouldn't It Be Loverly." I was captivated by what I heard.

Because I have a good ear, I was able to instantly sing one song for them then and there, which seemed to please them.

Shortly afterward, I was also asked to do an audition for the legendary Richard Rodgers, who was casting for his and Oscar Hammerstein's new show, *Pipe Dream*. I went to a theater with Lou Wilson and handed the pianist my audition piece, "The Waltz Song" from *Tom Jones*. I had been asked to sing something other than a song from *The Boy Friend* . . . something more vocally challenging.

I was the sole person auditioning that day. The theater was dark, with only the work lights for illumination; it felt cavernous and unfriendly. I stood on the stage, trying to see where Mr. Rodgers was sitting in the auditorium. I belted out the opening cadenza of my song as strongly and loudly as I could.

Mr. Rodgers came up onto the stage afterward and introduced himself. "That was absolutely . . . *adequate*," he said. Then he smiled. "I'm teasing. Thank you so much for coming and singing for us."

We chatted for a few minutes, then he said, "Have you been auditioning for anyone else?"

"Well, yes," I replied. "As a matter of fact I've been speaking to two gentlemen, Mr. Lerner and Mr. Loewe, who I believe are putting together a musical based on Shaw's *Pygmalion*."

Mr. Rodgers looked at me for a long moment, then he said, "You know, *if* they ask you to do it, I think you should accept. If they *don't*, I wish you would let us know because we would be happy to use you."

I will never forget that moment. What amazingly generous advice from one of the most eminent men in the world of musical theater.

I was more nervous singing for Mr. Rodgers than I was meeting Messrs. Lerner and Loewe. It was heady stuff and it may seem, as I tell it now, that I was a little blasé about it all. I was aware how incredibly fortunate I was to be considered for these roles, but I was only just becoming familiar with the mores of Broadway and how high-powered it all was. I was young and green—an innocent abroad with blinkers on; a young girl from Walton-on-Thames who was, more often than not, preoccupied with matters of family. How could I recognize the enormity of the opportunities that were coming my way?

I could not know at that moment that I was about to undertake one of the most difficult, most glorious, most complex adventures of my life, or that I would be guided through the daunting forest of self-discovery by several of the kindest, most brilliant giants one could ever hope to meet. But I am running ahead of myself.

AMAZINGLY, THE OFFER to appear in *My Fair Lady* came through. Despite the fact that this time I would have to accept the two-year contract—and perhaps because Richard Rodgers had already bestowed a blessing upon the project—I agreed to it. Besides, I think Charlie Tucker and Lou Wilson would have strangled me if I quibbled in any way. But the forthcoming production seemed to tower over me, and it was probably just as well that I was blind to the enormity of what lay ahead.

The thought that I would be coming back to the United States within three months made my return home doubly precious. The pack-up was exhausting: there were trunks to fill with clothes, memorabilia, and gifts for the family. Other boxes had to be put in storage for my return, and there were good-byes to be said to the company. Strangely, I remember nothing about my last performance in the show.

Neil came down for that last weekend, but the night before my departure I was so weary that I fell asleep on him. I woke in the middle of the night to find him sulky and morose. He had been expecting a tender and loving farewell, and I had completely passed out from fatigue.

When I finally boarded the plane the next day, I had a breakdown of sorts. I suddenly felt freezing cold, then broke out in a sweat with a knife-sharp pain in my bosom. I've only experienced that feeling twice in my life, both times from complete and utter exhaustion.

By the time we landed in London, I was feeling a little better. My family was thrilled to see me, and it was a lovely time of telling tales and visiting with everyone. It was grand to see my siblings. Mum and Pop were indeed back together again, though I don't recall that I saw much of him. He may have kept his distance—and I was certainly busy.

Soon after I returned to England, Neil followed. I believe he had a job offer. I knew in my heart that there was no point in discussing marriage anymore. We saw each other a few times in London, and I remember a taxi ride when we both agreed it was over.

Tony Walton had returned home from Canada in late 1954. Subsequently he had been studying at the Slade School of Art in London and was also working part-time at the Wimbledon Theatre, providing him with a wonderful combination of idealistic training along with the basics—the nuts and bolts of practical theater.

I was invited to his twenty-first birthday party. I understood that he had a new girlfriend, and that took me by surprise. Although we had corresponded during *The Boy Friend*, it had never occurred to me there might be someone else in his life. (Pretty crass of me, given my own behavior with Neil.) But our friendship was so unique, the bond between us so unshakable; we were as much like brother and sister as anything else. I felt a part of his family, he of mine. This new girlfriend definitely seemed like an intruder to me. I went to his birthday celebration, but I don't remember her being there.

At some point, Tony and I repaired to his room to chat, and I asked him if he still had a record album of *Daphnis and Chloe*, which had been one of our mutual favorites. He put it on the phonograph, and hokey as it sounds, that music helped make it perfectly obvious to us both that there was still a great deal of feeling between us.

Everything about Tony felt so safe, so reassuring, known and loved. After the confusion of the year in America and the seesawing relationship with Neil, it was a huge relief to be close to someone I knew—and who knew me—so well.

I WASN'T ABLE to spend the entire three months at home. During the month of November, I flew to Los Angeles to appear with Bing Crosby in a television musical of *High Tor*, adapted by Maxwell Anderson from his drama of the same name. The music was by Arthur Schwartz, with lyrics by Anderson. It was my American television debut.

The trip to L.A. was pleasant enough, but it was a weird time in my life, almost a suspended moment. Lou Wilson planned to join me, but he could not get there until a couple of days after my arrival.

I landed at night in the vast, empty, sprawling city. My hotel was on the outskirts of Beverly Hills, with office buildings in every direction; no restaurants, no snack bars—nothing like New York or London. I began to unpack, and felt hungry. The hotel had no restaurant or room service, so I called the hall porter, who offered to send out for a sandwich. I didn't know where I was in relation to the city, and I couldn't imagine how I was going to get around. I was relieved when Lou arrived.

Arthur Schwartz and his wife took me under their wing. They could not have been kinder—treating me as a young protégée about to be launched on a waiting world. They wanted to show me off and have me meet as many people as might help my career. A dinner was held for me at their house in Beverly Hills. It was a big gathering and I was asked to sing a couple of the songs from *High Tor*. Arthur played for me, and though I felt shy, everyone was friendly and appreciative.

The television show was daunting, to say the least. I knew nothing about film, and I remember the early morning makeup calls, my inexperience with cameras and close-ups.

Bing had been told that I was twenty-four years of age—four years older than I actually was, because the producers felt (probably correctly) that he would have thought me too young for the role and would never have hired me. He was a pleasant man, relaxed and easy in his own skin.

One day David Niven visited Bing on the set and we sat together for a while. I listened as these two very attractive and charming men reminisced about their early years, and I have seldom laughed as much. They were truly funny, and kept topping each other's stories, which were witty and outrageous.

Many years later, my husband Blake made two films with David, and we often saw him at our home in Switzerland. We adored him. I don't know anyone who didn't.

Bing and I worked together well, though I felt my performance was very stilted. I was just readying myself to go home for Christmas, when Bing asked if I would like to go to the Rose Bowl with him and his family to see an important football game. I think he felt I might appeal to one of his older sons.

I replied, "Oh, it's terribly nice of you, Bing, but I've got a huge amount of packing to do. I think perhaps I'd better stay and do that."

He looked at me in total disbelief.

"I have tickets in the owners' box and my sons will be there. It's the playoffs—almost the biggest game of the year."

I looked at him blankly.

"Well, it's really lovely of you," I said. "But honestly, I do have to pack."

I was shy, and couldn't imagine what I would say to his sons, so I went home. What a dummy. What an experience that would have been.

Bing gave me a lovely little pendant on the last day of shooting: a pearl-encrusted angel, inscribed "Julie, thanks. Bing." Alas, *High Tor* was not a memorable piece, and received only lukewarm reviews.

CHRISTMAS WAS AT home, as was the New Year.

Alan Jay Lerner writes in his wonderful autobiography, *The Street Where I Live*, that most of the cast of *My Fair Lady* planned to arrive in New York a week prior to the start of rehearsals on January 3, but I delayed traveling there until the last possible moment, because I'd had so little time with my family since returning from *The Boy Friend* in September. Alan couldn't know the reasons behind my insistence on the delay, but I simply had to be home through the holidays, especially for Don and Chris.

Repacking with the knowledge that I was now going to be away for two years, my mind and emotions were in a state of chaos. The weight of responsibilities looming in every direction seemed more than I could shoulder. Though Tony had plans to join me in New York as soon as he could, I was once again deeply anxious about leaving the boys and my mother, and for such a long time. The situation at The Meuse had not changed. Who would keep them safe? Who would cheer them and help banish the bleak depression in the household?

I remember saying sad good-byes to the family at Heathrow Airport and boarding the huge Stratocruiser with Lou Wilson, who had been in London and was accompanying me back.

As our flight took off, I wept as if my heart would break. Lou seemed puzzled at first, then became quite concerned. I sat beside him and bawled my eyes out. I couldn't explain why, and I couldn't stop. It was a tidal wave of emotion.

The flight took about eleven hours, I think. The plane had fore and aft seating sections with stacked sleeping quarters in the center, much like berths on a train. I sat beside Lou and tearfully hiccuped my way through dinner, which I barely touched. I was grateful to climb into the narrow bunk, pull the curtains closed, and once more let go of my emotions.

THIRTY-ONE

D URING MY BRIEF stay at home, Alan and Fritz had come over to London, and I'd gone to see them in a hotel just off Bond Street. It was there that I first met Rex Harrison, who was to play the leading role of Henry Higgins. He was tall and thin, his clothes exquisitely tailored. He was sophisticated, with a clear sense of himself, albeit somewhat egocentric. He was definitely the center of attention.

We listened to the new songs that had been added to the show. *My Fair Lady* was taking shape wonderfully.

Alan Lerner told me that *My Fair Lady* was originally entitled *Fanfaroon*—a man who blows his own horn. The title *My Fair Lady* comes from the song "London Bridge Is Falling Down," those three words being the very last line of the ditty. Its melody can be heard briefly in the overture of the show.

I had been working on the music with Madame Stiles-Allen. She had recently donated the Old Farm outside Leeds to the Yorkshire College of Music and Drama, and had moved south to a pretty cottage in West Kingsdown, Kent. She prepared me for "Just You Wait," which is a dangerous song for the voice because it has to be sung so angrily, even shouted at times. Madame taught me, as always, to emphasize the consonants for vocal clarity and safety.

REHEARSALS FOR *My Fair Lady* were held at the New Amsterdam Theater on 42nd Street. Lou escorted me there the first day. I was once again staying at the Park Chambers Hotel, this time in a room of my own. I remember scanning the streets as we drove down Broadway, superstitiously looking for a sign, some omen that would give me the much-needed confidence to begin the marathon. Strangely, I saw not one, but three.

There was the "My Fair Lady Nail Salon," "Pygmalion Clothiers," and "Andrews Coffee Shop." Good!

The New Amsterdam had once been a grand and glorious theater, home to the famous *Ziegfeld Follies*. In its upper reaches there was a smaller rooftop theater.

I learned that when the *Follies* played in the main theater below, the chorus ladies went upstairs after the performance, removed most of their already scant costumes, and paraded on a glass catwalk above the tables of the elite club.

By the time we began rehearsals in 1956, both theaters were in terrible shape; the larger one was now a cinema. The upstairs was never used, run-down, filled with dust, an old empty space, though the little stage and remains of the catwalk were still there. But it allowed us enough room to put the show on its feet, and it afforded some seats on the floor area for the creative team to observe the rehearsals. It also gave us complete privacy. I believe our company was the first to use it after it had been shut for so many years. Since then it has been magnificently restored by the Disney Company and is the linchpin of the 42nd Street rejuvenation.

AND SO I come to Moss Hart. The great Moss Hart, the director of *My Fair Lady*, and later *Camelot*. The man who created six plays with George S. Kaufman; the man responsible for *Winged Victory* and for *Lady in the Dark* with Gertrude Lawrence; the man who worked with Irving Berlin, Cole Porter, Richard Rodgers, Kurt Weill, and wrote the screenplays of *Gentleman's Agreement* and the second version of *A Star Is Born*, to mention but a few of his many accomplishments.

There has hardly been a day since that era of my life when my thoughts haven't turned to dear Moss. He has been much in my mind during the writing of this autobiography. At times I have invoked his name aloud, asking for his guidance. I still sense him as a constant presence. How does one adequately describe a man who, over time, completely captured my heart? Hopefully, as these pages continue, he will emerge, and the reader will understand why it was that everyone loved him.

Simply, he was a well-built man, with dark, receding hair, full, gentle lips, piercing brown eyes, well-defined eyebrows, and surprisingly large ears. In retrospect, he looked a little like George Gershwin; they could have been brothers.

Moss's aura was compelling, his intellect witty and sharp, his nature endearing. He was a unique and magnetic man. He had a slight stoop and, during rehearsals, would pad to and fro in the "earth shoes" he had specially made for him. He often clenched a pipe between his teeth, though, to my knowledge, it was never lit. He had a penchant for antique cuff links and wore a gold signet ring. He was warm, friendly, funny, and he embraced us all. Indeed, he embraced the world, and all the good things in it.

On that first day of rehearsals, the upstairs theater at the New Amsterdam had been made ready for the initial reading of the play.

The cast members were seated on rows of chairs, arranged in a shallow semicircle, the principals sitting in the front. I sat with Rex, Stanley Holloway (playing Eliza's father, Alfred Doolittle), Robert Coote (Colonel Pickering), lovely Cathleen Nesbitt (Henry Higgins's mother), and Michael King (Freddy Eynsford-Hill).

Opposite us, long tables and chairs had been set up for the production team: Moss sat in the center, and Herman Levin (our producer), Hanya Holm (choreographer), Oliver Smith (designer of the glorious sets), Cecil Beaton (creator of the exquisite costumes), Abe Feder (lighting), and Franz Allers (maestro of the orchestra) sat either side of him—plus members of the production and stage management staff.

In retrospect, I cannot think of a more celebrated, talented, awesome team to helm one show. Almost everyone connected with the musical that day had a distinguished biography that would fill several pages in *Who's Who*.

Oliver Smith's sketches for the sets and some of Beaton's costume designs had been put on display for the company to see. Alan and Fritz sat at the piano to one side of the stage.

After some initial press photos were taken, we began the business of the first read-through. Moss read the stage directions; Lerner sang the songs. He wasn't exactly a singer, and one was never sure he was going to make the higher notes (". . . and ohhhh, the towering fee-ling" from "On the Street Where You Live" was a big hazard!). But he sang with conviction, and it is always riveting to hear a score interpreted by its author. Fritz played with enormous panache and gusto, smiling benevolently at everyone.

Our production stage manager, a bear of a man with a warm voice and comforting manner by the name of Samuel "Biff" Liff, was friendly, supremely professional, and patient. His two assistants, Jerry Adler and Bernie Hart (Moss's brother), were affable and gracious, and sat next to him.

I was acutely aware that Rex appeared at home in his role already. All the cast members read well. I, on the other hand, was absolutely unsure of a single line I uttered. I remember feeling oddly distant, like an onlooker watching the proceedings from afar.

I had no idea how to do a cockney accent. I don't know why I hadn't thought to study it before we began. Some idiotic part of me must have thought that I could wing it. A man called Alfred Dixon was hired as a dialect coach for me. I saw the irony of taking English cockney lessons from an American professor of phonetics—my own personal Henry Higgins!

Costume fittings for the show began almost immediately. I knew more about Cecil Beaton than I knew of Moss or Fritz or Alan. I knew that he was British, highly esteemed, and considered very grand; that he had created costumes for many British productions, including several Noël Coward plays; and that he was also a celebrated portrait photographer long favored by members of the Royal Family. I was pretty intimidated by him at first.

The costumes were being made at the Helene Pons Studio on West 54th Street. Helene was a diminutive Italian woman, very busy, very pressured, full of energy, and a little mother to me.

At one point in the show, I had to wear one costume over another in preparation for a very quick change between scenes. When Eliza returns from the glamorous ball, she is wearing a full-length black velvet cape, and one supposes she has her ball gown beneath it, but I was in fact underdressed with the skirt and blouse of a yellow suit. Eliza has a fiery argument with Higgins and storms out. There is barely time in the quick scene change to don the suit jacket and shoes and add a new hairpiece and hat for the scene that immediately follows.

The Helene Pons Studio was on the thirteenth floor of a skyscraper, and whenever there was a high wind, the building really swayed. One day in early February, I was fitting the yellow suit and the velvet cloak on top of it. Beaton was a taskmaster, and I had been standing a long time on a small dais while the hemlines were marked and the cloak pinned. Several seamstresses had been jostling and poking me. I felt the building swaying and I suddenly became unbearably hot. Then *I* began to sway, and I knew I was about to faint. I broke out in a sweat and had to lie down on Helene's couch. Beaton was not sympathetic.

"Oh *dear*," he complained, flapping his long, delicate hands in a help-less fashion. "Somebody *do* something. Get her some water or a fan."

AFTER MY BEAUTIFUL ball gown was made ready for the show, Beaton requested a photo session with me. I tried to give it my all—leaning against the balustrade in his studio as gracefully as I could, while he took lots of pictures.

"Lovely, lovely, lovely," he murmured in a slightly bored voice, his camera clicking continuously. Then again, "Lovely . . . *yes*, lovely."

I thought maybe I was making some headway and beginning to impress.

"Now give me a profile. Yes. Now look at the camera. *Lovely!* . . . Of course you are the most hopelessly *un*-photogenic person I have ever met."

Beaton sort of got my goat. Because we were both British, I quickly picked up on something: he was grander than he had any right to be. Maybe I sensed arrogance or hidden ambition. Certainly he acted like a snob.

I began to tease him a little, using my developing cockney accent to good effect when I felt he was being condescending or indifferent. And he liked it! I would glimpse the teeniest crack of a smile on his pursed lips and a slight twinkle in his eye when I deliberately flaunted a lower-class attitude. Eventually I believe we came to appreciate each other, and his glorious costumes made one forget everything else, anyway.

MOSS CHOSE A late afternoon and evening rehearsal schedule, which allowed time in the morning for all the other things we had to do. We began working every day at 2:00 P.M., took a break for dinner at 5:30 P.M., and then reassembled from 7:00 until 11:00 in the evening. Stanley Holloway and I kept up the British tradition of a cup of tea at 4:00 in the afternoon, and soon everyone was enjoying that welcome little break.

Alan was more often present at rehearsals than Fritz. Fritz was the cavalier who loved the good life, loved the ladies, and was by far the easiest of the three men to get along with because he was always laid back and charm itself.

Alan was very highly strung. He, too, was incredibly charismatic, gifted, and highly intelligent. He wore glasses, and the skin on his face was taut, revealing the good bones beneath. He smoked heavily and per-manently held a cigarette—lit or unlit—between his thumb and third fin-ger, twirling it constantly with his second finger.

As we moved further into rehearsals, I became aware that he some-times wore white cotton gloves. He had a terrible habit of nail biting—not that I ever saw him do it, but apparently he bit his nails down to the quick until his fingers actually bled, and the gloves helped prevent him from doing that.

Rex became increasingly demanding and desirous of Moss's atten-tion. He double-checked every line in the play, insisting that we stick to Shaw's original dialogue. If he suspected Alan had injected a line, Rex would shout, "*Where's* the Penguin? Where's the *Penguin?*" He would then pore over the Penguin paperback edition of *Pygmalion* while everyone waited patiently. "See!" he would say. "This is the correct line. *This* is what it should be."

Alan and Moss wisely allowed Rex his head in these matters, and Rex was undoubtedly right to tout the preservation of the original play, which is what gives *My Fair Lady* such a strong core.

"Where's the Penguin?" became such an oft-repeated cry that one day Moss and Alan presented Rex with a full-sized taxidermist-stuffed penguin, which made everybody laugh and eased the tensions.

I began blocking some of the musical numbers with Hanya Holm, our choreographer, a sweet-faced, slightly rotund little lady, who turned out to be extremely kind and rather a comfort to me, the only woman in the male-dominated production team.

Once I started learning the choreography and setting "Loverly" and other songs with her, I found her to be encouraging and warm, as were the dancers around me, and it was the one time I didn't feel inadequate.

But about two weeks into rehearsals, it became obvious to me and to everyone, that I was hopelessly out of my depth as Eliza Doolittle.

I watched the original film of *Pygmalion* with Wendy Hiller and Leslie Howard a couple of times, searching for clues that would help me with this character. I still had not mastered the cockney accent, and I'm not sure I ever got it completely right. I adapted to the songs easily, and if it hadn't been for them, I honestly think I would have been dismissed and sent home. I had heard of people being fired on the spot and replacements being brought in, and I dreaded that mortification.

I got the feeling from Rex's cold and ungenerous attitude that I wasn't making inroads with him and that he was, quite rightly, making a stink about this silly little English girl who couldn't manage the role. Apparently he once said something like "If you don't get rid of that c—, you won't have a show." Thank God, it was many years before I knew of that remark.

I wondered if Moss would have the time to focus his attention on me. Did he know how much I yearned for guidance? I was a blank slate looking out at the world—no knowledge, no assurance or opinion, no concept of how to create a character, how to shape it, form it, bring it alive. Right or wrong, it would have been good to have an idea, but I had nothing to draw on. I was inexperienced and painfully aware of it. The only thing I felt was that there was *something* inside me—some awareness of "smarts" and a yearning to be set free. I felt I could be Eliza, could find and understand her, if only someone would gently unravel the knotted ball of string in my stomach and pull it up and out of my head.

And that's where Moss's humanity came in.

Dear Moss. He later told me that he said to his wife, Kitty Carlisle, "You know, if this were the old days, I'd have taken her to the penthouse at the Plaza Hotel, locked the door, made passionate love to her all weekend, and she'd have emerged Monday morning—a STAR!"

Kitty apparently replied, "Well, darling, we know we love each other. If you think it'll do any good—go ahead."

Moss decided instead to dismiss the company for forty-eight hours and to work solely with me. How he came to believe that I was worth the effort, I will never know. Perhaps my singing and a certain stage presence—or the fact that I was English and an appropriate age for Eliza—gave him cause for optimism. Certainly he was no fool, and couldn't afford to waste time or be indulgent. I do have a sense that he recognized and empathized with a lost soul. He came from a background of poverty and difficult circumstances. He knew what it was like to yearn for a way out, and he had received help from mentors who cared. I suspect that his instincts were so attuned, so generous, that he understood and reached out to give me one big chance, in hopes that I had the equipment to cut it.

On the way to rehearsals on that fateful weekend, I felt like someone going to the dentist with an agonizing toothache. You dread the experience, yet things have gone so far that you must deal with the pain. You hope you may feel better when it's over.

Moss said to me, "Julie, you and I have some work to do, but there isn't much time for niceties. If we are to accomplish anything at all, this is going to be hurtful and difficult." I knew that his words were chosen out of care and decency, and I braced myself for whatever was coming my way.

For those two days, alone in the rehearsal theater with only Biff and Jerry to assist, Moss and I hammered through each scene—everything from Eliza's entrance, her screaming and yelling, to her transformation into a lady at the end of the play. Moss bullied, cajoled, scolded, and encouraged.

He yelled from the floor, "No! You're saying it like a schoolgirl! Give me more." And then again, "Louder! I want that angrier."

I screamed the lines at him.

He leapt onto the stage to show me what he wanted. He snatched

Eliza's purse from my grasp and whacked an imaginary Higgins. He showed me how Eliza might sit in the scene at Ascot, teacup held high, pinky finger extended.

There were moments when I became angry at him, hated him, in fact. Then I became tearful from sheer frustration or despair. But I fought back the tears, and Moss would give me a little break, after which we would return and have at it again.

By the end of the forty-eight hours, that good man had stripped my feelings bare, and disposed of my girlish inadequacy; he had molded, kneaded, and helped me become the character of Eliza. He made her part of my soul. We were both exhausted.

Later I learned that at the end of that weekend, when Moss returned home, Kitty asked him how I responded.

"Oh, she'll be fine," Moss replied wearily. "She has that *terrible* British strength that makes you wonder how they ever lost India."

ON MONDAY MORNING, we ran through the whole show with the principals. I knew that Rex and everyone else were watching me to see what the weekend had produced. I probably fell back 50 percent from nerves, but I also gained 50 percent, and from then on I was on my way. Rex appeared somewhat mollified.

I was now able to move forward with the foundation that Moss had given me, and little by little, I cemented the role. Once I gained confidence, I began to add my own touches and flourishes. But for every single performance of the two years that I played on Broadway, I never stopped working on Eliza. She is such a character, and I have never in my life had as good an acting lesson as Moss gave me that weekend.

THIRTY-TWO

POOR STANLEY HOLLOWAY had been waiting for his own chance to work with Moss, and he finally had a bit of a meltdown, even threatening to quit the show.

Moss spoke with him. "Look, Stanley, I've had my hands full with a leading man who's never done a musical before and a leading lady who's never played a dramatic role. You've done both, so take it as a compliment that I didn't get to you immediately."

We traveled to New Haven to break the show in. Our theater, the Shubert, was right next door to the hotel where the principal members of the company were staying.

The weather was terrible—snowy, blustery, frigid—and indoors, we were mired in the out-of-town madness that comes from the technical demands of putting a big show on its feet. Oliver Smith's sets were phenomenal, but his designs called for two large turntables, which were the bane of Biff's, Moss's, and the company's existence, because they were slow and lumbering and they seldom lined up properly.

Hanya Holm had created a ballet at the end of the first act—the grooming of Eliza: the manicuring of her nails, the styling of her hair, the fitting of her costume, the queue of tailors presenting fabrics. Eliza becomes more and more exhausted, pushed here and shoved there. It so mirrored my own experience—the fittings with Cecil, the work with Moss, musical rehearsals—that it was easy for me to identify with the ballet, but it was a gargantuan sequence to manage in the midst of an already physically challenging role.

Julie Andrews

It wasn't until we were in New Haven that we met and heard our orchestra. Needless to say, hearing the score with a full complement of musicians for the first time was thrilling beyond words. The overture alone will forever give me goose bumps. When I hear it now, it takes me straight back to the nights I sat in my dressing room listening to it, putting finishing touches to my makeup and anticipating the weight of the show ahead of me.

There are eight unison notes as the overture begins. Every time I heard them I would think, "Oh my God, we're committed now." I could sense the excitement of "I Could Have Danced All Night" or "Show Me" or "On the Street Where You Live." As the overture ends, the horns herald the curtain going up, and the set of Covent Garden and the Opera House is revealed, with patrons of the opera milling with cockney street vendors, all in their incredible Beaton costumes. The audience nearly always broke into applause.

Our Austrian maestro, Franz Allers, was a task master. He would tell the chorus, "I want it tuk-tuk-tuk-tuk," as in "Every-<u>Duke</u>-and-<u>Earl</u>-and-<u>Peer</u>-is-<u>here</u>; Every-<u>one</u>-who-<u>should</u>-be-<u>here</u>-is-<u>here</u>"—a staccato pronunciation. Everything had to be exact and clearly enunciated. He kept the show in immaculate shape, calling a vocal rehearsal every week during the run on Broadway, and he always had endless notes for the principals. When conducting, however, he was a gentle, benign presence in the orchestra pit, and his instincts were infallible as to what any performer needed on any given day.

The rehearsals in New Haven were a nightmare for Rex. Kitty had forewarned Moss that singing with the orchestra would knock Rex sideways—and it did, because suddenly he couldn't hear his melodies, everything sounded new, and he didn't know where his cues lay. Franz Allers worked with him almost to the exclusion of anybody else, but Rex was panicked and created a great deal of fuss.

Actually, he was innately musical. Though he didn't truly sing in *My Fair Lady*, he performed the songs in an original "speak/sing" voice—a first for Broadway, I believe—and he had an ability to float across the rhythm of his songs in a unique way. His panic stemmed from the fact that he had never done a musical, never sung with an orchestra.

We inched our way through the interminable tech rehearsals, which are all about the sets and lighting and getting it right so that stage management can cement the show and make precision calls night after night. Finally, we came to the first preview, a performance that is indelibly printed on my memory.

Word was out about the show, and all manner of agents, VIPs, and special guests were planning to attend. It was such a highly anticipated production that anyone who was connected in any way with a member of the company or with the industry was coming up to New Haven.

That afternoon a huge and unexpected blizzard hit the East. It snowed and snowed and snowed. Inside the theater, chaos reigned. The turntables on the stage were not working—maybe they never would work. Rex was frozen with panic. Hair, wigs, costumes, and quick changes were being worked on. Ernie Adler, our diminutive and forever up-beat theatrical hairstylist, was flitting from room to room, crowns and bejeweled hairpieces temporarily perched upon his head, clips between his teeth, combs in his hands.

My own hair was long, and pieces were added to it throughout the show as necessary. My first costume called for long, straggly curls beneath my shabby straw hat. Once Eliza was accepted into the Higgins household, I wore a long "fall" at the back of my head, attached with a velvet bow, followed later by a beautiful twisted chignon for the ballroom scene. I not only had costume changes, quick changes, the underdressing, but also hairpiece and hat changes, too.

On the afternoon of that first preview, Rex suddenly declared he wasn't ready to do the show. He was adamant. There was nothing to be done except to postpone due to "technical difficulties." The company was dismissed and told to go home or have a good meal or whatever. The annoying turntables continued to be worked on, as they still were not functioning.

The problem was that people were already on their way up to New Haven. In order to alert everyone who had left early to brave the storm, hourly bulletins were broadcast on the radio, advising theatergoers of the cancellation. Nevertheless, by six o'clock, hundreds of people had arrived and were waiting to collect their tickets at the box office.

The house manager of the Shubert threatened to expose the true reason for the cancellation, and Rex's agent persuaded his terrified client that if he intended to continue in the business, it was in his best interest to get onstage, do the show, and be done with it. Rex finally agreed. There was a mad dash to get the word out to the company that the show was going on after all. The stage management went crazy, for members of the cast had disseminated all over town. By performance time every one of them had been located.

REX WAS A basket case. I, on the other hand, went from not having known how to cope during rehearsals to finding my true strength. The old vaudeville training kicked in. The show must go on? I rose to the occasion.

It was a monumental effort, but I honestly feel that I spearheaded the company through the entire performance that night. I encouraged, pushed, and motivated Rex and did everything I could to help make the show work. Miraculously, the turntables grumbled but didn't falter, and, miraculously, the audience simply loved it. The show ran about three and a half hours, but we got through it.

When the curtain came down, I went to my dressing room utterly spent, and sat in front of the mirror, eyes glazed, in total silence.

Everyone rushed to Rex's dressing room to congratulate him. I slumped in my chair, thinking, "I don't believe we did it . . . ," at which point my door was flung open and Cecil Beaton flew in. The little hat that I wore with the yellow suit was lying on my dressing table. It was an oval shape and flat like a saucer. In the haste of pinning up my hair and the hat going on my head in the quick change, it had been put on back to front. It was the only thing that night that hadn't been done correctly. Beaton picked up the hat and slammed it onto my head. "Not *that* way, you silly bitch—*this* way!" he snapped. I nearly burst into tears.

Within two or three days, to my enormous relief, Eliza's transformation ballet was cut, along with one of Rex's songs, entitled "Come to the Ball," and a lovely ballad for Eliza called "Say a Prayer for Me Tonight." The latter was subsequently used in the film *Gigi*.

My entrance in the beautiful ball gown had originally been in the middle of the ballroom scene, with everyone waltzing and swirling in their own magnificent costumes. Consequently, my lovely gown wasn't having any impact.

Moss and Alan made a deep cut in the first act—the only piece of major surgery in the entire show. Instead of the ballet, Alan wrote a small scene, which perfectly—and brilliantly—solved the problem. Pickering and Higgins are in his study, dressed and ready for the ball, waiting for Eliza. They discuss how hard Higgins has been on the young girl, and Pickering wonders if she will manage the evening ahead. The door at the top of the study stairs opens and Eliza appears dressed in the shimmering gown, and to orchestral accompaniment, she walks slowly down the steps. Both men watch, mesmerized. Higgins is holding Eliza's wrap, and as she gets to the bottom of the stairs he drapes it over his arm, offers Eliza his other arm, and escorts her out of the study with Pickering following. The turntables revolve, the study splits open to reveal the ballroom.

The replacement of all the effort that had gone before with this one little scene was inspirational. It is the defining moment of Eliza's transformation.

I should mention one other important change that went into the show long before previews began. I had a very pretty song called "Shy," and originally Eliza sang it to show her feelings for Higgins. Alan Lerner realized that in Shaw's original play, the main characters never once speak of love. Therefore, he and Fritz created another song, the famous "I Could Have Danced All Night," which conveys all the affection and emotion Eliza feels, yet never once mentions the word.

WE OFFICIALLY OPENED in New Haven on February 4, 1956. Just before the show, I went to my hotel room in the late afternoon, and in my mailbox was a bulky envelope with a little note from Moss:

"Darling Julie, I think these belong more to you than to me."

Inside were two brass discs—a pair of ticket tokens to the Covent Garden Opera House that Moss had found many years ago and had converted into cuff links. In the old days, if one had a box at the opera, one presented a token and was shown to the appropriate seat.

The gift almost brought me to my knees. It was so unbelievably touching and appropriate. Not only were the tokens from my home country and the famous opera house featured in our play, but they were also from Moss—and I knew how much he treasured them. The fact that he had chosen to give them to me was the greatest accolade I could have imagined. I cherish them to this day.

We played New Haven for a week, with Alan, Fritz, and Moss continuing to tweak and refine every day. We received wonderful reviews. From there, we went on to the Erlanger Theater in Philadelphia, opening on February 15.

To my dismay, during both the New Haven and Philadelphia runs, my voice began to feel the strain. In those days, Broadway performers did not wear body microphones as they do today. General floor mikes were strategically placed along the footlights, and we had to project like crazy in order to be heard. At one point I almost lost my voice completely. I became terribly worried. But, miraculously, it bounced back of its own accord, stronger than ever. I subsequently found this to be true of all rehearsal tryouts. The paint is fresh, the sets are new, the atmosphere is dry from the wood shavings and dust flying everywhere. With rehearsals all day and performances at night, the strain on vocal cords is tremendous.

If one is lucky, and sensible (I was lucky, but not that sensible in those days), the voice goes through a kind of metamorphosis, first going into decline and then, bit by bit, strengthening again . . . much like the result of a workout day after day.

On opening night in New York City, I distinctly remember feeling like a prizefighter going into the ring; I was the correct weight, I knew what I had to do, my voice had returned, and.I was as ready as I could possibly be. It was the only time in my entire stage career that I have felt that way.

THIRTY-THREE

THE MARK HELLINGER Theater on West 51st Street was originally built by Thomas W. Lamb in the 1930s as a movie palace for Warner Bros. Herman Levin, our producer, took a gamble when he chose the venue as a home for *My Fair Lady*, since, before our occupation, it had been a bit of a white elephant and was situated a few blocks uptown from the main Broadway area. But it was a beautiful theater, especially the front interior of the building, the lobby being exquisite and ideally matching the elegance of our show. Though a little shallow backstage, it was one of the largest and best equipped of the New York theaters, and it had a seating capacity of eighteen hundred people.

Much later, in 1970, the Nederlanders purchased it, but after a string of flops, they leased and eventually sold it to the Times Square Church in 1989. Various parties have tried to reclaim the building as a legitimate theater in the years since, but to no avail—which is truly a shame, since Broadway must and should preserve every great theater that it can.

MY FAIR LADY opened on March 15, 1956. After more tech rehearsals, we had had one paid preview only, which the audience received enthusiastically. On opening night, Moss gathered the company onstage before the curtain went up. He gave a short, charming speech telling us that we were all wonderful, and if the audience didn't love the show—well, what did they know! He added, "I have only one thing left to say: God bless us every one . . . and screw Tiny Tim."

The audience *did* love us. The reaction at the end of the performance was as phenomenal as any I can remember. People rose from their seats, seeming to want to storm the stage in their excitement. There were repeated bravos and many curtain calls. The reviews the following morning were ecstatic. Broadway embraced us and took us to its heart.

I wish I could tell you every detail of that opening night. I cannot. I doubt that even Alan or Moss gave accurate descriptions of it. It was so stunning, so overwhelming, and I think we were all dazed from the effort and the extraordinary reaction afterward. Was there a cast party? Did I go to Sardi's? I think Lou Wilson was with me that night. My family sent telegrams from home, of course, as did Charlie Tucker.

Tony Walton and I had been exchanging Dictabelts when I was out of town with the show. This was a new way of corresponding at the time. We would record our voices onto a plastic roll inside a compact little machine known as a Dictaphone, and send each other the roll in an envelope on an almost daily basis. Alas, the Dictaphone is defunct these days, and there is no way to gauge what I relayed to Tony in terms of that opening night, but he remembers that the recording was euphoric.

The high of the opening was followed by the immediate pressure to make the cast album, which we recorded a week later, on a Sunday. More stress on the vocal cords, more exhaustion—because we gave it our all and we didn't have a day off.

Our press department was bombarded with an assault of epic proportions from the media. All the daily papers, evening papers, and magazines wanted their own photo calls, and there were long nights after the final curtain came down when the company stayed on in the theater. Suppers were brought in; we changed scenes and costumes endlessly. Each session was a marathon for the photographers as well as the cast, and each shoot required discipline and as much conservation of time and effort as possible. Many a night we didn't get to bed until three A.M. or later.

THUS BEGAN THE great learning period of my life. Knuckling down, working, discovering what it is like to be in a great show and a very long run. I divide the experience into four distinct sections.

Right after the opening, one feels as if one has never learned a single line of dialogue. For the first three months there are panicky moments when, because you've had your head down for so long, nothing has been totally absorbed and it's almost as if you have to relearn the play: "Is this the right line here? Is that what I meant to say?" Then you really cement it.

The next three months of the run are pure enjoyment; fleshing out the role, giving it the best you have, playing with it, finding depth.

The following three months, one searches for anything to keep focused: listening to countermelodies in the orchestra that you've never heard before, reworking a line for better effect or finding something new.

The last three months are sheer slog: everything you can think of to concentrate, to be disciplined, to bring to bear all that you have learned.

And I had another year to go after that!

Overnight, it seemed, tickets to the show were like gold dust. The advance sales were tremendous. We heard that a couple had received a pair of tickets anonymously in the mail. Though they had no idea who had sent them, they decided to take advantage of the generous gift. They came to the theater, had a wonderful evening, and went home to discover their house had been burgled. The burglars had left them a note saying, "*Hope you enjoyed the show.*" Pretty creative, if you think about it!

The first weeks of a show's run, audiences consist mostly of theater parties. These are audiences who have paid over and above the ticket price to benefit some charity, and patrons arrive stuffed with pretheater goodies and drinks, and are a little annoyed at having paid through the nose. They are inclined to sit on their hands with the attitude, "You're a hit—show me!"

In the case of *My Fair Lady*, our theater parties continued for almost three months, and though word was out about how good our show was and those audiences did indeed enjoy the performances, there was a marked difference when we finally began playing to regular houses. Then we *knew* we really were a hit.

I recall the wonder I felt whenever a great audience reacted to Eliza's outburst at the end of the Ascot scene. She is trying so hard to be a lady, but in the excitement of being at the race track, she completely forgets herself and encourages her horse by yelling at the top of her voice, "Come *on*, Dover! Move your bloomin' *arse*!" It was an extraordinary experience to feel an entire audience rock back in their seats as one body, with total surprise and helpless laughter.

TONY ARRIVED IN New York City in the middle of April. He sailed over on the *Queen Mary*, and Lou Wilson and I went down to the docks to meet him. He moved into the room next to mine at the Park Chambers, and from then on we were inseparable. He came to see *My Fair Lady* immediately (a matinee performance), and he described the afternoon as being "magical."

I couldn't count how many times he saw the show in all, but he visited often and would sometimes walk through the pass door separating the backstage area from the front of the theater to watch a favorite moment.

Rex was dating his future (third) wife, Kay Kendall. She was a good actress and comedienne; generous, beautiful, fine-boned, a thin delicate nose, long legs, and an exquisitely small waist. She was all heart, all fun.

She and Tony were the "bachelors" (the theater widow and widower, if you will) flung together by the circumstance of their respective partners working nonstop in a Broadway show. Many evenings Tony and Kay would saunter off together for some jolly escapade, and afterward, they would tell Rex and me all about it.

I began to observe Rex at work, and was filled with admiration for his talent. He had an instinctive sense of timing. If somebody coughed or made a sound in the audience, his senses were so attuned that he would adjust accordingly and hold a certain line or repeat it. His technique was outstanding, and he moved like a dancer, sometimes on his toes or drawing his entire body up much like a human exclamation mark, his arms above his head for emphasis.

He continued to worry about hearing the orchestra correctly. Higgins's last song in the show, "I've Grown Accustomed to Her Face," was sung downstage, outside Higgins's house. The song begins softly, and Rex insisted that no scene change could be made behind him until the tempo of the song picked up and the orchestration was fuller and louder. That way, nothing distracted him or interfered with the quiet moment.

One night a frayed rope holding a flat, which was stored in the flies of the theater, came apart. The heavy piece of scenery swung sideways, then fell at an angle, skewering the stage with a terrible crash, just behind the painted scrim where Rex was standing. The scrim ballooned forward from the draft, splinters and debris spilling out beneath it.

It just so happened that not a single person was backstage at this moment, because of Rex's edict that the scenery not be touched. Nobody was hurt—which was a miracle. But the crash was horribly loud, and the orchestra came to a grinding halt, Rex came to a grinding halt— then, with great presence of mind, he said to Franz Allers, "Well, come on, *come on*—give me that bit with the 'clarionet.'" The audience burst into applause, the show picked up again, the stage management hastily cleared the broken set behind the drop, and we finished the show.

Rex and Kay occasionally invited Tony and me to the country house that they had rented. It was lovely to get away on a Saturday night after the two shows and to have a decent rest in fresh air, except that life at the Harrisons' was anything but peaceful. Everything was a drama.

One evening Rex was discussing with Tony the merits of a little painting by the French naïve artist Bombois that he had just acquired.

"I bought it because I like it," Rex said to Tony, "but what is it about the artist that makes him so special?"

Tony offered whatever insight he could, but was distracted when Kay walked in covered from head to toe in mud, leaves, and twigs.

"What on earth have you done?" Rex was astonished.

"I was walking the dogs and I fell in a bog in the woods," she declared.

"Rubbish," said Rex. "You did it to make an entrance."

Kay just smiled.

Everything about their lives together seemed heightened, crazy, funny. Tony and I enjoyed being observers.

Another time, they invited us to join them and then completely forgot that they had done so. Tony and I were packed and ready, but Rex and Kay didn't appear. We found them just as they were exiting the stage door. Trying to be casual, we asked, "Are we on for this weekend?"

They apologized. "Oh sorry, not possible this weekend. We completely forgot."

We went to see a movie instead.

MOSS VISITED OFTEN after we opened. He burst into my dressing room once in a brand-new Aquascutum raincoat and said with considerable glee, "Want to see something? Ta-da!" He opened the coat as if to reveal some dirty postcards. The inside was lined with mink.

He explained, "I just bought Kitty a new fur and told her it was a shame to waste the old one, so I decided to use it."

He loved money, loved what he did with it. He relished it in an appropriate way, delighting in his good fortune.

HOOKED ON AMERICAN milk shakes and occasional boiled potato sandwiches (my favorites), I became somewhat overweight. Moss said tactfully, "You're looking a bit broad in the beam, darling, particularly in the last dress."

"I know it, Mossie!" I confessed. "I've been wondering what to do about it."

"I have an infallible diet," Moss replied. "I do it all the time. Just halve your portions. If you normally have two potatoes for dinner, cut it down to one. If you normally have one potato, cut it in half and relish it all the more. That way you don't deny yourself a thing."

It worked beautifully, and I slimmed down.

BIFF LIFF CALLED the show from a tall desk in the wings. He would stand wearing headphones to cue the lights, sound, and scenery. If I had a moment, I would give him a hug, and he would acknowledge me with a nod and a smile as he busily got on with the show. While he was preoccupied, I would very gently remove his tie clip or sneak the wallet out of his back pocket. Later he would pretend to look for it and I would magically produce it. I am sure eventually he was on to me, but he allowed me to play the silly game anyway.

The company had bonded out of town, but now the real friendships began.

Robert Coote, who played Colonel Pickering, fondly called me "Baby Doll," which then became shortened to "BD." He would burst into my dressing room before the show calling, "BD, BD! Hello, BD. How are you today?"

I'd be hurrying to get ready, but I always stopped to chat for a moment.

Coote would continue, "I walked around the Central Park Reservoir this morning and then I had a *wonderful* swim at the Athletic Club." He would give himself a hearty slap on the diaphragm. "Then I had a good lunch . . . ," and he would describe it in detail. Everything with "Cooter" was about physical fitness and health. He'd inhale deeply and say he was feeling fit as a fiddle, and indeed, with his ruddy cheeks and sparkling eyes, he looked it.

Stanley Holloway was always adorable, as was his wife, Lainie. The two were inseparable. She was blond and petite, and Stanley was forever hail-fellow-well-met. He had a booming voice, probably because he was a little deaf. We shared the same birthday, and would celebrate together. The couple had a son called Julian, now a well-known actor in his own right.

Cathleen Nesbitt, who played Henry Higgins's mother, was a woman of grace and beauty. She had actually played a small role in the 1938 film version of *Pygmalion*. Beaton had dressed her exquisitely in the show, with frills about her wrists and gloves on her hands. You would never have guessed that she suffered dreadfully from rheumatoid arthritis. The great love of her life had been the poet Rupert Brooke, who died tragically in the First World War. She often talked about him.

When she heard about the Dictabelts that Tony and I sent each other, she said, "Oh, if *only* Rupert and I had had that opportunity! I would have him with me still."

I HAVE NEVER really liked to know before a performance who is in the audience, and in those days it was especially intimidating.

Laurence Olivier saw the show one night, and came backstage to see Rex. He stopped by my dressing room and informed me that although

I gave a lovely performance, I needed to speak louder and project more.

The playwright Terence Rattigan was often present—Noël Coward, too, both being close friends of Rex's and Kay's.

Ingrid Bergman came. She was tall, radiant, and natural, and while she visited me, she asked if she could use the "john" in my dressing room. For days afterward I didn't want to sit on the hallowed seat!

Helen Keller attended a performance and came backstage. The entire company was bowled over by her. She was probably in her sixties by then. She could neither see nor hear the show, but her interpreter relayed the entire performance to her by signing on her hand. Helen conveyed to me in a halting voice that she identified with Eliza, because she had so many problems herself with language. It was deeply moving.

The great opera singer Maria Callas came to see us. Afterward, she asked me how many performances I did a week.

"Eight," I replied.

"How do you *do* that?" she was genuinely amazed. "How do you survive? At the height of the season I sing maybe two performances a week or, at the very most, three. You do *eight* shows a week, night after night, and *two* on Wednesdays and Saturdays. Not only that, but you sing *and* you speak, which means you have to keep changing your vocal placement."

She was truly impressed, and I was grateful for the acknowledgment of how hard we were all working.

THIRTY-FOUR

M Y MOTHER CAME to New York in early spring. She traveled over
with Charles Tucker, and it was a pleasure for me to spoil her and
try to give her a good time.

Oddly, I don't recall her reaction to seeing me in *My Fair Lady*. I am
sure she loved the show itself, but I don't remember any embrace of
delight, or pride in my achievement. Looking back now, I think she was a
little weary, bewildered, and absent; perhaps because of seeing New York
for the first time, but most probably from the effects of the stress at home.

Charlie, on the other hand, was over the moon . . . proud, ebullient.
He squired Mum around New York when I was at the theater. He announced that he was going to buy me the fur coat he'd predicted I
would one day have, and he took me and my mother to a discount place
on Seventh Avenue and bought us each one. Though animal rights
activists will rightly shudder at this, he chose a classic design for me that
was practical and quite weatherproof. It suited me, and back then I loved
the feeling of luxury when I wore it.

EVENTUALLY *MY FAIR LADY* took its toll on me, and on my voice.
The role was so demanding, and the shows when I didn't have to pace
myself vocally were rare.

About five months into the run, I began to notice that, though I would
commence the show in fine voice, about two-thirds of the way through the
evening, my vocal quality would weaken. A few weeks later, my voice
would last for perhaps *half* the show before again losing strength and

sounding fainter. After a few more weeks, my vocal strength lasted a mere quarter of the way through the show. It was puzzling and worrying; I had never experienced anything like it before.

Rex was having vocal problems as well, and at one point had to be out of the show for a few days.

Though I was in trouble myself, I could not be off at the same time as Rex. Audiences would have been appalled if two leads were absent. Anytime a prominent cast member is out, the rest of the company assumes the burden and the balance shifts.

Rex's standby, an actor called Tom Helmore, was brought in. He had been preparing the role of Higgins, but he'd never actually worked with the principals, so he rehearsed with us all day Tuesday before going on that evening and then all morning Wednesday before the two shows.

Somehow we made it through Tuesday night, though neither Tom nor I was doing well in the vocal department.

During the matinee the next day, Helmore lost his voice. It descended into his boots, until he became incomprehensible. He had been drilled and pushed too hard, and his overstressed vocal cords simply folded on him.

By the evening's performance, he could only manage a whisper. He confided to me backstage, "It's funny, I feel *so* much better!" I think he was referring to his ability to play the role. Nevertheless, I could not hear him and neither could the audience. Their astonishment was palpable. Patrons began to drift out of the theater.

I was pulling everything I knew out of the hat to keep the show going. I replied to everything that Tom said in such a way that the audience understood what he had said to me.

I arrived at the song "Just You Wait," and *my* voice was by now so fatigued that when I reached the middle of the song—". . . *one day I'll be famous* . . ."—a sound came out of my throat like nails scraping on a blackboard. I thought, "Oh my God, I am in *terrible* trouble." I could still speak, thank heavens, and "Just You Wait" is a song that, in a pinch, can be talked instead of sung . . . so I did just that.

The scenes that follow are a montage of Eliza working with Higgins on her speech lessons. There are several blackouts in this sequence to suggest the passage of time, but they were not long enough for me to get offstage to alert management of my dilemma. Poor Tom Helmore couldn't be heard at all, I could not sing, and still we had "The Rain in Spain" to do and I had "I Could Have Danced All Night" immediately after that. I knew without a shadow of doubt that I would not be able to manage it.

During each brief blackout, I sent word via members of the company.

"Tell Biff that I have also lost my voice! Please ask him to do something. I will not be able to sing 'I Could Have Danced All Night.' Tell him to trust me."

They dutifully did so. I received no response, and the show wove inexorably through the lessons montage. In every blackout as we regrouped, I kept saying, "Did Biff hear me?"

"Yes, he heard you."

"Well, *please* tell him to believe me!"

Still no response.

I talked my way through "The Rain in Spain," thinking, "In one minute I'm going to be as mortified as I have ever been in my whole life." I didn't have the guts to stand before the audience and say, "I am so sorry. I, too, have lost my voice." With a lifetime of discipline and training, I just couldn't stop a show, break character, and talk to the audience without management's permission, and I knew I could not perform "I Could Have Danced All Night" as a talk-song. It is purely melodic with a big, high finish.

Tom Helmore, Cooter, and I sank onto the couch as "The Rain in Spain" ended, and I thought, "This is it. This is the worst moment of my life."

Suddenly, miraculously, Biff and Jerry Adler appeared on either side of the stage, walking the huge front curtains to a close.

"That's it, folks," Biff said to us. "We are shutting down for the night." He slipped through the curtains and addressed the audience, explaining that, as they were obviously aware, Mr. Helmore was having vocal difficulties. Refunds or exchanges would be processed.

Biff told me later that he had heard my vocal dilemma and had received my messages, but that protocol required him to dash to the front of the theater and ask the house manager's permission to phone Herman Levin, our producer, and get *his* permission to shut down the show. Hence, the agonizing delay.

I went back to my dressing room and leaned against the door, feeling as if the hand of God had come down and plucked me from a fate worse than death in the nick of time. No one was around. It was the middle of the evening, still quite light outside, and no other shows had let out yet. The theater was eerily silent.

The following morning, the press simply mentioned poor Tom Helmore and the fact that he had a very bad cold. There was not one mention of my vocal troubles. Amazingly, Tom went on again for the next few nights, and with some decent sleep, I, too, recovered enough to manage three or four more performances until Rex returned, though I was out of my mind with worry. Finally, I took time off and my understudy went on.

I went to see various specialists.

One doctor told me there was nothing wrong with my throat. "It's a little pink, but that's all. You're fine."

I asked him, "Then how come I can only sing for a quarter of the show before my voice weakens?"

"Well," he replied, "the cords are a little tired, but they're not *red*, they're just pink. There's nothing for you to worry about."

Another doctor—one recommended by Alan Lerner—gave me a complete physical, then suggested that perhaps my problem was sexual. "Are you and Tony having physical relations? Maybe you shouldn't kiss or hug or overstimulate each other for a while."

No point in continuing to see *that* medical genius!

Eventually I saw a dear man called Dr. Rexford, an Austrian, old-school, knowledgeable throat specialist. He took one look at my cords and said, "No wonder you're having problems. You have *acute* vocal fatigue. If, for instance, you hop on one leg for the longest time, it will eventually weaken. You rest it overnight and it might be a little better, but hop on it again the next day and it will become weaker *sooner*. That is what has been happening to your cords."

Dr. Rexford prescribed ten days of rest, and at that very moment, my father came to visit. It was difficult for me, because I hoped to give him a wonderful time, but I had to rest and remain silent. I was a basket case of anxiety, nerves, and tension, knowing that so much of the show rested on my shoulders. I knew I had to return to performing as soon as possible, and that I still had more than a year to go before completing my contract.

Dad immediately assumed that what I needed was country air. His solution was to take me to Central Park, rent a skiff, and row me around the lake talking quietly to me all the while. I remember looking at him with affection, thinking, "Dad, you're a darling, but I don't think this is really going to do it for me." But it was dear of him. He tried so hard to bring me back to nature and its soothing, healing qualities.

I began to visit Dr. Rexford every Saturday morning. He would check my vocal cords, pulling my tongue out so far that I became expert at relaxing my muscles and I seldom gagged at the mirror that was halfway down my throat. He always gave me a vitamin shot—B-12 and B-Complex—which was painful since he insisted on keeping his old needles and re-sterilizing them, rendering them horribly blunt. He would then sit at his piano and make me vocalize with him. He employed an awful falsetto voice, demonstrating what he wanted from me vocally, but he knew his craft.

The instinct, when one is in self-preservation mode, is to grab the cords and make a harsher, harder sound. If in fact you do *not* rub them together abrasively, but let them relax and use a good deal of breathy air as the sound comes through, it can stand you in good stead.

I hyperventilated so much trying to follow his advice that I nearly passed out onstage once or twice, but I learned some invaluable techniques for getting through a show: as much humidifying steam as possible in my apartment and my dressing room, no alcohol, no ice, vocal rest, of course—and NO talking on the telephone, especially first thing upon waking.

Midweek was always the hardest time for me. To this day, I still think of Wednesdays as "Black Wednesdays." I would be in the theater early to prepare for the matinee. After the performance I would nap in my dressing room—always making sure that my upper half was propped up against pillows, as the blood rushes to vocal cords and thickens them if you lie flat, especially after having used them. I would then eat a light meal and get ready for the second show. I would not leave the theater until midnight or after. I barely saw daylight on a Wednesday.

Doing two heavy shows on one day can slam you down in terms of fatigue. I would gradually pull myself back up for the Thursday evening performance, and by Friday night would feel a little better. Saturday arrived and with another two shows I would be flattened once again. I could relax on Sunday, but by Monday evening we started the process anew.

At the bottom of 51st Street, the New York docks are situated on the Hudson River, and the *Queen Mary* or *Queen Elizabeth* Cunard liners departed for England around noon on a Wednesday. I would be in my dressing room, applying my makeup for the first show of the day, and I would hear the great ship's horn as the tugboats guided one or the other out to sea. The sound always made me feel sad. The liners represented freedom and home, and I longed to be aboard and sailing away in the fresh sea air.

I started seeing Dr. Rexford on Wednesday mornings as well.

REX, TOO, FELT the strain of eight performances a week. He also became a little bored. To keep himself amused, he would do mischievous things.

We'd be doing the lessons montage, and he'd suddenly pull down a trombone that was on the wall and blow it in my ear. I'd jump out of my skin, though he always made it seem as though it was part of the action.

Later I'd ask, "What did you do *that* for?"

"They wouldn't have put it there if they hadn't wanted me to use it."

Or he would take up the box Brownie camera that was set decoration and ad-lib, "Hold it!" and pretend to take a photograph of me.

Cooter did a fair bit of ad-libbing, too, upping one or two lines to three or four, then five or six. He could bluster on forever, and backstage we would raise eyebrows and say, "Oh Cootie," as he "milked" a monologue for several minutes.

For some reason, about three months after we opened, I started to get the giggles onstage. I have no idea what actually sponsored this appalling lack of discipline, but I could not help myself. When this occurred, Rex would look at me in total surprise, his eyebrows raised high, and from sheer nerves, I giggled all the more. I'm ashamed to admit that at times it got so bad I could barely speak my lines. If I didn't look at Rex, I managed pretty well, but he was so unpredictable with his expressions and the things he might do, that the minute I got onstage with him, the slightest thing would set me off. I can only guess at the extent to which my nerves were frayed. Was Rex setting me up? Did he sense my awe and fear of him? Did I sense his irritation with me? Who knows!

I prayed in my dressing room before the show, "Please God, *don't* let me be such a wimp. *I do not wish to giggle.*" It took me about six weeks to get over that idiotic phase.

"*THE RAIN IN SPAIN*" was a high point in *My Fair Lady*. Eliza has finally spoken flawlessly, and there is great excitement. Higgins picks up a cloak, Pickering pretends to be a bull and charges the cloak, then Higgins swirls Eliza in his arms for a mad tango, at the end of which they all fall back onto the couch with laughter. At this moment applause usually stopped the show, and there was time for a brief sotto voce exchange between Rex, Coote, and me.

One night we had a particularly unresponsive benefit audience. Rex murmured quietly, "Bunch of *twats*."

I'd never heard the word "twat" before, and assumed it meant "twit" or "fool." I echoed him gaily, "Yes. Twats, twats, twats! You're absolutely right."

The two men looked at me as if I had lost my mind.

Later I asked Tony about it and he tactfully said, "No, no, darling, that's not the same word at all . . . ," and he explained.

Not long into the run, I became aware that Rex had a rather windy stomach. I expected that much of his balletic "dancing" stemmed from attempts to clench through gaseous moments.

One night his timing was impeccable.

In the penultimate scene of the show, Eliza runs away to Higgins's mother's house. Higgins barges in and confronts Eliza, and she launches into a long speech about the difference between a lady and a guttersnipe;

i.e., it is not how she *behaves* but how she is *treated*. All Rex had to do at this point was pace up and down at the back of the scene. He didn't have to say a word.

On this particular evening, as I finished my speech, Rex released a veritable machine-gun volley of pent-up wind. Members of the orchestra heard it—every musician looked up to the stage in bewilderment; even the first few rows of the audience heard it. There was a shocked silence, and at that precise moment Cathleen Nesbitt, as Mrs. Higgins, had the line "Henry, dear, *please* don't grind your teeth."

It was outrageously funny. The orchestra roared with laughter. I could not look at Rex, and every single line I uttered in the scene after that had a double meaning.

HIGGINS: Eliza, you ungrateful wretch, you talk about me as if I were a motor bus.

ELIZA: So you *are* a motor bus; all *bounce* and *go* and *no* consideration for anyone!

By now Rex had a devilish look on his face. Cathleen was trying to disguise her mirth, and as usual, I was a basket case of giggles.

Eliza's song "Without You" follows this dialogue, and I could see the lyrics coming at me before I sang them: "*No*, my *reverberating* friend, you are *not* the beginning and the end!"

I took so many pauses in that scene trying to contain myself that the show ran over by about ten minutes.

I found myself punching Rex during the curtain calls.

"How could you *do* such a thing?"

He pulled at his tie and straightened it. "I'm sorry, *I'm sorry*! I was always a windy boy—even when I was young."

Another night Rex lost one of his capped teeth. I was suddenly faced with this gap-toothed actor, trying to work the object into the side of his mouth for later retrieval.

It's very hard to keep a straight face when things like that are going on.

There is a moment in the show when Eliza hurls Higgins's slippers at him. I have never been able to hurl *anything*. I don't have the appropriate flick of the wrist or the elbow or whatever it takes. If I try to throw a tennis ball, I somehow manage to end up on my backside. So the slippers would hit Rex on the head, or smack him on his bum, or worse, they'd disappear completely into the horn of the megaphone that was part of the scenery—all of which Rex used to full advantage. He would turn and look at me with total outrage—especially if I hit him on the head—and the giggles would rise in my throat all over again.

I learned to sing and perform through every kind of difficulty: rain, shine, air-conditioning breakdown, leading man having problems, my having a sore throat, giggles, headaches, disasters backstage.

Alan Lerner once said that a long run in one very good role is probably better training for an actor than performing repertory week after week. One can really hone one's craft and find out what works, what doesn't, and why.

THIRTY-FIVE

IN OCTOBER OF that first year of *My Fair Lady*, I celebrated my twenty-first birthday. Charlie Tucker flew over for it, as did my mother and also my girlfriend Susan Barker.

Charlie hosted an after-theater birthday supper upstairs at the famous 21 Club. Lou Wilson was there, and Rex and Kay, "Cooter," and Cathleen. Stanley and his wife were invited, of course, as it was his birthday, too.

There was a large U-shaped table so that we all sat facing each other. I was next to my mother. It was her second visit to the States, and for some reason, she was in a foul mood. I do not know what caused it. She certainly drank a lot that night, and single-handedly, she made my twenty-first birthday an absolute misery. All through supper she scowled and barely spoke. It was embarrassing and sad to see her so disturbed.

Trying to engage her in conversation, I whispered, "Doesn't Cathleen look beautiful tonight?"

"Yes," she replied in an icy tone, "and she's *such* a lady, with *such* good manners," implying that I had none.

When we finally returned to the Hotel Park Chambers, Tony felt moved to say something. As he said good night, he added, "Please, Barbara, try not to hurt Julie any more."

It was the first time I had ever heard him speak to her that way. It was a brave thing to do because he was not in her good books—nobody was.

As she and Charlie were preparing to depart for Britain, he said, "Julie, your contract with me has expired. I'd like to renew it."

I was miserable that my mother was leaving with so much unresolved. I knew she was probably miserable, too. I replied, absently, "That's fine."

"No need to look at it. It's the same as it's always been," he said. "Just sign."

Later, when I went over the document with Lou Wilson, I discovered that Charlie had raised his already large commission by a considerable amount. Lou was appalled, and I felt betrayed. I had signed the paper, so the damage was done, but unfortunately that incident changed forever the tenor of Charlie's and my relationship.

After they departed, Tony and I settled into a quieter way of life. Technically, he wasn't allowed to work since he had to wait to take the United Scenic Artists of America exam in order to join the union, and that exam was offered just once a year. He began looking for a job anyway.

His passion was the theater, and Oliver Smith, our brilliant set designer, was exceedingly kind to him. Impressed by Tony's portfolio, he invited him to his house in Brooklyn Heights and counseled him regarding the theater, the union, and how to proceed.

The same was true of our lighting designer, Abe Feder. He was a short, stocky fellow, built like a tank. He nearly always walked around with a good Cuban cigar clenched between his teeth. He, too, was a legend on Broadway, a larger-than-life personality, wonderfully charismatic, chock-full of ideas and good humor. In addition to his theatrical experience, Abe was a renowned architectural lighting designer and had illuminated vast projects like the World's Fair, Rockefeller Center, the Empire State Building, and the United Nations, among others.

Abe provided Tony with introductions to several major magazines, including *Vogue, Harper's Bazaar,* and *Playbill.* Tony's very first assignment in the U.S. was to design caricatures for *Long Day's Journey into Night* starring Fredric March and Florence Eldridge.

TONY AND I attended some wonderful parties.

Moss and Kitty Hart were the best hosts in New York. Their evenings were charming and sophisticated, their guests extraordinary, the dialogue sparkling. There were trays heaped with food and the champagne flowed. At the height of the festivities, someone played the piano and Moss and

Kitty would entertain us, singing witty duets. They were marvelous together, and seemed really to enjoy the fun.

Stephen Sondheim was a young, up-and-coming talent. His lyrics for *West Side Story* had earned him instant recognition. I met him for the first time at a luncheon party. Despite his celebrity, he was sitting alone at one side of the room—terribly shy, but innately intelligent and charismatic. We struck up a conversation and my heart instantly went out to him.

Just around the block from the Mark Hellinger was the Alvin Theater, and a play called *No Time for Sergeants* was playing there. A group of us were coming out of our theater one day, and we stopped to chat with members of the play's cast. Someone said to me, "Do you know Roddy McDowall?," indicating one of the actors.

My knees practically buckled. Here was my fantasy hero from *My Friend Flicka*! I had never imagined that one day I might meet him.

"You don't know it," I said to him, "but we're *sort* of married."

He looked at me, puzzled, and I explained my girlhood fantasies about him, the ranches, and the horses. He loved my story. I told him that if I could find one of the original deeds that I had made, I would send it to him. I *did* find one—and he kept it in a beautiful lacquered box on his desk.

Roddy was a devoted friend to a great many people, and he was loyal to a fault. I always hoped he would write a book about his life and the people he knew. When asked why he didn't, Roddy replied, "I have too many friends. I know too much. I couldn't."

Tony and I began to entertain a little. We had moved out of the Park Chambers, and Lou had found for us a tiny ground-floor apartment on East 65th Street. We thought it must once have belonged to a high-class call girl, because we kept getting phone calls at all hours of the night asking for this particular woman. The flat certainly had all the trappings: purple and gold curtains, speckled mirrors, comfortable but over-decorated furnishings.

We sometimes made weekend trips to a lovely little inn by a lake on the west side of the Hudson River. It got us out of the city, and I was grateful for the rest and relaxation. We'd walk in the woods or take a boat on the lake.

EVERY YEAR, EACH show on Broadway gives one extra performance for the Actors' Fund of America. This benefit is usually done on the actors' day off. When it is your company's turn, you perform seventeen performances in two weeks without a break. Every actor, every gypsy on Broadway comes to see the show, especially if it is a hit, since it is the one night that working colleagues can catch up with what is currently playing. These are simply electric evenings, the kind one never forgets.

Our Actors' Benefit was a knockout success. We could not progress smoothly through the show because of the constant ovations. Our entrances were greeted with roars and applause, screams, whistles, shouts. Practically every number stopped the show. It was phenomenal.

I discovered that on important nights such as these, my nerves would take over and my heart would beat as if it were about to jump out of my chest. I would also feel somewhat light-headed.

Many years later, I discovered that I suffered from very low blood sugar—thus, when under stress, the only thing supporting me was adrenaline. I was eventually able to compensate for this by having high-protein meals and occasionally sipping liquid protein during the show. It made all the difference to my stability and energy, and I wish I had known more about it in those early days.

Tony and I went to see the Actors' Fund Benefit of *West Side Story*, which was our closest and biggest rival. It was a miracle of a show, from the first downbeat of the overture to the last note of the evening. As *My Fair Lady* was to song and book, *West Side Story* was to song and *dance*. The two shows were equal titans. I became friends with Chita Rivera, who played Anita, and her boyfriend, Tony Mordente (who later became her husband), as well as with Carol Lawrence, who played Maria.

REX'S CONTRACT WAS up at the end of November, and Edward Mulhare (who had subbed when Rex took vacation time earlier in the year) was brought in to take over the role of Higgins. Mulhare was almost the spitting image of Leslie Howard, who had played the role in the film version of *Pygmalion*.

In spite of the difficulties I'd had with Rex, he was so charismatic, such a brilliantly faceted diamond, and so fascinating to watch, that when he left the company, I missed him very much.

He lived his life in the grand manner; he oozed style. I missed his power, his presence, and of course, he always kept me on my toes. I can't remember who said this, but someone made a cogent remark: "No matter how big a shit Rex was, the truth is he cut the mustard—and for that, one forgave him everything."

Suddenly, though, there was a new dynamic. Once Rex departed, the weight of the show seemed to fall on me.

Mulhare certainly looked the part, and he did a good job playing Henry Higgins, but I don't think I ever really got to know him. Rex had been so flamboyant; Mulhare was more guarded and private.

TONY PASSED HIS union exam and got a job designing the sets and costumes for Noël Coward's *Conversation Piece*. He came home with hilarious tales about Noël and the auditions.

Two Noël Coward productions were being prepared simultaneously, and auditions for both were held in the same theater at the same time. The great master would sit in the center of the auditorium, one production company on the left of him, the other on the right. The manager for the auditions would come onstage and say, "This gentleman is auditioning for . . ."

One day a man rushed onto the stage and said, "I understand that there's a gigolo in your play, Mr. Coward," and before anyone could reply, he continued, "so I thought I'd show you my physique." He stripped naked, except for his bright red socks, and just stood there. Both production teams were stunned. There were a few stifled giggles but otherwise total silence, and the stage manager hesitated, wondering what to do. Everyone glanced at Coward for his reaction.

Suddenly his immaculate English voice called from the auditorium, "Er . . . turn a little to the *left* please!"

I LEARNED SO much about the theater from Tony. I would complain about the enormous hats Beaton had designed, and the forced perspective of the sets that made it difficult to pass through doorways and nar-row spaces. Tony would gently point out that there is only so much room on a stage, and that false perspective is utterly essential, indeed part of almost every theatrical design. Stages are often raked, couches and beds are foreshortened, doorways and rooftops have proportions much smaller than audiences might imagine watching from the audito-rium. As I observed Tony at work through the years, I learned to respect very much the designer's craft.

I said to him one day, "I wish my nose wasn't so big. I'd like a small, retroussé nose like, say, Vivien Leigh."

"Nonsense," he replied. "You have a lovely nose. It doesn't disap-pear into the scenery. Gertrude Lawrence had a large nose—and look what it did for her!"

I never complained about it again.

As I have mentioned, Tony often watched our show, and he helped me resolve something that had been puzzling me. There were times when I felt that I had given a pretty good performance, yet Tony would indicate that it was merely average.

There were nights when I didn't think I was good at all, but Tony felt I had done a terrific show. What made it more difficult to understand were the special nights when I "threaded the needle," so to speak: I *felt* good, I *was* good, and the audience hung on every word.

When I spoke to Tony about this, he said, "I think in the first instance you are sometimes too busy watching yourself and saying 'Aren't I doing this well?' Your focus is turned inward. In the second instance, when you don't feel up to par, you are concentrating so much on getting through to your audience that you lose the awareness of self and your focus is on sending it out to them instead. That's the night when you think you're bad, but in fact you're very good. The third case is when you have found the exact level of health, generosity, and technique."

Is it ever perfect? Hardly. But that rare magical performance, when one "threads the needle," is nourishment for the soul. It is the reason, ultimately, why one strives over and over to capture the feeling again.

THIRTY-SIX

IN JULY AND November of 1956, I made two appearances on *The Ed Sullivan Show*, the biggest weekly variety show on television at the time. Sullivan's ratings were so high that he attracted top performing talent from all over the world.

I certainly wasn't a headliner, and my appearances were not particularly noteworthy, but they were important for two reasons: I was exposed to a vast viewing audience across the country, and, more importantly, I sang songs from *My Fair Lady*. These, together with scenes from *Camelot*, which I performed on his show in 1961 with Richard Burton and Robert Goulet, are the only filmed records that exist of my performances in both musicals.

Nowadays there is always archival material taken of any show on Broadway, but for so many years, nothing was recorded on film or tape (except for bootlegged footage that no one will own up to). The tiny snippets of shows that were captured on television in that era are like gold dust to people who are interested.

I made a brief appearance on a television special with Rex called *Crescendo*. It featured an amazing cast—Ethel Merman, Peggy Lee, Benny Goodman, Diahann Carroll, and the great Louis Armstrong. Our paths crossed briefly. I had completed my segment and Louis was just commencing his. His energy seemed boundless. He clasped the famous trumpet, wiped the sweat from his brow with a big white handkerchief, and grinned at me. He said, in that delicious growl of his, "I seen you in that *My Fair Alligator*." Made perfect sense to me.

IN 1957 I made two record albums. One was for Angel Records, and was called *Tell It Again*, a collection of unusual children's songs composed and arranged by a blind eccentric named "Moondog." He was the equivalent of an English "busker," playing various instruments on the corner of 54th Street, near Broadway. He was brilliant, funny, and a little daunting—for he sported a long beard and dressed in loose robes, open toed sandals, and a Viking's helmet. He also carried a spear. He was definitely not crazy, but certainly unique. His music was sophisticated and original. Some of his rhythms were in five-fourths and seven-eighths, which I found challenging, never having sung them. Martyn Green, a man famed for his performances in Gilbert and Sullivan, shared the album with me.

The second album I made that year was for RCA Records and was entitled *The Lass with the Delicate Air*. Irwin Kostal was the arranger/conductor, and it was the beginning of an extended collaboration. We made another album together, and later he was arranger/conductor for the films *Mary Poppins* and *The Sound of Music*.

The Lass with the Delicate Air was a collection of English ballads, and though I think RCA hoped I would choose pieces that were more popular, I was very keen to record the songs, since I had an instinct that there would come a day when these sweet minor classics would not be as easy for me to sing.

IN MARCH, I had an altogether different experience. I was invited to play the title role in a live broadcast on CBS of Rodgers and Hammerstein's *Cinderella*. This was an original musical created basically for me, and I felt incredibly fortunate. It coincided with a two-week vacation that was due me from *My Fair Lady*.

A wonderful cast was assembled. The legendary theater couple Howard Lindsay and Dorothy Stickney were to play the King and Queen; Edie Adams, the Fairy Godmother; the hilarious Kaye Ballard and Alice Ghostley would play the Ugly Stepsisters; Ilka Chase would be the Stepmother; and a newcomer at the time, Jon Cypher, was to play the handsome Prince.

Our director, Ralph Nelson, had a fine reputation for many prestigious shows, but his concept for *Cinderella* seemed a little odd. He hoped to make the story appear as real as possible, which was unusual given the fairy-tale nature of the piece and the endless possibilities he had for magical effects—pumpkin-to-coach, Cinderella's transformation from rags to riches, and so on. He may have been limited because we were, after all, doing *live* television; the night we performed was the night we aired across America, and trick photography would have been difficult.

I thought the songs were very pretty. I loved the ballad "In My Own Little Corner," and a song called "Impossible," which I sang with Edie Adams.

Edie had an air of sparkling sweetness about her. She was dating the great comedian Ernie Kovacs at the time, and they subsequently married.

Kaye Ballard and Alice Ghostley were wonderful foils for each other. Kaye's character was so strong and bossy, and Alice's so giggly and silly. Jon Cypher was very good-looking, and had a pleasant singing voice.

Howard Lindsay and Dorothy Stickney were the dearest couple. Married in real life, they had been the stars of one of Broadway's longest running plays, *Life with Father*. On lunch breaks they would sit on the set, side by side on their scenic thrones, and eat their sandwiches out of brown paper bags. Howard was an effervescent, diminutive man, and Dorothy was pretty and equally diminutive. Tony and I became great friends with them.

They owned an exquisite mill house in New Jersey, close to the Pennsylvania border, and they invited Tony and me to stay with them one weekend. We drove out in their car, which Dorothy's cook had stocked with fruit pies and wonderful casseroles.

We arrived in the cool of the night at this beautiful stone cottage. The property had a rustic charm, and there was an herb garden ringed by a white picket fence. Hammocks were strung between the trees and a bubbling brook made sweet music. Everything about the place was comfortable. There were glowing table lamps and soft couches covered in floral patterns. There was a screened patio, and one could eat alfresco and not be bothered by mosquitoes. Tree frogs, crickets, and cicadas would buzz and hum.

We visited Howard and Dorothy several times, and they were wonderful hosts. Tony and I would rest, read, and take leisurely walks. Howard would disappear into his study to write. Dorothy would putter in her kitchen.

Eventually the Lindsays allowed Tony and me the use of the cottage for a quiet vacation. I remember one weekend when we walked midst the riotous colors of autumn and the far-off hills were covered in a misty haze. Deer came down to the little stream to drink, and rabbits scampered in the grass beneath the trees. It was a safe and lovely haven.

REHEARSALS FOR *CINDERELLA* progressed, and we soon brought the production to the floor of the television studio from which it was to be aired. There were technical problems to be resolved, many cameras to be rehearsed, and for the actors, there was much waiting around.

I chatted a lot with our floor manager, a charming, shy, and extremely capable young man. I asked him what he would be working on after *Cinderella* was finished.

He said, "Actually, I don't think I will be doing television much longer."

When I inquired why, he said that he was close to realizing a long-held dream of providing free Shakespearean performances in Central Park for the general public. I thought of the hard work he must have done to get something so unusual off the ground. I also wondered if his project could ever be successful. I remember wishing him luck. His name was Joseph Papp.

His vision, of course, soon became a proud reality at the Delacorte Theater in Central Park and at the Joseph Papp Public Theater in New York.

ONE DAY I was waiting in the wings of our set, and I happened to be whistling. (When I am nervous, I always whistle. I'm good at it, and directors have used it from time to time . . . . I whistled in *Mary Poppins*, and in

My Fair Lady and *Camelot*.) I was standing there and, I do not know why, I whistled a few bars of a song called "The Last Time I Saw Paris."

A voice behind me said, "I really meant that when I wrote it, you know." I turned around and was face-to-face with Oscar Hammerstein.

"Oh gosh, Mr. Hammerstein," I stammered. "I'm ashamed to say I had no idea that was *your* song."

He said, "I was so devastated when Paris fell to the Germans during the war, and remembering the city as I once knew it, I felt compelled to write that lyric."

I realize now that in those days I walked with giants: Alan, Fritz, Moss, Rodgers and Hammerstein, Joe Papp . . . Why didn't I think to ask the hundreds of questions that haunt me today whenever I think about them? I suppose I was too busy finding out who *I* was.

LIVE TELEVISION WAS daunting. We were performing a musical show, yet, unlike theater, there were cameras doing a slow dance around us at all times (and in those days, they were much bigger); people were pulling cables out of the way, and we were trying to ignore all the chaos of a working crew while attempting to convince our audience there was no one around but us actors. That's where Joe Papp was so helpful, because he smoothly directed traffic on the floor, cued the actors in terms of where we had to be, how long before we were on camera, and which camera was being used.

The most difficult part for me was the transformation scene when Cinderella, clothed in rags at one moment, is wearing a beautiful ball gown the next. Since Ralph Nelson wasn't using magical effects, this was achieved by a camera panning down to my foot to reveal my sparkling shoes. Then, while someone was furiously pinning a new hairpiece and crown on my head and draping a cape around my shoulders, the camera slowly panned back up. By the time it reached my face, the transformation was complete. It was risky, especially on live television. There were so many people working on me, and I was trying hard to stand still and accommodate them, yet make it work for the cameras so that it all looked appropriate and effortless.

The coach to the ball was actually half a coach, so that cameras could appear to be inside it. The whole contraption was rocked back and forth as Edie Adams and I bounced our way to the ball singing "Impossible." It was one of the highlights of the show.

There were commercial breaks, which helped with some of the costume changes, but once on-air, it was a pretty hectic all-or-nothing exercise.

Two days before the airdate, we recorded a cast album with a twenty-eight-piece orchestra for Columbia Records, which was to be released the day after the telecast. I have no idea how the albums could have been pressed and made ready so quickly.

Robert Russell Bennett created the lovely musical arrangements, and it was thrilling to work once again with the man responsible not only for creating the arrangements for *My Fair Lady*, but also the great spacious sound so evident on many Rodgers and Hammerstein shows—*Oklahoma*, *South Pacific*, *Carousel*. The orchestra rehearsal was a total joy.

We filmed our two dress rehearsals as a backup in case of some disaster or major breakdown.

The night of the telecast, just before we aired, some "good friend" said to me, "You realize that possibly more people will see this show on one night than if you played in *My Fair Lady* for fifteen years." It was not exactly what I needed to hear at that moment.

I was later told that more viewers watched *Cinderella* than any other show in television history. The evening went fairly smoothly, and we all did the best we possibly could, but for me, it felt a little lopsided: too rushed, and without the smooth polish we could have had if filmed and edited for a later date. It was an incredibly hard job, but a great learning experience. It took me years to realize the enormity of what we actually pulled off that night.

THIRTY-SEVEN

MY FINAL PERFORMANCE in *My Fair Lady* on Broadway was on February 1, 1958. Although my contract in New York was up, I had by this time agreed to play Eliza for another eighteen months in the London production. Rex and Stanley would be recreating their roles as well. We were to begin rehearsals on April 7.

Before I left New York, however, I did two more television guest spots in January and February: *The Big Record* hosted by Patti Page, and *The Dinah Shore Show*. Dinah was warm and welcoming. I did a number from *Showboat* called "Life Upon the Wicked Stage" with Dinah and Chita Rivera, who was also a guest.

We were choreographed by an endearing, energetic man called Tony Charmoli who, nearly twenty years later, choreographed my own television series, *The Julie Andrews Hour*. Crazy world!

SALLY ANN HOWES was to take over the role of Eliza on Broadway, and Anne Rogers, who had created the role of Polly in *The Boy Friend* in London, was scheduled to play Eliza with the American National Tour of *My Fair Lady*.

As my contract drew to a close, there was a big fuss from Actors' Equity Association about Anne being granted a work visa in the United States. Tony and I knew Annie fairly well because of our shared paths in *The Boy Friend*. It transpired that one of the people creating the problem about Annie's permit was a British actor—albeit a U.S. resident—playing a minor role in *My Fair Lady*.

The rumor flew around our company, and dislike for the perpetrator was pretty intense. If true, we couldn't believe that someone so blessed to be in the U.S., and who was enjoying its wonders and those of *My Fair Lady*, could be so tough on a fellow performer. Happily the problem was resolved and Annie duly arrived.

She's a North Country lass, wonderfully spunky and forthright. Tony and I embraced her immediately upon arrival, and she went into rehearsals and then out on the road with the touring company.

I was filled with mixed emotions during my last week on Broadway. I was saying good-bye to dear friends and to New York City. I had no idea when or if I would be back. I was relieved to be free of the tremendous pressure of eight performances a week. I was tearful yet grateful, exhausted yet exhilarated.

FOR TAX REASONS, Charlie Tucker advised that I not enter the United Kingdom until the first of April, when the new fiscal year would begin. Because I so badly needed a vacation, it was decided that I would spend six weeks traveling in Europe, beginning in Paris.

Packing up was chaotic. There was much to sort, clear, and organize, many shows to catch up on, farewell dinners, and the final departure from our odd little apartment. Two weeks later, on Valentine's Day, I flew to Paris.

Tony stayed behind, as he still had work to do, and he moved in with some friends for a few extra weeks. We planned to meet in Europe as soon as possible.

I could not believe the feeling of instant ease that Paris gave me. I felt as if my temples were being gently massaged, and that harmony and balance were being restored to my world. I remember asking Tony later, "What *is* it about Paris that is so soothing?"

His answer surprised me. "I think it's to do with the proportion to your eye," he said. "In New York, everything is above you—you're in the canyons, so to speak. In Paris, you look out over rooftops—you can see your world, feel on top of it, be in control."

The sense of his words resonated even more when, years later, I lived in Switzerland and, again, experienced the feeling of tranquility looking out over the chalet rooftops and watching the toy-like trains run up and down the mountains.

Paris certainly was the perfect city in which to recover from two years of hard work. I reveled in it, luxuriated in it.

Charlie Tucker met me there, bringing Mum and Pop with him. Donald had just joined the merchant navy, and Chris was still at school. We stayed at the small Hotel Castiglione on the Rue Faubourg St. Honoré. We went sightseeing and had long, elegant lunches and dinners. We took the elevator to the top of the Eiffel Tower, and saw Versailles. Mum and I went to a Dior fashion show and had fun shopping on the boulevards.

One evening we went to see Edith Piaf in concert. She came onstage wearing a simple black dress and flat slippers, no makeup, frizzy hair. The moment she began to sing, she was mesmerizing.

Charlie Tucker and Pop departed, and Mum left a couple of days later, having had a lovely time. We got on famously, and her recent displeasure with Tony seemed to have vanished. I was sad to see her go. Dad and Win, Johnny, and Celia came over in her place. The English rugby team was on their flight and about to play a big international match with France. Dad was ecstatic—more thrilled to meet the team than he was to see me, I believe! He had struck up a conversation with the English captain, Eric Evans, and offered him house seats to *My Fair Lady* in London—already impossible to come by in the skirmish over the advance sales—in exchange for six tickets to the match. He had a deal!

Unfortunately, our tickets were in the French section of the Colombes Stadium, and we were rooting for the Brits. I was screaming my head off, yelling, "Go, England!" and Dad kept nudging me in the ribs because we were getting terrible glowers from the French supporters all around us.

The family and I climbed the 365 steps to the top of one of the towers at Notre Dame, where we had a spectacular view of the city. We got tickets to the Lido and saw a glittering revue. We strolled around the vast Louvre Museum. What a glorious holiday it was.

When they returned home, Pauline Grant arrived. She and I went to Zurich, then on to the tiny country of Lichtenstein, where we walked and rested.

Tony finally joined us, and we spent a few days in Arosa. Pauline returned to London, and Tony and I journeyed on to Venice, seeing the famed city for the first time.

We stayed at the wonderful Hotel Danieli; took gondolas along the canals; explored the Basilico San Marco; visited the galleries, where we saw exquisite Canaletto and Guardi paintings; ate at Florian's; and admired the gem of an opera house, the Teatro La Fenice. Venice could not have been more beautiful, and we marveled how, in the blustery March weather, it seemed to adjust its coloring—pink, terra-cotta, and white in the sun, and mauve, blue, and gray when it was overcast.

In that most romantic city, I developed a large fever blister on my lip, which dampened our ardor and ruined every photo Tony tried to take of me!

We ended our holiday in Klosters, Switzerland, where we met up with Tony's family for one last week, returning to England on Easter Sunday, April 6.

The very next day, rehearsals for the English production of *My Fair Lady* began. We had about four weeks to pull the show into shape.

OUR PRODUCER, IN partnership with Herman Levin, was a gentleman called Hugh "Binkie" Beaumont, the head of H. M. Tennant. His shows always reflected style and class. He was sophisticated and witty, probably the most powerful producer in the West End, and his knowledge of theater was impressive.

Charlie Tucker felt that I could not commute every day from Walton-on-Thames, as it would have been too exhausting for me. So during the rehearsal period, I stayed at the Savoy Hotel, which was within walking distance of the famous Theatre Royal, Drury Lane, in which *My Fair Lady* would be playing. I had a small, enchanting suite overlooking the Thames and the Houses of Parliament.

While there, I did an interview for a theater magazine with a bright and charming young man by the name of Leslie Bricusse. Today he is the award-winning composer and lyricist of such classics as *Stop the World— I Want to Get Off*, *The Roar of the Greasepaint—the Smell of the Crowd*, *Doctor Dolittle*, *Goodbye, Mr. Chips* . . . and of course *Victor/Victoria*, to mention but a few. Our professional and personal lives have continued to overlap throughout the years, and he and his beautiful wife, Evie, remain two of Blake's and my closest friends to this day.

ONE OF THE first things I had to adjust to, once *My Fair Lady* was up on its feet, was a slightly different pitch in the sound of our orchestra.

"Pitch" is the perceived fundamental frequency of sound, and our musicians seemed to play the score of *My Fair Lady* with a slightly brighter, shinier resonance; not a different key, but a lifting of sound, perhaps to give it greater clarity. This could have been something to do with the acoustics in our theater, or perhaps our conductor, Cyril Ornadel, preferred that particular tonality.

I was actually told by Alan Lerner that I was singing a little flat, which really irritated me since I was proud of having a good ear and I believed I *never* sang off-key. In this case, though, the songs I had been singing for the past two years felt as if they had been transposed a whole tone higher. I had to really listen to myself, and the orchestra, and eventually I adjusted to the new frequency—but for the first couple of weeks, it was quite distracting.

If memory serves, rehearsals were at the Drury Lane Theatre itself, the very place where, seven years before, I had seen the production of *South Pacific*. The theater and the Royal Opera House, Covent Garden, are two of London's historic structures, and they lie almost within a stone's throw of each other.

Strolling to work each day from the Savoy Hotel through the old Covent Garden market was a joy for me, seeing the sheds and the booths and the tall desks where the clerks stood to negotiate prices for their produce: fish, vegetables, flowers.

In those days, the market was a hive of industry, especially in the middle of the night when the growers sold to retailers, who then rushed the fresh goods to their own establishments in time for the morning shoppers. The entire wholesale market was relocated to Nine Elms in 1974, and Covent Garden is now a very upscale area.

When I walked there on a matinee day, there were always still a few barrow boys tidying up, wheeling their carts amid piles of debris left from the predawn selling. Sometimes they would recognize me and smile and wave, calling, "Welcome back, Julie" or "Hello, girl!" It felt good to be home.

Tony and I decided that, since I was probably going to be in the theater for the next eighteen months, we should make my spacious, high-ceilinged, and wainscoted dressing room as charming and comfortable as possible.

Charlie Tucker gave us a modest budget and we went shopping, purchasing a good dressing table and matching stool, a big, long couch, plus some George Moreland prints in gilt frames—which were much too expensive, but which looked lovely on the damask-covered walls.

There was a little mirrored alcove in the room that had been converted into a small bar, and in the months that followed, I delightedly watched my dad take charge of it, playing the grand squire—as if to the manner born—when his friends came to see the show.

The advance word on *My Fair Lady* was tremendous, and we all felt that we could not possibly live up to it. The press was talking about the musical as the biggest, best, and most extraordinary ever to hit London, and we worried we might be riding for a fall.

Moss, Alan, and I were walking away from the stage one day, after a rehearsal. I was a little ahead of the men, and Alan suddenly said, "I wonder what hidden depths lie within our Julie?"

I looked back at him. He was smiling at me, teasing, in a way. I think he was implying that though he knew me, he didn't really know me. I supposed I still appeared a little glacial at times.

I managed a jokey reply, but inside, I was yearning to say something pertinent and truthful. I wanted to let him know, "I'm in here, Alan. Believe me, I hear you. I'm in here."

Kitty Hart did not fly over to join us until rehearsals were well under way. Moss drove to the airport to meet her, with his brother, Bernie Hart, accompanying him.

Bernie told us later that the moment Moss and Kitty embraced, they just stood in the middle of the busy crush of people, oblivious to everyone, their heads together in silent communion. He thought it one of the most loving, tender moments he had ever seen.

Sadly, Fritz Loewe did not make it to London for the opening. He had suffered a severe heart attack a week prior to the commencement of rehearsals and was not fit enough to come. Fortunately, he who so loved life and all its delicious temptations, recovered well, and the setback did not cramp his style in any way.

Our preview performances were packed, and audiences responded enthusiastically.

The night before we opened, Tony and I exited the stage door at the end of the evening well after midnight and were surprised to see a long line of people going all the way around the theater, with bedding and chairs on the pavement.

I asked, "What's happening here?"

"We're queuing for the opening night gallery seats . . . ," "They go on sale in the morning!", "We have to queue now if we want a good seat," they replied.

Tony and I stood and chatted with them for a while, and as we departed, I called out that I hoped they would enjoy the show.

The following evening, April 30, my dressing room was so full of flowers, I could barely move. There was an extraordinary bouquet from Charlie Tucker that was the most magnificent azalea plant I have ever seen, but the most endearing gift of all was a simple wooden Covent Garden flat tray, filled to the brim with bunches of dewy, fresh, sweet-smelling English violets—Eliza's flowers. My lucky flowers.

When I opened the card it simply said, "*With love from the opening night gallery queue.*" They had apparently made a collection among themselves and purchased the violets from a Covent Garden vendor. That gesture meant more to me than I can possibly say.

THIRTY-EIGHT

THE OPENING NIGHT of *My Fair Lady* in London was more restrained than the one on Broadway. The gallery crowd being an exception, the audience seemed a little staid by comparison. Noël Coward was there, along with many other celebrities, most of whom had seen the show in New York. Of course my family was there, too, except for Donald and Chris. Perhaps there were not enough available tickets.

It felt as though everyone in the audience was holding his or her breath, hoping that the show was as good as the advance word. We gave a solid performance, and received a grand ovation, but for me, the evening lacked a certain charge.

I returned to the Savoy with my family, phoned my brothers, and sat on the floor in my suite with my shoes off, tired and relieved that it was over and done with.

Win had been looking for a decent coat to complete her opening night ensemble, and she found just what she wanted in the Ockley Jumble Sale for sixpence. It suited her, and her budget, admirably. She had spent most of the previous night altering the sleeves and taking up the hem. Upon arrival at the theater, she deposited the coat in the cloakroom, and it cost her ninepence: more to hang it up than to buy it. We laughed a lot that night.

The reviews for the show were excellent, with just a few minor carps here and there. It may not be true, but I heard that the critic from the *Daily Express* panned us in the first edition of the newspaper, and that

Lord Beaverbrook, who owned the *Express* and had loved the show, insisted the review be a rave. Indeed, by the second printing, it was.

Two nights later, there was a small private reception at the Savoy, and my mother informed me that my biological father would be present. He was going to see *My Fair Lady* and wanted to say hello to me. At the party, I received the slight impression that he hoped to "come aboard," so to speak; to claim some sort of relationship. I didn't like his attitude, and certainly didn't like him horning in on something that should have been my dad's province. So, though polite and, I hope, decent, I was a little distant with him. It was the last time I ever saw him.

Many years later, he wrote me a good letter, short and to the point, saying that he was aware that I knew of our connection and that if I cared to discuss it, he would genuinely welcome the opportunity. I thought about it for a long time, and finally replied—asking him to understand that since this could possibly hurt the man I considered to be my father, not to mention my siblings, it might be better to leave the situation as it was. He must have understood, for after that I simply received an annual Christmas card with his signature. I appreciated the gesture. I subsequently heard that he'd passed away.

ON MAY 5, Her Majesty Queen Elizabeth and her husband Prince Philip attended a performance of *My Fair Lady*, which, in my opinion, was much more glamorous than the opening night. The theater was festive, the royal box bedecked with flowers. Our performance shone. Afterward, the Royals spent time with Alan, Moss, and Binkie Beaumont, then came backstage and greeted the company. Her Majesty said that she had loved the show, and Prince Philip lingered and chatted, particularly to Rex. They must have passed on their enthusiasm to other members of the Royal Family, for on May 22, HRH Princess Margaret came to see us.

Probably the most meaningful performance we ever gave was when Sir Winston Churchill came to see the show. We all knew he was in the audience, and we understood that he would not come backstage to visit because he was elderly and in frail health. He had requested that a copy of our script be sent to him, and he read it in advance. Our entire company played that performance of *My Fair Lady* for him and him alone—this extraordinary man whom we loved, admired, and respected so much.

THREE MONTHS AFTER we opened, the stress of eight performances a week began once again to take its toll on my voice. But this time I knew what to do. Every Wednesday and Saturday I visited a fine ear, nose, and throat specialist, Dr. John Musgrove, whose offices were on Harley Street. He was dashing, British to a fault, always attired in a morning suit, and he was exceedingly good to me.

I continued to have throat infections from time to time, and Dr. Musgrove decided that my wisdom teeth should be removed as soon as possible since they were impacted. It took some arranging, but I went briefly into the London Clinic, had all four of the offending teeth extracted, and was back in the show three days later.

It was also essential that I have my tonsils removed, but that operation would have to wait until the work in *My Fair Lady* was over.

Dr. Musgrove kept my voice maintained, as Dr. Rexford had in New York City, and I could not have survived without his help.

ONE SUNDAY NIGHT, Tony and I were visiting his family in Walton-on-Thames. We were having a quiet supper by the fire. Life was very good indeed, and Tony and I were sitting side by side on a low footstool, balancing our dinner plates on our knees. We looked at each other and smiled, and I honestly don't know how it came about, but one of us whispered to the other, "We should get married soon." And then, "Should we mention it now?"

So we suddenly said, "We were just talking about getting married."

I thought the Waltons would explode with joy. They opened a bottle of champagne and toasted us. It was as if we had truly announced our engagement, whereas we were simply floating it out there as a thought. But from then on everyone assumed that we were formally engaged, so that was that.

Not long afterward, Tony and I received an invitation to attend a Royal Garden Party on July 17 at Buckingham Palace. What a thrill—but what should I wear?

There was a designer called Rachelle who had made some of my dresses when I was touring in the early years. She was impoverished and totally hopeless at keeping her books. More often than not she asked for a loan, but she was a good designer and fitter, and she had good seamstresses working for her. I found some black-and-white printed silk material, and she designed and made me a lovely afternoon dress, which I wore with a wide-brimmed, black straw hat.

As we were driving to the palace, I thought of the days when I would say to my mother, "Do you think I'll ever get to have tea with the Queen?"

The atmosphere in the garden at Buckingham Palace was cheerful but formal. There was a huge marquee beneath which strawberries and cream and tea and scones were being served. White tables and chairs dotted the lawn, and people were milling about waiting for Her Majesty to arrive.

Suddenly, Tony and I were approached by Her Royal Highness, Princess Alexandra, the Queen's cousin. She was approximately my age, and she stopped and chatted with us for a while.

"I'm so pleased about your recent engagement," she said. "I wish you both every happiness."

I was startled that she knew, since we had only just announced it publicly.

I RECEIVED A phone call from the secretary to Sir Victor Sassoon, hotel magnate and businessman. Would Tony and I care to join him for lunch at Claridge's? We were intrigued.

At the luncheon, Sir Victor—suave, elegant, and silver-haired—asked me if I would object to the use of my name for one of his racing fillies. He had originally wanted to use the name "My Fair Lady," but that had been already taken. I had no objection, and we had a pleasant time together. The filly was sired by Pinza, the famous Derby winner. When Sir Victor found out that Tony and I had recently announced our engagement, he gave the horse to me as a wedding present. I was stunned.

She was stabled in Ireland, and I never, ever saw her. Her papers were passed on to me, however. Sir Victor explained that she didn't have the speed required for the track, but that she would make a fine brood mare because of her good genes. So he had the filly "covered"—impregnated—and when he handed her papers to me, she was supposedly already in foal. I thought this was all extremely generous.

There were complications with the birth—or she never conceived—I cannot remember which, so she was "covered" again, and then I received word from the stables that something else had not gone as planned. Months later, after having paid considerable expense for a horse I had never seen—and with no sure knowledge that any offspring had survived, or even been born—we began to feel that something odd might be going on. None of us had any knowledge whatsoever of horse breeding, and we had left the filly's care in the breeder's hands. Charlie Tucker was overseeing it all for me, and he finally suggested that we sell the little mare, as she was costing me so much. I wanted to fly over to Ireland to see her at least, but there seemed no convenient time. Sadly, my namesake was passed on to someone else. For all I know, there may be several fine breeding lines out there, all foaled by my little filly.

FROM JULY 22 through July 25, I made a recording of Rudolf Friml and Herbert Stothart's famed operetta *Rose Marie*, with the glorious baritone Giorgio Tozzi. We were accompanied by the New Symphony of London under the direction of the esteemed Broadway conductor Lehman Engel. He had conducted *Fanny* and *Wonderful Town* on Broadway, as well as several Gilbert and Sullivan operettas. He was meticulous, consummate at what he did, and he helped me rise to the challenge of pure operetta. I enjoyed the whole experience. What astounds me is how I fitted it into my busy schedule. No wonder I occasionally had vocal problems.

UP TO THIS point in my life, I had muddled through with things like answering my correspondence and noting down appointments, chores, laundry, dry-cleaning pickups, etc. Charlie Tucker paid all the main bills for me. I had a modest checking account, and submitted receipts and check stubs to him on a monthly basis. But life was becoming so full, and I really needed someone to help me sort it out.

Charlie interviewed a lady called Alexa Weir. She was single, middle-aged, dressed rather severely, and had a stiff carriage, but she had a quiet sense of humor and was obviously very competent. She took over my life—lock, stock, and barrel. I had an inkling that she had been requested to report my every move to Charlie, but I was grateful to her, for she took a big load off my shoulders.

She was at the theater most performances, and kept note of my house seats and who was requesting them. She became my "personal dragon"—the buffer between me and nearly everyone else. She dealt with my fan mail, kept the flowers in my dressing room fresh, and shopped for whatever I needed.

It was obvious that I couldn't stay at the Savoy Hotel forever. Alexa's entrance into my life coincided with Charlie finding me a lovely little apartment at number 70 Eaton Square, in Belgravia. It had a small kitchen, two bedrooms, one bathroom, and a living room, and tall windows throughout that furnished good light and a view the length of the square.

Tony and I moved in together (much to Charlie's annoyance), and it was a perfect abode for the two of us.

We went to Harrods and bought some furniture, including a small Steinway piano, which Charlie grudgingly allowed. I didn't have a dishwasher or anything practical, but I did have a grand piano, and it had a glorious tone.

The building had a superintendent named Bob Chatwin. He was a dour but decent man who lived in the basement apartment and managed the boilers, the general cleaning, and made sure all the brass on the doors was polished. We saw him once in a while, but we saw a great deal more of his wife, Becky.

She was tiny, almost dwarflike, rotund, and bespectacled. She was, in fact, technically blind and entitled to a white stick, which she disdained to use. She was also the cleanest, most forthright lady, a small dynamo. Number 70 Eaton Square was her world.

I would hear my letterbox flapping, and when I opened the door, Becky would be on her knees trying to peer in to see if anybody was home. She knew the details of every tenant in our building; she was nosy, she was a gossip, and I loved her.

"I can tell when something is dirty," she would say. "I *feel* dust."

She would run her soft little hand in a slow, sure movement across surfaces, and could sense with her fingertips if something wasn't clean.

"I can teach you how to clean your house in five easy moves," she said to me. "You'll need a stiff, short-handled brush, a very *soft* short-handled brush, a vacuum cleaner, and a duster."

Getting on her hands and knees, she showed me how to work around the base of the wainscoting with the stiff brush. With a sharp flick of her wrist, she would lift all the dust and lint from the edges of the carpet about a foot into the room. She used the soft brush to wipe every top surface: picture frames, doorways, shelves, window casings, and so on. She vacuumed up whatever was on the floor, and at the very end she would go over all the important surfaces with her soft duster.

She taught me how to wash a pile of dishes efficiently in a very small sink. I'd fill one of the dirty saucepans with hot water and suds, creating in essence a second sink, and throw in all the cutlery, then I would run the hot water in the main sink, dip a long-handled scrubbing brush into the soapy pan, wash a plate, rinse it under the tap, and set it out to dry. I learned to do everything in rotation; glasses first, plates next, then cutlery and, last of all, the saucepan that had been soaking all along. Becky's tuition was helpful, since housekeeping was something I didn't have time for.

Becky's main task was to clean for the English lord who lived in the apartment above us—Viscount Margesson. He was tall, dignified, and had a wonderful plummy voice. Becky idolized him.

I asked her if she knew a good laundry. She replied that I needed a personal laundress, and that she had a friend by the name of Olive Faigan who would be just the ticket.

Olive had worked in a professional laundry, and was superb at ironing and pressing. She came into our lives, and I have never had my wardrobe or my linens better cared for.

Becky wasn't finished with us, however. She arranged for Lord Margesson's valet, a Mr. Cole, to spare Tony a couple of hours a week. This quiet gentleman would come and collect Tony's clothes, and they would be returned by day's end, steamed, pressed, and spot-cleaned.

This was the perfect built-in godsend for a working couple. I remember the delight with which I viewed my wardrobe. I could pick out any dress and wear it instantly, thanks to Olive, Mr. Cole, and sweet Becky, who wrapped us, my home, and my housekeeping, into one perfect package.

Tony had been asked to design a production of a musical by Sandy Wilson, of *The Boy Friend* fame, called *Valmouth*. His sets and costumes for it were exquisite. He had commandeered our second bedroom as a workroom/study for himself. As the months went by, my attempts to keep that room tidy became more and more futile as pads, pencils, inks, drawings, models of sets, memorabilia, and reference books filled every available nook and cranny. My dad built some bookcases for us in our front hall, which helped a little. He also gave us a house-warming present—a hand-turned wooden fruit bowl, which I still treasure.

THAT SUMMER, I had a consultation with the designers at Madame Tussaud's Wax Museum who, because of the success of *My Fair Lady*, were making a wax model of me as Eliza Doolittle. Photos were taken, not only of me but of my costumes, and I stood for extensive measurements of my entire body and face.

A gentleman came to our new apartment with six long, leather-bound jewel cases under his arm. He flung back the lids with a flourish and revealed pair after pair of glass eyes, all different colors and staring in all directions. He proceeded to hold up one eyeball at a time, comparing it to my own.

"No, not quite bloodshot enough," he would say. Then "No, not quite yellow enough."

It was bizarre.

ONE MATINEE AFTERNOON, Paddie O'Neil—the big, brassy blonde from my early vaudeville days—suddenly showed up at our stage door during the performance. I had not seen her for years. For some reason, Alexa was not around. Not wishing to be snooty, I suggested to the stage doorman that he send her to my dressing room. I had a very brief moment between scenes to make a quick costume change and to say hello to her. I could not fathom why she had come to see me.

She said she was just in the neighborhood. As I changed and fixed my hair and makeup, I said, "I'm so sorry, Paddie, but I'm due onstage."

Then she did something rather scary. As I moved to leave the room, she deliberately tried to delay my exit. Leaning nonchalantly against the dressing table, she held me at the door with her questions.

I kept saying, "Paddie—I *must* go," and she said, "But just let me add one thing," or "Oh, *one* more question . . ." There was a smile playing around her mouth, as if she hoped I would miss my entrance and she was enjoying herself.

Eventually, I just dashed for the stage. When I returned, she had gone.

I can only think that the envy or the sadness in her must have been all-consuming. Who knows what she was thinking or feeling that day.

I CAME DOWN with a terrible cold and was out of the show for a few performances. When I recovered, I remember thinking it was essential to get myself back into shape; this was the moment to be fitter than ever before. I decided to do a really good, vigorous workout.

I stretched, but obviously did not warm up enough, for as I moved on to the heavier exercises and attempted one that was fairly strenuous—a swing to the right, a swing to the left, and a swing all the way round—I flung myself into it, and at the first rotation, threw my back out completely. I simply could not move. I was due back in the show that night, and wondered if this was something that I had done subconsciously to avoid returning. I literally dragged myself to my bed and lay there in agony.

It was lucky that my brother, Johnny, was with me. He was doing his obligatory two years in National Service, but was on a break and had traveled up from the country for a visit. He phoned Tony's father, Dr. Walton, telling him my dilemma, and the good man promised to drive up to London and give me an adjustment as soon as he was finished with his patients.

I lay on my bed for several hours, completely unable to move, my back in an excruciating spasm. Eventually I developed a terrible need to relieve myself, but I couldn't possibly make it to the bathroom. I called Johnny.

"I'm desperate," I explained. "There's a bucket in the kitchen. Maybe if you brought it in . . . ?"

With agonized groans and many contortions, I succeeded in using it. I think Johnny and I bonded as never before, and we still laugh about it.

Dr. Walton arrived and maneuvered me onto his table. With a long massage and a great deal of manipulation, he helped me become mobile once again. He had never had reason to treat me before, but after one look at my back he said, "You know, you have a nasty curvature of the spine—a scoliosis." It was the first I'd heard of it. Dad W. felt that it was probably congenital. Thank heavens for his good care, guidance, and tuition about it—for in the years since, it has continued to plague me, and I've had to make accommodations for it such as special stretching exercises and adjustments to my shoes. Several days, several treatments, and some relaxing pills later, I returned to the show.

THIRTY-NINE

Tony and I purchased a miniature gray poodle puppy, and we called her Shy. She was a sweetly feminine little dog. Once she was housebroken, she went with us everywhere.

She would listen to me vocalizing at my piano and would throw her pretty head up, her mouth slightly pursed, and howl to the skies. I discovered to my surprise that I could almost make her sing scales. It was all very cute, but also somewhat annoying because I could not get on with my practice once Shy began to vocalize, so I would place her in the corridor while I did my scales. I'd hear her scratching at the door, then I'd see her little black nose appear beneath it and hear a lot of breathy huffs and puffs. I would say, "Shy," in a warning voice and she would try her best to contain herself, uttering muffled scales in a tiny voice until she could stand it no longer—at which point she would let go again with a full-throated howl.

She was a honey of a dog.

WHILE TONY AND I had been in New York, we had stayed in touch with the lovely ballerina Svetlana Beriosova. Once we returned to London, we received an invitation from her to attend her wedding reception.

We were happy to go, and were immediately greeted by the groom, Mohammed Masud Raza Khan, whom we had never met. He welcomed us and ebulliently enfolded me in his arms.

He was the son of a wealthy Pakistani land-owner. He was tall and strikingly handsome, with dark flashing eyes, a mustache, and a head of long thick hair. He had a full, slightly drooping lower lip, which was seductively pouty—a subtle indication perhaps of his addiction to cigarettes.

Masud (or Sudi, as we later called him) could not have been more friendly or attentive. I had the uncharitable suspicion that his effusive overture was because he thought I was someone important in the theater since *My Fair Lady* was the hottest ticket in town.

Sudi and Svetlana quickly became our close friends, and we saw them often. Sudi was a complicated man, a psychoanalyst of some brilliance and renown. He became a very important influence in my life, inspiring and encouraging me many years later to enter into analysis. He was gentle and kind to me, and as our friendship developed, I seemed to be the only woman in his life that he didn't wish to tear to shreds. I suppose I wasn't a threat. He could be quite abusive to Tony and to Svetlana, but they knew him well and took it all with good grace. Sudi was just being Sudi.

We spent many evenings at their apartment in Knightsbridge. They lived in Hans Crescent, almost next to Harrods department store. The flat was a little dark, but had large rooms and very high ceilings. It was sparsely furnished. There were good lithographs on the walls and a few photos and a huge collection of books, which were Sudi's passion. He would make trips to Paris and bring back his latest acquisitions with glee, spending a great deal of money on beautifully bound editions, which were proudly displayed in glass cases.

Sometimes he and Svetlana would get into an almighty row, and Tony and I would wait patiently until they got themselves out of it. Svetlana would argue passionately, though she adored Sudi. I grew to realize that though brilliantly cerebral, Sudi was not always emotionally healthy. His personality seemed split right down the middle, as if he was totally trapped between the cultures of east and west; one half being the imperious son of a land-owner, the other a well-trained London-based analyst, a disciple of D. W. Winnicott, the great psychoanalyst whose papers he eventually helped to edit.

In the years since his death, there has been considerable scandal surrounding his methods of work with his patients. His academic writings, however, are lauded throughout the psychoanalytic world, and I'm fairly certain that he was a better theorist than he was a practical psychoanalyst.

Sudi did not believe in bathing. He felt it robbed the skin of its essential oils, so every day he cleansed himself by using oil on his body. He was always immaculately dressed, often wearing a velvet smoking jacket with slippers to match. A cigarette would droop from his soft, half-opened lips, and ash would spill all over his elegant clothes. As life went on, it seemed that he moved further and further out toward madness, but when we knew him, he was still powerful and relatively in control of himself.

He told us initially that he was a prince—the love-child of his father's thirteenth wife. Many years later, we discovered this to be untrue. He said that, as a child, if he didn't win a card game he had the power to have his fellow players' hands cut off. Tony and I were struck by this bizarre statement, and wondered if he invented his outrageous stories— and if so, why?

Svetlana was loving and dear, her laughter nearly always present. She would supervise the simple fare at the table—mostly steak, vegetables, baked potatoes—cooked and served by their houseboy. She was everything that I yearned to be: dedicated, disciplined, with a pure, clear work ethic. She seemed to want for very little in life, and kept her needs to the barest minimum. She attended ballet classes every day; she never complained, never put on airs; and with her Russian, triangular face, she was exquisitely beautiful. A core of integrity was evident in everything she did.

Whenever we could, we attended her performances. Several ballets were created for her by the great Kenneth MacMillan, then a young, up-and-coming choreographer. We saw her dance *Giselle* and *Sleeping Beauty* and *Swan Lake*. She was always superb, a little more imposing than some dancers because of her height—and she was a good actress, as well.

We had dinners with John Cranko, another brilliant choreographer, who created *Prince of the Pagodas* for Svetlana and later became Artistic Director of the Stuttgart Ballet.

It was a heady time for us all. We were part of the young artistic scene in London, and we were drawn to each other for many reasons. I could think of no more wonderful evening than to attend a performance of the ballet at the Royal Opera House, then go to a restaurant or back to Svetlana's and Sudi's apartment for supper. Often other dancers from the Royal Ballet joined us, as well as writers, analysts, actors, and directors, and we would talk until all hours on all subjects.

One day Sudi said to me, "When you next come to the ballet, you're going to be sitting beside a great friend of ours. You will love her."

With some distrust I slid into my seat on the appointed evening and found myself next to an attractive dark-haired woman named Zoë Dominic. She was a photographer—for many years the exclusive photographer of theater, ballet, and opera for the London *Sunday Times*. Her work was brilliant. By the end of that first meeting we had, indeed, bonded. Zoë, Svetlana, Sudi, Tony, and I became inseparable.

Sudi was shopping in Harrods one day. The store was crowded, and at the counter, a woman pushed in front of him. Sudi drew himself up to his full height and addressed her courteously.

"Madame," he said. "The good lord has given you an advantage over me. He has made you a woman. But if this salesperson serves you before he serves me, I shall personally tweak his nose." It was classic Sudi.

Svetlana and I were in Harrods one afternoon, when she asked if I would like to come back to her flat for some tea.

It was tempting. "Oh that's lovely of you, Svetlana," I replied, "but I should probably just go home and have a rest and prepare myself for the show."

"How stupid of me, Julie," she gasped. "I forgot you had a show tonight . . . and of course you must go home and rest. You *must*."

The implication in her words was that art must always be given the first priority.

Maybe it was because the words were hers, or maybe they were simply spoken at the exact moment I was ready to hear them, but I suddenly became aware of a newer, deeper purpose to my craft and to what I was doing. I always appreciated that my singing voice was a special gift, to be acknowledged with gratitude, but now I felt that my whole being could be used to give something *back*—to share my appreciation for the gift more fully.

Most of my early life, during those vaudeville years, my work was—

well, work. It was what I did. And in my youthfulness, it never occurred to me that when I appeared onstage, I could perhaps make a small difference. I now began to develop a sense of fulfillment in the doing—in the attempt to convey joy and to bring pleasure to people; to help them transcend their everyday worries and problems for the few hours that they are a part of the theater experience. I was finding reasons, motivations, a deeper core—and an answer as to why I was given the gift in the first place. Whatever the inspiration, the small exchange with Svetlana that day was life-altering.

FORTY

To describe now what theater means to me, and what the work feels like, is difficult. One is usually so busy attempting to find answers and hone them into honesty, focusing on the moment and its progression, sending it out and finding the well of energy that it takes. My feelings about it shift and change on any given day.

In the moments of preparation and the gathering momentum toward curtain time, there is a tingle of anticipation when the flute calls and the trumpet answers, when voices are raised in practice and passages of song, when the Tannoy squeaks and disembodied instructions echo through the corridors, the orchestra moves into the pit and the musicians check their pitch.

Backstage, midst all the hustle and bustle and the hum of chatter from an audience, there is a sudden moment of absolute silence, and one is aware that the conductor has raised his baton. The overture erupts; there is no turning back.

Once in a while I experience an emotion onstage that is so gut-wrenching, so heart-stopping, that I could weep with gratitude and joy. The feeling catches and magnifies so rapidly that it threatens to engulf me.

It starts as a bass note, resonating deep in my system. Literally. It's like the warmest, lowest sound from a contrabass. There is a sudden thrill of connection and an awareness of size—the theater itself, more the height of the great stage housing behind and above me, where history has been absorbed, where darkness contains mystery and light has meaning.

Light is a part of it . . . to be flooded with it, to absorb it and allow it through the body.

The dust that has a smell so thick and evocative, one feels one could almost eat it; makeup and sweat, perfume and paint; the vast animal that is an audience, warm and pulsing, felt but unseen.

Most of all, it is the music—when a great sweep of sound makes you attempt things that earlier in the day you might never have thought possible. When the orchestra swells to support your voice, when the melody is perfect and the words so right there could not possibly be any others, when a modulation occurs and lifts you to an even higher plateau . . . it is bliss. And that is the moment to share it.

One senses the audience feeling it, too, and together you ride the ecstasy all the way home.

There's that word again. Home.

Then I think there is no more magical feeling, no one luckier than I. It is to do with the joy of being a vessel, being used, using oneself fully and totally in the service of something that brings wonder. If only one could experience this every night.

It is as great as sex . . . that moment before climax. It is as overwhelming as the mighty ocean. As nurturing as mother's milk to an infant. As addictive as opium.

IN FEBRUARY OF 1959, a second recording of *My Fair Lady* was made at Abbey Road Studios in London. The original Broadway album was recorded in monaural sound, since that's all there was in those days, but stereophonic sound came onto the scene, and the record industry had to reinvent itself. It was essential that we make a new album of our show.

The English company with, I believe, a slightly augmented orchestra, went into the studios—and I am so glad we did. I think Rex, Stanley, and I gave better performances on the second album. I had settled into my role, I knew what I was doing, and though there are still things that I wish I had thought to add, the stereo recording is light years better than the original, and is the one officially used today.

*

REX DEPARTED FROM the show at the end of March. He and Kay threw a party for the cast after his last performance, and once again I was unhappy that he was leaving. There is always a subtle shift in a company when original members have to move on. Audiences still see the show they are meant to see, but within the company there are small changes in the balance of the whole, and there are adjustments to characters and their importance. There's a slight feeling of abandonment for the people left behind.

The actor Alec Clunes took over the role of Higgins, with all the attendant rehearsals to help ease him into the show.

Tony was working hard. In 1959, he was involved in four theatrical productions in London, and I delighted in watching him create and develop them. The first was a play by Peter Coke, entitled *Fool's Paradise*, for which Tony did both sets and costumes. It starred an elderly actress, Cicely Courtneidge. Tony would arrive home after her costume fittings, smiling and a little puzzled. "I don't understand it," he said. "I cannot fit her dresses properly. Her tummy shifts every single day!"

He did scenic design for *The Pleasure of His Company*, by Samuel Taylor, and I had the enjoyment of watching a couple of rehearsals and sitting in the audience on opening night. Coral Browne starred in the play and I marveled at her style, wit, and glamour.

Next came *The Ginger Man*, based on the book by J. P. Donleavy, and starring Richard Harris. In addition to designing the sets and costumes, Tony helped produce this play. We became friendly with Donleavy. He was a little wild in those days—athletic and mischievous, quirky, yet cagey. It was hard really to know him, though Tony saw much more of him over the years. He had a sort of country squire look and wore good Irish tweeds and jackets with leather patches on the elbows.

The last production in 1959 was a revue called *Pieces of Eight*, for which, once again, Tony provided sets and costumes. Much of this revue was written by Peter Cook and Harold Pinter, with a song or two by an unknown composer named Lionel Bart, later of *Oliver!* fame. It starred the outrageously gay and funny comedian Kenneth Williams, much beloved by English audiences, and was directed and choreographed by a young man called Paddy Stone. I worked with

Paddy myself several times over the years, most notably when he did the choreography for the films *Victor/Victoria* and *S.O.B.*, in which he also appeared.

To this day, I can recall and quote passages from some of the sketches in *Pieces of Eight*. Kenneth Williams, playing an old newspaper seller, is talking to his friend, the owner of a Chelsea bun-and-tea stall—one of those on wheels, with an awning. After chatting about everything under the sun, the newspaper seller declares, "So the *Evening Standard* was the last to go."

His friend, after a pause, says, "Then that went, did it?"

"Yes..." Another, longer pause. "...like a *shot*!"

In March, there was an exhibition of Tony's work at the Hazlitt Gallery in St. James. When we arrived for the initial opening, Sir John Gielgud was there, strolling around looking at the art. His reputation for malapropisms was legendary in show business. I was a big fan of his, and having never met him, I approached him and explained that I was the artist's fiancée and thanked him for coming.

Gielgud recognized me.

"Oh, how do you do?" he said, extending his hand. "You have often enjoyed my work. I *mean*...!"

In a flurry of embarrassment, he exited the gallery.

TONY AND I decided that May 10 would be our wedding date. Having been in *My Fair Lady* in London for a year, I was due a two-week vacation in May, which fitted in nicely with our plans.

Charlie Tucker swung into action and booked me an appearance on *The Jack Benny Show* in Los Angeles, probably in order to obtain finances to pay for the wedding. I understood the necessity, and it made sense to use the trip to the U.S. as an excuse for a honeymoon.

Contrary to tradition, I asked Tony if he would care to design my wedding gown. He said he would love to. He also designed my wedding band.

Because of the impromptu nature of our engagement, I never had an engagement ring, but Tony had given me a beautiful little brooch while we were in New York, the same size as a ring, in the shape of a laurel wreath. My wedding band was an identical circle of laurel. It was made by Cartier and was engraved inside.

I decided to ask Tony's sister Carol and my sister, Celia, to be my bridesmaids, and I asked Aunt Joan to be my matron of honor. Noel Harrison, Rex's son, was Tony's best man. They had attended Radley College together and had been friends for years.

WHILE WE WERE busy with our wedding plans, Charlie Tucker got it into his head that a painting of me as Eliza Doolittle should be commissioned. He chose Pietro Annigoni, who had done many portraits of members of the Royal Family.

Annigoni was an arrogant man, the epitome of the temperamental artist. He demanded total dedication and punctuality.

Photographs were taken of me wearing Eliza's flower girl costume, and he placed them around his studio to study them while he worked, but he also needed several sittings with me. Since I was performing in the show, organizing the wedding, and having fittings for my gown, life was rather hectic, and it was difficult to slot everything in.

The inevitable happened, and I arrived late at his studio one day. He was so miffed that he locked me out on the street. I could see the curtain twitching at his upstairs window as he peered down at my discomfort, so I knew that he was home. Charlie Tucker had to phone him and beg him to continue the portrait.

The finished painting of me as the flower girl is wonderful. Annigoni captured the essence of Eliza. What is rather extraordinary is that in the background there is a half-hidden poster with the words *The Sound of . . .* How prophetic!

Charlie Tucker owned the portrait. It hung in his office for many years, but when he no longer represented me, he put it up for auction. By that time I was married to my present husband, Blake, and he arranged for a friend to go and bid on it. I heard that Charlie asked whether this friend was bidding on my behalf, and he seemed happy when the fact was confirmed. I am thrilled to own it, and it hangs in my home.

*

RACHELLE WAS TO make my wedding gown, and she informed us that the best selection of material was to be found in Switzerland. Somehow we were able to make a brief trip to Zurich, and we chose a bolt of exquisite white organza sprinkled with embroidered white roses. We found as well some lovely water silk taffeta that was made into a pretty evening dress for *The Jack Benny Show*. Rachelle also made the dresses for the bridesmaids and the maid of honor, and they, too, were designed by Tony.

My wedding gown was beautiful. It was ankle-length at the front and had a high roll neck and long sleeves. Tiny buttons secured it at the back, and there was a long train.

I had no wish to modify the gown once the wedding was over, so I carefully packed it away, hoping that perhaps one day it might be used by a daughter. I remember Olive Faigan helping me fold it into a box with sheets of tissue and many mothballs, and I hoped it wouldn't become yellowed. It survived well, and many years later, to my delight, all the buttons and the lovely embroidered roses were incorporated into our daughter Emma's wedding dress—which Tony also designed—when she got married.

Tony and I wished to be married at St. Mary's Church, in the parish of Oatlands, near Walton and Weybridge. The church is picturesque— the prettiest in the area. Its lichen-covered gate has a little V-shaped roof over it, and a country path leads up to the church doors.

Our minister, the Reverend Keeping, was a charming man, kind and gentle in our meetings with him.

On one occasion we were introduced to the organist who would be playing at the ceremony. He announced proudly that he had "the finest organ in the south of England." Tony and I couldn't look at each other, and later relayed the story with relish.

It wasn't enough that I was born in the adjacent village; I had to prove residency in the parish of Oatlands in order to obtain the permit for us to be married at St. Mary's. We decided that I would move into the nearby Oatlands Park Hotel for the better part of six weeks.

Charlie Tucker was none too happy that I was getting married. I think he felt that Tony wasn't old enough, sophisticated, or wealthy enough for me. Some rather unusual things began to happen which left me feeling a bit paranoid. I can't prove that Charlie had anything to do with them, but I'm fairly certain that he did.

Out of the blue, a gentleman called Carl Lambert contacted me. He was a psychiatrist with offices on Brook Street in Mayfair, and he claimed he had been commissioned to write a series of articles on the subject of fame for *The Times* of London. After several persistent phone calls, and Charlie assuring me it was a good thing to do, I agreed to the interview.

I met the doctor occasionally for lunch. He was Austrian, charismatic, elegant, and erudite. Our conversations covered many subjects. For our final interview he asked me to go to his office, where I lay on his patients' couch. I remember that I wept copiously, telling him a little about my early life. He touched my forehead gently when the session was over. In spite of all our meetings, no articles were ever published.

About two weeks before the wedding, Charlie Tucker held a supper party at the Savoy. Pauline Grant was there, and I was invited to join them.

At the table was a dynamic young man who went out of his way to be attentive. I'd never met him before, but it seemed that he was more than interested in me, and I confess he was a fascinating dinner partner. His focus was on me throughout the entire meal, and afterward he escorted me to the elevator as, for some reason, I was staying in the hotel over-night. He kissed me—quite deliciously, I might add—and said, "I wish you weren't marrying Tony."

He told me he was returning to South Africa on business within a couple of days and wished he didn't have to leave. He said he would be in touch with me. I received a beautiful bouquet of tuberoses from him, and then, strangely, I heard nothing more.

My guess was that he had been asked by Tucker to loosen my resolve concerning marriage to Tony.

Charlie's attempts to control every aspect of my life were starting to become awkward, and though exceedingly grateful to him, I began to grow uncomfortable with his managerial style and the manner in which he represented me.

Charlie's reservations notwithstanding, the wedding ensued.

FORTY-ONE

MAY 10, 1959, dawned clear and sunny. I spent the night before the wedding at The Meuse. I had been nervous for several weeks, but on this day I felt calm and happy.

Dressing for the wedding became quite hilarious. Aunt Joan was in a tizzy, dashing about asking, "Does my gown look all right? What about my hair?"

I remember standing in the big living room at The Meuse, where we had placed a full-length mirror so that we could all check ourselves. I was alone, fully dressed and ready to go. Aunt was flitting all over the place, Mum was off finding her stockings. I looked at myself in the mirror and thought, "Well, here I am! It's my wedding day—I wonder if they'll get around to *me*?"

Dad arrived in the limo, looking spiffy in his rented morning suit and top hat, and we headed for the church.

One of the things I felt most grateful for that day was that I knew Tony as well as I did. Making such a huge commitment is daunting, to say the least, and to know that I was marrying my dearest friend was a great comfort—a safe, sure feeling.

As we approached the church, the lane was lined with well-wishers who had come out to support their hometown girl. There was a large phalanx of press, but once inside the church, we were able to keep it to just family and friends.

It was fun to see my mother and Win all dressed up. Pop was sober, and I sensed no danger that he was going to be difficult. Uncle Bill was an elegant head usher assisted by Tony's brother, Richard, and my brothers, John, Donald, and Chris. Tony's mother was pretty as ever; the fleet of great-aunts were ruddy-cheeked, robust, and looked extremely matronly.

THE CEREMONY ITSELF was lovely. Afterward we drove to the Mitre Hotel, an old and charming establishment on the water's edge opposite Hampton Court Palace. The river was sparkling, and the view of the palace, glinting in the sun, was magnificent.

Tony and I stood for a long reception line. Among the nearly three hundred guests were Svetlana and Sudi, Zoë, Charlie Tucker, Lou Wilson, Maggie Smith, Stanley and Lainie Holloway. Toasts were made, the food was delicious. The many-layered cake was cut and pieces saved for absent friends. Speeches were delivered, funny and loving. Photographs were taken.

Binkie Beaumont had given us a complete set of antique Chinese blue and white china: terrines, cups, saucers, sauce boats, milk jugs, a teapot, and plates of many sizes. My mother privately gave me a lovely silver rose bowl. She said she wanted me to have a gift that was just from her. It started a tradition, and I gave my daughters similar personal gifts when they got married. Moss and Kitty sent an engraved silver cigarette box. Neither of us smoked, but it looked elegant on our coffee table.

God knows what chaos we left behind us—the clearing up, and all the wonderful gifts that were delivered to our apartment.

I had reserved a room at the hotel in order to change for our flight to Los Angeles to tape *The Jack Benny Show*—and suddenly it was all over. In a blur of hugs, kisses, flash cameras, and rice, Tony and I departed for the airport.

We slept on the flight and I remember opening my eyes just before landing. I looked at Tony in the seat beside me. He smiled.

"*Help!*" I said to him in a very small voice.

He nodded, knowing what I meant.

The festivities were over; we were married and heading into the unknown.

WE STAYED AT the Beverly Hills Hotel, and quickly made the acquaintance of Bud Yorkin, the director of *The Jack Benny Show*. Among other things he was renowned for having directed the Emmy-winning Fred Astaire TV specials, which were so stylish and elegant.

Phil Silvers was a guest on the show, and just before the finale of the special, he said, "Julie. You are on your honeymoon . . . I have a favor to ask. May I dance with the bride?" and we waltzed together. He was a darling man and wonderfully funny.

Jack Benny was kind and generous. He took us out to dinner one evening and afterward said, "Come back and see my house."

Opening the front door, he called, "Mary—we've got friends." His wife was upstairs, and was obviously not happy about the unexpected visitors, because she never came down.

One night after rehearsals, Bud Yorkin and his then wife, Peg, took us to one of the famous nightclubs on the Sunset Strip. A stripper named Candy Barr was appearing there. She was all the rage at the time, had an extraordinary body, and was a wonderful dancer.

By the time we got past the huge bouncer at the front door and arrived at our seats, the music was pounding and she was just ending her first session, already completely naked. I'd never seen a stripper in my life. I took one look at this lady dancing so erotically and I had to sit down rather quickly. Once I got my naïveté in check, we had a terrific evening.

Our friend Edie Adams, married by now to Ernie Kovacs, invited Tony and me to a cocktail party at her house. It was pretty sumptuous, and the guests included some of the most important people in Hollywood.

I remember seeing Jack Lemmon talking to the director Blake Edwards, the latter seeming handsome and charismatic, if perhaps a trifle arrogant. If I had known then that almost eleven years later I would be married to that extraordinary gentleman, I think I would have fainted dead away. (I think we *all* would have!) But I was on my honeymoon with Tony, and Blake and I at that time were ships passing in the night.

As honeymoons go, it was somewhat lopsided—more of a working vacation, what with the fittings, the rehearsals, and the taping of the show. We never lolled by the hotel pool or had much chance to be together on our own. But still it was fun.

The Jack Benny Hour aired on May 23, the same day that Tony and I flew back to England, so we were unable to watch it.

The following day, I went back into *My Fair Lady,* and thus began our married life.

FORTY-TWO

A<small>LTHOUGH MY CONTRACT</small> in London was for eighteen months and I was due to leave the show in October 1959, I actually left on August 8, two months early, because by then I was exhausted and as neurotic about my voice as I could possibly be.

I was seeing Dr. Musgrove on Wednesdays and Saturdays, taking injections of vitamins, having "diathermy" on my throat (a method of heating tissue electromagnetically and ultrasonically for therapeutic purposes), having the poison in my tonsils suctioned, trying in every way to keep myself going.

Performing for two years in New York and sixteen months in London—not to mention all the rehearsals and being out of town—had been a marathon. I never knew on any given day whether my voice or stamina would hold up for me. Most of the time it did, but I was always a basket case of nerves.

We received word that Annie Rogers was back in town after her tour of the U.S. in *My Fair Lady*. She had already been contracted to take over from me, and Charlie Tucker ascertained that she would be willing to start a little sooner if we could arrange it.

Charlie and I went to see Binkie Beaumont.

My guess was that he would say that I had to stay in the show and fulfill my contract, but I underestimated him. The case was put to him; since Annie was willing to begin, could I possibly depart two months early? He looked at me and he looked at Charlie. Finally he said, "Look, I will grant you this permission, *but* . . ." He stabbed a finger at Charlie.

"I do *not* want you making that young lady work for the next three months. I want you to *promise* that she will have every chance to really rest and recuperate."

I felt as if the cavalry had arrived, and I hugged him. How dear of him to so completely understand.

When I finally ended my run in *My Fair Lady*, it was as if I emerged from a long, narrow tunnel into the bright sunlight. The world was suddenly in Cinemascope, and I had a life once again. I had tremendous affection and fondness for the show, and I received a wonderful send-off from the company . . . but the relief was overwhelming.

Like Rex, I threw a party for the company, and my diary entry for that week simply says, "Lovely, *loverly* end to show—very sad but very glad, too. People *so* sweet and kind."

The experience of that show will forever remain in my bones. There is a line from the song "Just You Wait," in which Eliza imagines the King declaring, "Next week, on the 20th of May, I proclaim 'Liza Doolitle Day.' " Every May 20, I still receive cards from friends and fans.

Often I am asked how I felt about not landing the role of Eliza in the film version of *My Fair Lady*. I know Alan hoped that Warner Bros. would cast me, but eventually the role was given to Audrey Hepburn. At the time, I completely understood their choice. Warner Bros. needed a big name for the marquee, and although I had starred on Broadway, that was a very small pond compared to the rest of America and the world. In later years, I did wish that I had been able to record my performance somehow, somewhere, for posterity—or at least for my grandchildren. Audrey and I became good friends, and one day she said to me, "Julie, you *should* have done the role . . . but I didn't have the guts to turn it down."

A FEW MONTHS prior to my departure, Alan and Moss asked me to read an extraordinary book based on the Arthurian legend, called *The Once and Future King*, by T. H. White. They hoped to make it into a musical, and asked if I would play the role of Queen Guenevere.

Tony and I read it cover to cover, adored it, and embraced the idea, though I couldn't imagine how Alan and Fritz could manage an adaptation, since the book was actually a compilation of four complete novels.

It seemed a monumental task, but nevertheless it was scheduled for production a year hence.

Charlie almost kept his promise to Binkie, and for the next two months I did not work. I saw friends and family, went shopping, had my hair done. We went to the theater and to the ballet—but mostly I just took it easy.

That month we received the devastating news that Kay Kendall had died from leukemia. It was sudden, and deeply sad that such a bright light had left us so soon.

We escaped to Paris for a weekend in October and, later, went down to Oxford for a week, where *Pieces of Eight* was doing a pre-London tryout.

IN LATE OCTOBER of 1959, I began work on a four-part series for the BBC called *The Julie Andrews Show*. We would tape one show a week. Pauline Grant was the director, Kenneth MacMillan the choreographer, and Tony designed the settings. It was decided that not only would I sing and entertain, but I would also try some celebrity interviews. My guests included Vic Oliver, Richard "Mr. Pastry" Hearne, the comedian Kenneth Williams, and Pietro Annigoni.

While we were brainstorming ideas, Pauline said, "Why don't we try to get the author T. H. White for an interview?" Since I was contracted for *Camelot*, it seemed like an absolute must.

We heard that Mr. White was a recluse, living on the remote Channel Island of Alderney, and that he probably would not consider coming to the mainland for something so trivial. The offer was made anyway, and to our astonishment and delight, he accepted. (Later, when we asked him why he agreed to appear, he said it was because he knew nothing about television and wanted to learn how the cameras worked and what happened on the set.)

It was arranged that I would pick him up after he had checked into his hotel. I remember driving him around Hyde Park Corner, by Apsley House. As usual the traffic was going in all directions, and he said, "My goodness, London is busy. How do you drive through all of this?"

Living as a hermit on his little island, I think he was amazed and bewildered at the crazy tumult of London life.

Within days, Tony and I fell in love with this endearing, professorial man. He looked almost exactly like Ernest Hemingway, though Tim was taller. His beard was a little yellow from cigarettes. He had a fine head of white hair, and his wardrobe was mostly corduroy and casual, though he often sported a startling red bow tie.

He came onto our studio set and pottered around, and when we finally did the interview, he sweetly put up with my asking him some pretty banal questions. I was nervous about interviewing people, and wasn't very good at it. He really seemed to be enjoying himself, however, and even if he wasn't, he would never have shown it. Tim had a personal code of honor that required him to behave as decently to everyone as the medieval knights in his wonderful book.

I mentioned to him that I was soon to have my tonsils removed.

"You must come and stay with me!" he cried. "The sea air will be great for your recuperation. Please come to Alderney—I would love that!" We promised we would try.

We ended up with four fairly good shows, the final episode airing on Christmas Eve. Also in December, I appeared in a midnight gala at the Lyric Theatre on Shaftesbury Avenue, to raise funds for the thousands so calamitously affected by the collapse of the Malpasset Dam in Frejus, France. It was an all-star lineup, with American and British stars.

Those who could sing or dance did so. The actors made the introductions, and it was my good fortune to be introduced by Sir Ralph Richardson. We had never met, but I admired him enormously.

When it was time for my appearance, he made a fairly grand speech, then announced in his unique voice, "On these 'Lyric' boards it is my pleasure to now introduce the one, the only, the sublime . . . Miss Julie *Anderson!*"

There was dead silence as the audience tried to fathom who this person might be. I walked onstage, lamely whispered "*Andrews*," and sang whatever I was supposed to sing.

The next day I received a small bouquet of violets from him and a letter written on a large piece of stationery with just two words per line.

"Dear Miss Andrews," it said in the smallest handwriting, *"I am so sorry that I did not introduce you correctly last night but my car was towed away and I'm afraid I was not my usual self. Please accept these flowers as my apology."*

The year ended with another performance of *Cinderella*—but this time I was happily attending Prokofiev's ballet at the Royal Opera House and Svetlana was dancing the title role. The evening was unforgettable.

FORTY-THREE

A ROUND CHRISTMASTIME OF 1959, something that had been nagging at the back of my brain came into focus. I had been uneasy about my brother Chris for quite a while. With Donald away in the merchant navy, my youngest sibling was now more alone than ever. The Meuse was run-down, gloom permeating every room. Mum was absent and at the pub most lunchtimes and evenings. The "local" was her crutch, and the lovely pianist who once had such a fine technique was now merely a bar entertainer thumping at the keys, her drinking cronies encouraging her lifestyle. Pop had a succession of jobs, first selling cash registers, then working at Hotpoint and, finally, Greenshield Stamps, so he, too, was not around very much. Aunt, now divorced from Uncle Bill, continued to teach, but she eventually moved her school into the village hall and took rooms for herself down the road. The studio at the back of our house, and the little bungalow, fell into disrepair.

The toll on Chris was evident; he was now thirteen, pale, abstracted, and if not already there, heading for a major depression. I suddenly realized that unless he got away, the conditions he was living in would have a lasting effect.

I found a good boarding school, Pierrepoint House, in Frensham, Surrey, and in late March, Chris sat for the entrance exam and passed it with flying colors. His first semester would be in the fall. Mum and Pop were thrilled, and though I sensed Chris might be homesick and anxious (though there was little to be homesick about), anything was better than staying where he was. Certainly he would be stimulated and in a better environment.

In late January 1960, I went back to New York to tape a two-hour prime-time variety special for CBS called *The Fabulous Fifties*, which chronicled the most popular theater, movies, books, and music of the decade. Even though Rex and I were no longer doing *My Fair Lady,* we filmed scenes replicating the rehearsal process. I was shown working with Alfred Dixon, the dialogue coach who helped me perfect my cockney accent, and that scene segued into my performing "Just You Wait." Rex did a sketch about his singing with an orchestra for the first time. The special received an Emmy for outstanding variety programming.

I also appeared in a live, colorcast production of *The Bell Telephone Hour*, a classy and prestigious series. The episode was entitled "Portraits in Music," and was hosted by the poet Carl Sandburg.

Knowing that we would be heading back to New York at the end of the summer for *Camelot*, my hope was to return to London and spend a few months just being Mrs. Tony Walton. There was also the matter of my tonsils, and now seemed the best possible time to have them taken out. But Tony and I had to miss the wedding of Princess Margaret and Tony Armstrong-Jones at Westminster Abbey, to which we had been invited.

I went into the London Clinic and had the operation, which, at age twenty-four, was complicated and quite painful. Then, as we had promised Tim White we would, we headed to the island of Alderney so that I could recuperate in the bracing sea air.

We flew across the English Channel in a small passenger plane and landed on a tiny airstrip in the middle of a cow pasture. Tim met us at the airport, such as it was, in his "country squire" wagon, and we drove to his house at Connaught Square, in the village of St. Anne's.

The island was simply magical, a mile and a half wide by three miles long, with tall cliffs at one end; heather, gorse bushes, cobblestone streets, and gaily painted stone cottages; and a sweet harbor and lighthouse down on the flat end. From almost every vantage point, one could see the sea.

Because of its strategic location in the English Channel, it had been heavily fortified over the centuries with Roman, Georgian, Victorian, and finally German structures—forts, gunneries, bunkers, lookouts—as well as being honeycombed with tunnels and storage vaults. Most of the latter were now being gradually reclaimed by nature, grown over with wild blackberries, nettles, grasses, and thistle.

Tim was indeed a recluse. Born Terence Hanbury White in Bombay, India, in 1906, he had moved to England with his parents at the age of five. He had been a teacher and head of the department of English at the famous boarding school, Stowe, in Buckinghamshire. After several years there, he retired and lived in a small cottage on the school estate to pursue his writing, and the falconry he loved. It was there that he wrote the first volume of his magnificent work, *The Once and Future King*. He lived in Ireland for a while, but in 1945, he moved to Alderney.

Tim's house was actually two stone cottages made into one, with a small rocky garden and a swimming pool in the back. He told us that because a "great star" was coming to stay with him (me!), he had put his house in order. It was freshly whitewashed, and he had completely redecorated in a sort of mini-Versailles style. There were twinkling plastic chandeliers and wall sconces, new fixtures, throw rugs, and laundry baskets. He was very proud of his decorating skills.

When we went down to the kitchen on the first morning to make a cup of tea, we found everything painted a fire-engine red, including the fixtures and fittings. The cupboards were filled with sticky spice jars in horrible condition, grubby tins, sauces, and greasy packets of this and that. Piles of old manuscripts were stored in his oven and stacked under the overhead grill, and the dilapidated fridge was bare. I immediately set about cleaning everything, and threw out as much dated food as I dared. Tim obviously never used his kitchen.

We learned that he was taken care of by a woman called Maisie Allen and her husband, Archie, who was in charge of the waterworks on the island. They lived in an old house on Victoria Street, the narrow cobbled road that ran through the village. Poor Archie had a rigid neck and had to turn his entire body left or right to look at anything. Maisie was a warm soul, sensible and honest as they come. She tolerated Tim's occasional verbal abuse, put up with his moods, and I suspect, like all of us, was bewitched by this wonderful author. He would go down to the

Allens' for lunch every day, so all he had to do was make a pot of burned coffee for himself in the morning.

Tim seemed very fond of me, and he was amazingly perceptive. I had a habit of boosting my own morale, albeit in a humorous way. After completing a chore, I was inclined to state, "I think I did that rather well, don't you?" He quickly cottoned on.

"Let's pay Julie a compliment before she pays herself one," he'd say with a teasing smile, or "Let's tell Julie she's pretty today . . . pretty Julie!"

He had a big, floppy red setter dog named Jenny (after Guenevere) whom he adored, and she was extremely pregnant. When she finally whelped, Tim said, "We'll leave Julie alone with Jenny because she needs to see this. She'll be having a baby of her own one day." I watched Jenny give birth to ten beautiful puppies. Tim found a home for every one of them.

He seemed to love having us for company. He delighted in showing us his world, driving us everywhere, stomping across fields and along the beautiful beaches. He showed us the thirteen forts and castles—one of them of Roman origin—built at strategic places on the island, some restored and privately owned, others in ruins. We explored the German gun emplacements left after the Nazi occupation during World War II. We climbed down a precipitous cliff to a rocky beach called Telegraph Bay.

Tim had huge mood swings. On a good day, he was the best companion you could ever ask for. Anything you wanted to know, Tim was the one to tell you. He knew everything about the universe: the stars, nature, fishing, sailing, geology, history. He *was* Merlin: wise, thoughtful, caring, dear.

But there were black days, when he was appallingly rude to people. And when he was drunk, it was best to leave him alone. There is a legendary story that some people knocked at his door late one stormy evening.

"We are collecting for Jehovah's Witnesses," they said, timidly holding out a tin cup.

"Then you've come to the right place!" Tim declared, grabbing the cup. "I *am* Jehovah!" And he shut the door in their faces.

One day, Tony deliberately and provocatively asked Tim why he hadn't written anything since *The Once and Future King*.

"Of course I've written!" he snapped. He stomped off and sulked in his room for the rest of the day.

The following morning he came into our room, his large velour dressing gown flapping around him, and threw long, thin ledgers onto the bed.

"You think I haven't been writing?" he sneered. "Read those!" Then he disappeared again.

Tony and I pored over the pages all day and way into the night. They were a treatment of *Tristan and Isolde*, an outline for a huge novel, which, alas, he never completed. It was riveting stuff—all his notes, the details in the margins.

Another time he was in his room far too long, sodden with depression. We kept calling, "Tim, are you coming down?" "Tim would you like something to eat or drink?" No response. Being new friends, we were not sure what to do.

Tony found some Dylan Thomas poems recorded by the author, so he put "Do not go gentle into that good night" on the old phonograph and turned the volume up very loud. After the poem was over, there was a long silence. Then Tim's choked voice bellowed, "PUT IT ON AGAIN!" Tony played it again—and again—and eventually Tim came downstairs.

I believe Tim may have been an unfulfilled homosexual, and he suffered a lot because of it. He drank a great deal—mostly Pernod, especially in the winter—but was sober all summer, and there was a reason for that. There was a young man whom he adored, and he talked to us about him endlessly. His parents allowed him to visit Tim every summer, and Tim lived for those times, teaching the boy how to fish, swim, sail, hawk, what to read. I do not think the relationship was ever consummated, but the lad's parents became worried and he was eventually forbidden to see Tim. It broke Tim's heart and made him very bitter.

OUR VISIT CAME to an end and Tim drove us back to the little airport. On the road, we passed three small white semidetached cottages. A "For Sale" sign hung in one of the windows.

"There you are, Tone!" I pointed at it. "That's what we should do. We should buy that cottage and then we can come back whenever we want."

As we arrived at our apartment in London, the phone was ringing. It was Tim. "You know that house you saw?" he said. "Well I bought it. Do you want it?" I was stunned. "It's all right, you don't have to have it," he added quickly. "I can sell it in an instant."

"Tim . . . I'll get right back to you," I stammered. Tony and I conferred excitedly, and then I called Charlie Tucker. The price was £2500. Charlie said, "You can't afford it." But Tim had made this kind effort, and I couldn't believe that we wouldn't get a loan from the bank. Very grudgingly, Charlie allowed it. I think he thought us completely mad and irresponsible. We pooled what little savings we had, and "Patmos," as the cottage was called, became ours.

It transpired that Tim hadn't bought the house at all! Wily fellow that he was, he had merely told the seller that he thought he had a customer. Patmos became our tiny second home, and we adored it. It was a lucky purchase, for so many happy things came about as a result of it: holidays that the entire family and friends enjoyed; the purchase in Alderney by Ma and Pa Walton of their retirement cottage (not that Dad Walton ever truly retired); and my sister Celia met her first husband in Alderney. Tony and I had the place for many years, and eventually deeded Patmos to our daughter, Emma, on the occasion of her twenty-first birthday. Now so many of the grandchildren enjoy the island.

Earlier that year, knowing that I would be traveling a great deal, we placed Shy in our vet's superb kennels in Kent. We decided that, to keep her occupied, we would breed her. She gave birth to five adorable puppies and we gave one of them to Svetlana and Sudi. They named him Khalu, and he became their cherished companion for many years.

THAT SUMMER, WE spent two weeks in Juan les Pins with the Waltons. Mum and Dad W. rented an apartment on the promenade with easy access to the beach. Tony and I had a lovely, lazy time with them, swimming, sunbathing, shopping, and taking leisurely dinners in the evening at the local restaurants.

After they departed, we stayed on in the South of France, joining Svetlana and Sudi in Monaco and spending the next two weeks at the glorious Old Beach Hotel out on the peninsula. Our circular room was right above the rocks overlooking the Mediterranean, so the sound of the surf was constant and heavenly. We took breakfast in our room and made tea in glasses with one of those filaments that heats the water. One exploded in the bathroom one day, and I hurriedly cleaned up before the hotel staff got wind of it.

Svetlana went to the marketplace every day, which was quite a long walk. She knew Monaco well, because her father had been ballet master there for many years. Occasionally we all went to the market with her and watched her pick out cheeses, fruits, salamis, long baguettes, wine, and flowers. Every item was carefully selected by her, handled, smelled, tasted. We would go down on the beach and stuff ourselves with our delicious picnic lunch, and follow that with a good siesta. We were compatible friends, and there was not a moment's discomfort between us.

Svetlana took at least two classes a week at the excellent local ballet school. I was amazed at her discipline. She said she simply *had* to do it or she suffered later.

I slept and sunbathed to my heart's content. I lay on the beach and got a lovely tan. Stretching out on my stomach, I would undo the back of my bikini top to avoid strap marks, and one day, having fallen fast asleep, I was completely doused by a wave from the incoming tide which was chillingly cold on my warm back. I shot up with a scream, only to realize that my top was still lying on the ground.

It was a glorious holiday, and I feel sure that the relaxed, carefree summer was one of the reasons I never missed a performance during the eighteen months I was in *Camelot*.

As Polly Browne in *The Boy Friend*, with the "Perfect Young Ladies" *(l. to r.)*: Millicent Martin ("Nancy"), Dilys Laye ("Dulcie"), Ann Wakefield ("Madcap Maisie"), and Stella Claire ("Fay"). *Eileen Darby Images, Inc.*

Polly Browne again, in the second act costume. *Photofest*

First rehearsal of *My Fair Lady*, with *(l. to r.)*: Rex, Alan, and Fritz. In the background: far right, Maestro Franz Allers; behind Alan and Fritz, Moss Hart; behind Moss, Jerry Adler, our assistant stage manager. *Photofest*

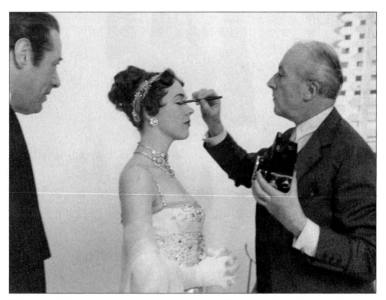

With Cecil Beaton at his personal photo shoot. Rex on the left; I'm wearing Eliza's ball gown. *Billy Rose Theatre Division, The New York Public Library*

Eliza Doolittle, Act 1, Scene 1, *My Fair Lady.*
Billy Rose Theatre Division, The New York Public Library

With Rex in the "Lessons" sequence, *My Fair Lady.*

"The Rain in Spain," *My Fair Lady.*
Billy Rose Theatre Division, The New York Public Library

Dad on the lake in Central Park.
Julie Andrews Family Collection

Publicity photo for Rodgers and
Hammerstein's *Cinderella*, with
Hammerstein on the left, Rodgers in the
center. *Photofest*

At the Savoy Hotel, following the opening night performance of *My Fair Lady* in London. In the background *(l. to r.)*: Charlie Tucker and Aunt Joan.

Julie Andrews Family Collection

The same evening, with Charlie Tucker and Pauline Grant.

Julie Andrews Family Collection

Meeting HM Queen Elizabeth II backstage, following the London performance of *My Fair Lady*. Stanley Holloway on my left, Rex on my right, Prince Philip, Duke of Edinburgh, next to him. *Julie Andrews Family Collection*

Pietro Annigoni's portrait of Eliza Doolittle.
Julie Andrews Family Collection

Arriving with Dad at St. Mary's Church, Oatlands, for the wedding. *Imageworks*

Tony and me at the Mitre Hotel following
the wedding. *Julie Andrews Family Collection*

With Lou Wilson. *Friedman Abeles*

Camelot first read-through *(r. to l.)*: Roddy McDowall, Robert Coote, Richard Burton, me, Robert Goulet, David Hurst, Michael Clarke-Laurence.

Billy Rose Theatre Division, The New York Public Library

At rehearsals for *Camelot*, with Richard and Moss.
Billy Rose Theatre Division, The New York Public Library

Observing *Camelot* rehearsals. *Billy Rose Theatre Division, The New York Public Library*

With Richard, after the opening night of *Camelot*.
Billy Rose Theatre Division, The New York Public Library

With Moss Hart. *Photofest*

Arthur and Guenevere, Act 1, Scene 1, *Camelot. Neal Peters Collection*

With Robert Goulet as Lancelot in *Camelot*.

Billy Rose Theatre Division, The New York Public Library

In *Julie and Carol at Carnegie Hall*, performing "Big D" from *The Most Happy Fella*. *Neal Peters Collection*

With T. H. "Tim" White, in Alderney. *Julie Andrews Family Collection*

With Svetlana Beriosova. *Copyright © Zoë Dominic*

With Rudolf Nureyev. *Copyright © Zoë Dominic*

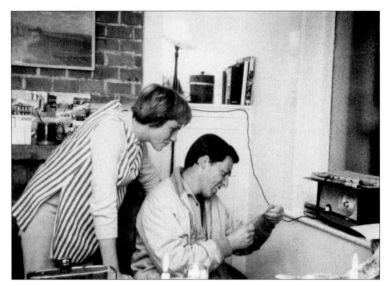

With Tony, at Patmos in Alderney, very pregnant. *Julie Andrews Family Collection*

With Emma Katherine Walton, a few days after she was born.
McCabe/Express/Getty Images

FORTY-FOUR

J UST BEFORE DEPARTING for New York, I drove down to Ockley to spend a day with Dad, Win, Johnny, and Shad. It was a Sunday, and Dad was playing cricket for the home team. He was passionate about the game and played every weekend that he could. He often said how much he wished I would come and see a match.

The family sat on the grass under a tree, Leith Hill in the distance providing a perfect backdrop for the village green and its smooth-as-velvet cricket pitch. We lazed and chatted and watched the game progress, the afternoon heat, the click of the ball, the occasional cry making one inclined to nod off. But when Dad came out of the pavilion and walked onto the pitch, we all perked up. He looked dashing in his whites, and I am sure he was acutely aware of our presence, and he must have hoped to play a respectable game. Indeed he did. The runs began to mount up: thirty— forty—would he make fifty? Johnny and I looked at each other; we were in an agony of expectation and nerves. Forty-eight, forty-nine—we held hands—and suddenly fifty runs were on the board. Good old Dad!

We felt hugely relieved and happy. Clapping enthusiastically, we heard "Howzat?", and at fifty-one, Dad was bowled out. But by then it didn't matter. We piled into the pavilion for tea. Win was helping out that day, as she often did, her homemade cakes and cookies set out for all to enjoy.

That evening, over drinks and dinner at the pub, it was sweet to watch Dad, a pint in his hand, flushed and rosy, chatting up the afternoon with us and his pals.

The local garage owner, another cricket enthusiast, had promised every Ockley member who made fifty runs or more a half gallon of free petrol. Dad duly got his.

It was one of those pastoral, English summer days, perfect in every way—and I will always remember it.

TONY AND I departed for New York in late August. We traveled with Shy, and immediately moved into a sunny, furnished apartment overlooking the East River. It was very different from the dark little ground-floor flat we occupied during *My Fair Lady*, and the view of the river with tugs and cargo barges plowing up and down and the 59th Street Bridge close by was a soothing pleasure.

My assistant, Alexa, was with us. She had her own room in the apartment, and she quickly got to work, finding us a young lady named Lilly Mae, who cooked and cleaned for us, and going on shopping blitzes, buying necessary bits and pieces for our comfort and a new typewriter for herself. Tony commandeered our small study and made it his work studio. I began costume fittings for *Camelot*.

From day one, we kept up a steady stream of correspondence with Tim White, and he with us, and our letters were filled with enthusiasm for all that was happening concerning his wonderful book and its becoming a major Broadway musical.

A fine cast had been assembled. Richard Burton, the charismatic theater and film actor, was King Arthur. Robert Goulet, a Canadian newcomer at the time, who had a magnificent baritone voice, was Lancelot. Robert Coote played the bumbling King Pellinore, and Roddy McDowall was the evil Mordred. Though his role was not large, Roddy had lobbied passionately for the part, and would brook no argument, wanting to come aboard for the joy of it and to be with chums. John Cullum, now a star in his own right, was a member of the chorus, and an actress called Mel Dowd played Morgan Le Fay. Once again, Hanya Holm was our choreographer, Franz Allers our maestro, and Abe Feder our lighting designer. A lovely gentleman named Robert Downing was our stage manager, and Bernie Hart assisted him. I was among good friends.

*

REHEARSALS BEGAN IN New York on September 3, 1960, and members of the company worked once again in the rooftop theater of the New Amsterdam on 42nd Street, while the principals rehearsed and blocked the show at the old 54th Street Theater.

As with *My Fair Lady*, I superstitiously looked for omens as I drove to work that first day, and I spotted a couple, so it seemed all was in our favor. Good!

Moss had kindly invited spouses and close friends of the principals to the reading, so including the sixty-odd members of the production, there was quite a crowd sitting in the audience.

Oliver Smith's luminous designs, which brilliantly evoked the illustrated manuscripts of the Middle Ages, were on display. Moss had asked Adrian, one of the most eminent names of Hollywood costume design, to conceive the wardrobe for the show. He was the first of several casualties suffered as the show progressed. He died from a heart attack before completing his work, but he had designed the bulk of it, and his original exquisite sketches were also on display. A devotee and assistant of his, Tony Duquette, was brought in to oversee the costumes and to design the remainder.

The first reading was truly exciting. I was introduced to Richard Burton, and was immediately enthralled, as was everyone present, by his charm. He was simply one of those charismatic people who attracted the attention of every man, woman, child, or animal the moment he walked into a room. Richard *was* King Arthur—his voice a magnificent instrument, mellifluous enough to make any woman swoon. It was a major part of his unique appeal. That, and his piercing gray-green eyes and full, beautiful mouth.

Alan and Fritz performed their lovely songs that day. The melodies were regal and evocative, and I marveled at Fritz's ability to write for any genre: *Brigadoon* (Scottish), *Paint Your Wagon* (Western), *My Fair Lady* (English/cockney), and now, with *Camelot*, a sense of the Age of Chivalry. Alan's lyrics were, as always, superbly crafted, with meticulous attention to the "voice" of each character.

Moss, ever warm, funny, and welcoming, presided over the event as if it were a party. And it was a party, in a way. Everyone was happy to be present.

Tony attended the read-through and loved what he heard, as did Richard's wife, Sybil. She was an attractive, petite Welsh woman with a lovely countenance, her chin tilted high. She had an easy, outgoing air. Roddy knew just about everyone present, and it was exciting to see him again. Robert Goulet, devastatingly good-looking, was probably as nervous as I that first day, but he was instantly friendly.

We all knew we had monumental work ahead of us, for the musical was a hugely ambitious piece. *Camelot* is a tragic three-way love story; Arthur, Guenevere, and Lancelot care deeply for each other. The king hopes to use his power, his sword, and his intellect to create a better world for mankind. "Might for Right" is how he describes it, and Lancelot and Guenevere support his vision. Arthur is aware of his wife's and Lancelot's mutual attraction, and though pained by it, he tries to turn a blind eye, since he loves them both so much. All three friends do their utmost to remain steadfast, but the presence of Arthur's illegitimate son, Mordred, who wants the throne for himself, is their undoing. He contrives to bring their idyllic world to an end. By the finale of the play, Guenevere is to enter a nunnery, Lancelot is banished, and Arthur is left on the battlefield to pass on his dream to a young page named Thomas Mallory, who will one day write the great book of Arthurian legends. He exhorts the young man to run, run as fast as he can, away from the conflict, saying, "Don't let it be forgot, that once there was a spot, for one brief, shining moment, that was known as Camelot." It was grand theater stuff, and for those of us who remember, the theme was adored by John F. Kennedy, and it came to symbolize his presidency.

That first reading of the musical ran far too long, but we all felt its enchanting potential.

Like an exquisite tapestry that captures the heart of anyone who gazes upon it, *Camelot* cast its mantle over us all, binding and enfolding craftsmen, actors, musicians, technicians. There was an indefinable, yet indelible, aura about the show that sprang from the book and its important themes of chivalry, honor, love, idealism, and hope.

We were to be tested many times as the weeks passed, and we gave of ourselves over and over again.

What was obvious as rehearsals continued was the marked difference between Act I and Act II. The play begins so lightly. The first scene is a mini-play in itself, and is beautifully constructed. There is a joyous romantic feeling to the first act, but the second act descends into darkness as it tells of the disintegration of the Round Table, and the show's ending is heart-wrenchingly sad. This is what Tim's extraordinary book is all about, but there was a concern that audiences might not like being led down one path, only to find themselves on another.

In the original work, Guenevere was not chaste. She and Lancelot had a passionate love affair—though they were guilty and miserable about deceiving Arthur. During the five weeks that we rehearsed, it became obvious that Richard (Arthur) was so damned attractive that Julie (Guenevere) was going to be roundly despised by all if she transgressed. This was not helped by my virginal, squeaky-clean image. Robert Goulet was undeniably attractive as Lancelot, but there was no doubt that the piece was not going to work unless Guenevere remained faithful to Arthur despite her passion for Lancelot.

The script was therefore revised, and oddly, it served to make the outcome of the play stronger and even more tragic. The evil Mordred schemes and plots against the three friends, and in spite of their attempts to remain faithful and hold everything together, he still manages to entrap the would-be lovers and bring about the downfall of Arthur's kingdom.

One day during rehearsals, Moss approached me.

"You're a bit quiet, Julie," he said. "Are you planning to sing that softly all the time?" I knew what he meant. I had been gently easing my voice back into a daily routine.

"No, Moss," I replied. "I think the effort of *Fair Lady* was so huge that I became neurotic about my voice. I'm just testing the waters and making sure it's there for me. I know it will strengthen in time." Mercifully, it did.

Richard was having no such problems. His singing was a revelation; those warm Welsh tones, honed by years of Shakespeare, gave him an enviable vocal ease. The first time I heard him sing Alan's beautiful ballad, "How to Handle a Woman," I simply melted, and there was hardly a night during the run when I didn't pause to enjoy his rendering of the gentle phrases and lovely melody.

SVETLANA CAME TO New York with the Royal Ballet, and Sudi was with her. They attended the last run-through before we departed for Toronto, which was where we were to begin our out-of-town tryout. Afterward, a happy, four-part letter went off to Tim White:

Saturday 24th September 1960

EXULTATION. We had the unique privilege of attending Julie's run through of CAMELOT this afternoon. In order of preferences, after we had gloated in the glorious lightness and abundance of Julie, the contained weightiness of Burton's Arthur, and exulted joyously and tearfully in the subtle aestheticism and emotion of Camelot, we suddenly recovered our wits and recollected the mammoth human who is the real father and mother of it all— TIM JEE. (Sudi)

Thumbs up! There will be never a dry eye or a louder cheer than on the first night of CAMELOT for which after we have congratulated and thanked Julie and Burton and all concerned, we must once again thank you. (Svetlana)

. . . The run through today felt quite good—and although we need to cut at least one hour from the show—it means that (with luck) the three hours left will be really something! Tons of love. (Julie)

. . . They wrote this last night while I was at the theater. I was absent due to VALMOUTH lighting . . . We open officially October 6th. I've just seen my heavenly Julie off for Toronto. SO IT BEGINS. And how tense and exciting it all seems. (Tony)

As Tony indicates in the letter, he was recreating his lovely *Valmouth* designs for a New York production, so he was unable to travel with me to Canada.

Camelot was to inaugurate a brand-new theater in Toronto called the O'Keefe Centre, and this posed its own set of unique problems. The theater had an enormous auditorium, the stage seemed vast, the acoustics had yet to be tested, the orchestra felt miles away, and the audience somewhere beyond that. Everything smelled of sawdust and fresh paint, and workmen were constantly hammering, drilling, installing seats, carpets, and lights—doing all the last-minute things in the rush to be ready for our opening.

To complement Oliver Smith's glorious scenery, Abe Feder decided to use airport floodlights in order to throw enough illumination onto the stage to create the brilliance of the ancient *Book of Hours*. Abe's lights were banked in tiers between the flats on either side of the stage, and when one walked onto the set, and was blasted by an additional barrage of light from the front, the result was a visual blackout. We simply couldn't see a thing; there was such a blur of brightness that we literally had to look at our feet to get our bearings, and had to be careful where we were going. We got used to it over time.

I occasionally went to sit in the front of the theater during the odd moments I wasn't needed. The combination of Oliver's sets and Adrian's costumes, superbly lit by Feder, was so breathtakingly radiant, I felt, and still believe, that I was seeing one of the most beautifully designed musicals ever.

Richard had a personal dresser on the show, who was a good friend and had worked with him before. His name was Bob Wilson. He was a stunning looking man, tall, quiet, tactful, decent. He knew all Richard's idiosyncrasies. Bob's wife, Sally, was a dresser also, and since I, too, needed someone to help me in the theater, it made great sense to all concerned that she come aboard and work for me. Sally was a godsend, a calming presence who kept my life sane.

Tony managed to fly up to Toronto for the last tech rehearsal, and the opening night. But, alas, he had to leave again immediately, to return to his own opening of *Valmouth* in New York City. He then flew to London, where he had designed a sequel to the revue *Pieces of Eight*, this one entitled *One Over the Eight*, again starring Kenneth Williams.

Moss made several attempts to cut our show before we opened, but even so, the first performance of *Camelot* ran almost four and a half hours. The audience was exhausted, and so were we. Tim's huge book was proving more difficult to condense than anyone thought. The following day, Moss, Alan, and Fritz made even deeper cuts.

Hanya Holm had created a superb ballet in the second half, a dance of the animals in the forest scene. Tony Duquette had designed the costumes for this, and he had chosen mostly earth tones, mustards and oranges, and the radiance of the show was suddenly diminished by the drab colors. Moss ended up cutting the ballet altogether, but even that did not lessen our running time by much, and we continued to play overlong.

Our press in Toronto was not overly enthusiastic, but most seemed to agree that the show looked and sounded grand and had potential, and that Burton was perfect as King Arthur.

People flew up from New York to see us, and word soon spread that our musical was more than a little top-heavy, but our company still felt optimistic. A show out of town is a work in progress, and we knew that we had something very special to offer.

A young lady by the name of Joyce Haber came from *Time* magazine to do a cover feature article on Lerner and Loewe. This was their first stage musical since *My Fair Lady*, though they had brilliantly conceived the film musical *Gigi* in the meantime. There was acute interest as to whether they would strike gold again.

Joyce Haber was friendly. She wanted interviews with all the principals, which she got, and she stayed with us for the better part of two weeks to observe and note every detail of the out-of-town process. Led first and foremost by Richard, we opened our hearts and welcomed her into the company.

Moss extended an invitation to Richard and me, Roddy, Mel Dowd, and Robert Coote, to come to his hotel suite one evening after the show. He explained that he had been writing his autobiography, and asked if we would indulge him and listen to a couple of chapters. Would we!

I remember sitting on the floor in his suite, my back propped against a sofa, listening to Moss, who was perched stiffly on a dining chair in front of us all, reading the first chapters of his wonderful memoir, *Act One*. I marveled at his writing style and his ability to capture the spirit of the thirties on Broadway, about which I knew relatively nothing.

On subsequent rereadings of his book, it occurs to me that what he read that night was almost identical to the version that was eventually published. He hardly changed a word.

WE CONTINUED TO work hard in Toronto, rehearsing and adapting to Moss's cuts almost daily, as well as performing our regular eight shows a week. Franz Allers drilled the orchestra and chorus mercilessly, and the results showed. We all continued to shape our characters and tried to help the potentially lovely musical fall into an easy rhythm and a seamless whole.

Then disaster struck.

Alan was suddenly hospitalized for internal bleeding from a perforated ulcer. It is surprising that none of us was aware of his problems at the time, though Moss must have known. We were all so preoccupied and busy with the show.

We later learned that Alan had been suffering a great deal of stress, due to the failure of his fourth marriage and the fact that his wife had taken his beloved young son, Michael, to Europe. There was the added strain of working at all hours on *Camelot*, and because of the necessity to keep going at all costs, Alan had taken medication for depression and anxiety, and the results had wreaked havoc with his intestines. He was in the hospital for ten days.

Moss held the fort in Alan's absence, and announced to the press that our opening on Broadway would be delayed by two weeks, due to Alan's indisposition. Moss was always an inspiring presence, but I remember that he, too, did not appear to be his usual creative and ebullient self.

On the day Alan was discharged, he was standing by the hospital elevator and saw a patient on a gurney being wheeled into the room he had just vacated. To his horror, he was told that it was Moss, and that he had just suffered a heart attack. It was devastating.

This was not Moss's first attack. He'd had one several years earlier. Now it was likely he was going to be in the hospital for quite a while. The company was not made fully aware of just how sick Moss was. We were told that he was in the hospital, and I believe we thought he had a serious case of the flu. We hoped he would be well enough to join us again by the time we arrived in Boston.

Moss sent a message to Alan, asking him to take over the reins of the production. Alan spoke to Fritz, who felt that a new director should be brought in immediately, thus freeing Alan to proceed with the necessary rewrites.

Alan spoke to Richard, and then to me. Richard and I both felt that Alan was the appropriate person to take the helm until Moss was better. Having just come out of the hospital himself, Alan was on the horns of a dreadful dilemma. He wanted to honor Moss's request. He felt fragile, and knew how much work the production needed. How could he continue to rewrite and direct as well?

Fritz kept pushing him to consider bringing in an outsider. I'm sure he, too, was feeling a little fragile.

We had one more week to play in Toronto, and Alan wisely decided to give himself and the company some breathing space. He let us play the long version of *Camelot* for the rest of its engagement in the city, and vowed to continue work on it once we were in Boston. Meanwhile, the search began for a director who might understand our immediate problems, but ultimately the idea proved to be impractical, since the hope was that Moss would soon be well enough to return to us.

The *Camelot* company was heroic. Spearheaded by Richard and his amazing charisma, and helped, I hope, by my own demeanor and optimism, plus Roddy's professionalism and Robert's enthusiasm, we all struggled and forged ahead without complaining through the last difficult week. We were tired and frazzled; we were worried about Moss; we supported whatever Alan thought best. We wanted our production to win out in the long run. There was an incredible bond within the company; everyone had such a decent heart and believed in the message of Tim's wonderful book.

The production closed in Toronto, and we moved on to Boston. We had a few days' rest while our huge sets were trucked down and stuffed into the smaller space of the Shubert Theater there. The principals were mostly lodging in the Ritz Hotel, at the edge of the Common. Richard held a party in his suite nearly every evening. I think he had problems being alone, and there were several regulars within the company only too ready to bolster him and to drink with him every night, and sometimes into the wee hours. Plus, of course, a lady or two to dote on him, and hang on his every word.

I'm grateful that Richard remained professional with me, and didn't press his luck until much later in the run. In all honesty, had he turned his considerable charms on me early in rehearsals, I do not know what my reaction would have been. He was *that* attractive.

FORTY-FIVE

AFTER THE IMMENSE size of Toronto's O'Keefe Centre, Boston's Shubert seemed very small. We began rehearsals again, working in the lobby of the theater, or in the bar downstairs while the setup and technical work continued onstage. Alan gave us more cuts, and his assistant, Bud Widney, rehearsed with us when Alan had to write. We did not see much of Fritz, and I understood later that a nasty rift was developing between him and Alan. Luckily, we were all so busy with the show that we weren't aware of it.

How difficult it must have been—first for Moss (not to mention his distraught wife, Kitty) and then for Alan, who had to withhold so much information in order to keep optimism high in the very large company.

Tony was due to return to New York from London with Tim White. I'd been talking about Tim to the company for such a long time, and everyone was excited that he was coming to visit. I knew that he would be royally welcomed and spoiled. It was understood that Tim would not see the show until it was in proper shape, perhaps not until our formal opening night at the Majestic in New York. But, by an absolute fluke, Tony and Tim's plane was diverted to Boston's Logan Airport because of bad weather on the very day we opened there. Tony called to give me a heads-up, since, obviously, he and Tim would be in town overnight.

I phoned Alan. He very kindly understood the situation and suggested they come see the show that evening. With all that was going on, we seemed destined to fail in Boston, but an amazing thing happened. Because we had spent so many weeks projecting into the vast auditorium of the O'Keefe, our performance at the Shubert was strong and vibrant, and the show dazzled everyone.

We received favorable notices, which gave us all a much-needed lift. The company made a great fuss over Tim. He was very generous about the show and was in his element, stomping about backstage with all the pretty ladies of the chorus loving him up.

Alan had forewarned Tim that converting his beautiful and evocative tome to a two-and-a-half-hour show was "less a matter of dramatizing incidents than capturing the spirit." Tim was very supportive and gave Alan permission to do whatever he thought best. The following day, Tim and Tony set off for New York. I would be joining them in fairly short order.

Philip Burton, a Welshman who was Richard's mentor and surrogate father, was brought in to take over rehearsals and to help direct whenever Alan was unavailable. Philip, a teacher, had discovered Richard as a youngster, giving him vocal coaching and inspiring his love for the theater. Richard, whose original surname was Jenkins, had taken Philip's last name. It was Richard's suggestion that Philip help with *Camelot*, and since we continued to be plagued with problems, Alan was anxious to give his star this added sense of security. No one in the company objected.

After Tony and Tim left, I felt somewhat abandoned and very alone. I had no wish to be as social as Richard, and I was weary. On impulse, I bought myself a portable turntable and some wonderful albums: Rachmaninoff, Brahms, Chopin, Ravel. At the end of each day I found the music infinitely comforting, and helpful in reducing my stress.

With no sign of improvement from Moss, our opening in New York was postponed a further week, and when we finally reached the city, we learned that advance sales were solid, despite the fact that word was out we were beset by problems.

Joyce Haber's *Time* magazine article was no help. She had been so affable in Toronto, but her story about the show was a bit of a hatchet job and it surprised and depressed us all. Many years later, she did several hatchet jobs on me and my husband, Blake, prompting my remark, which Blake loves to quote, "That woman should have open-heart surgery—and they should go in through her *feet!*"

During our last week in Boston, Alan decided that Guenevere needed a new song to replace a protracted farewell scene with Lancelot. Alan conveyed to me that he wouldn't have the time to write the lyrics until just before we opened in New York. He asked how I would feel about that.

I am a quick study, and we had been adding to and subtracting from the show for so many weeks that I was now used to changing on a moment's notice. Plus, I couldn't refuse the chance of a lovely new song, and Alan was so stressed that I wouldn't have made waves even had I wanted to. I asked him to try to get me the song as soon as he could.

We had two paid previews in New York before our official opening, and the night before our first one, I received my song. It was called, "Before I Gaze at You Again," and it was a beautiful, simple ballad. Fritz had already had it orchestrated, so I learned it, it was quickly staged, and it went in that night. It has always held a special place in my heart.

Camelot opened on Saturday, December 3, 1960, at the Majestic Theater, New York. We limped into town and gave the show our best shot. Moss was unable to be with us, though by now he was out of the hospital and recuperating at home.

The reviews were adequate, but not great. It is my opinion that had *Camelot* come before *My Fair Lady*, it would have had its own success. As it was, there were many inevitable comparisons with that great hit.

Every critic had a different suggestion as to what *Camelot* needed. One thought it should have been treated more "vastly," another wished the unhappy ending had been omitted. Most seemed disturbed or puzzled by the difference between the acts. To an extent, we understood the reviews, but we were saddened, because with all our recent problems, we had never been able to refine the show the way it deserved. However, we never felt a negative response from our audiences.

After opening night, Alan came backstage and made us a promise. He told us that Moss was going to get better, and that he and Fritz were going to take a break. Within three months they would all come back and rework the piece. We believed him. We tried not to feel deserted, and we had just enough advance sales to see us through.

FORTY-SIX

TIM WHITE STAYED with us through Christmas, departing just before the New Year. Tony had moved his mass of paperwork and paints to a separate room in our apartment building, and Tim took over the study. It was great fun having him as a guest, and over the holidays he was like a child, opening his stocking presents, his beard quite soaked with tears as he delighted in every little gift.

He had agreed to write an article for *Vogue* magazine, describing his feelings about the show, and America, and why he came to visit. He wrote that he understood the need for changes in *Camelot,* that he wished to be kind to all of us who had worked so hard, and that he had always wanted to learn what Americans were like.

I'd never witnessed him in writing mode before. In anticipation, he paced and paced, not putting pen to paper until his thoughts were fully organized. When he finally began to scribble, the words poured out of him, and seldom needed correction.

I peeked around the study door one day. Tim was at the desk, his glasses on his nose, writing furiously.

"Just wondered if you'd like a cup of tea, Tim," I whispered.

He did not look up.

"GET OUT!" he said sternly.

I hastily shut the door, and never bothered him again while he was writing.

Tim loved coming down to the theater, and he would watch the show from a chair in the wings so that he could witness the action onstage and off. He simply adored Richard, teasing him, calling him "a great *ham*." He wrote a poem for him, which is a superb analytical assessment of the actor. He wrote one for me, too, in case I felt left out. At first, he intended to write a funny parody of Herrick's poem that begins, "When as in silks my Julia goes," changing it to rhymes about my knees and my nose. But then he changed his mind, not wishing to trivialize or hurt my feelings.

Instead, he wrote a beautiful poem, which I treasure:

> *Helen, whose face was fatal, must have wept*
> *Many long nights alone.*
> *And every night*
> *Men died, she cried, and happy Paris kept*
> *Sweet Helen.*

> *Julie, the thousand prows aimed at her heart*
> *The tragic Queen, comedian and clown*
> *Keeps Troy together, not apart,*
> *Nor lets one tower fall down.*

Camelot was still playing far too long each evening, and we all felt the strain, but working with Richard and Roddy and Robert was a total joy. Richard, like Rex in *My Fair Lady*, was such a consummate actor, and watching him, I learned something every night. We developed a gentle friendship.

The opening of *Camelot* is a surefire scene to play. Arthur is miserable that he has never seen his bride-to-be, and she is due to arrive at any moment. He climbs a tree and witnesses Guenevere running away from her entourage, equally miserable at being married off before she has had a chance to experience life. Arthur is smitten, and they meet. He sings to her about the wonders of Camelot, and his identity is revealed when his knights come to find him. Arthur explains how he took the sword, Excalibur, out of the stone, thus becoming king. It is a marvelous speech, and Alan's words brilliantly captured the tone of the original book.

Arthur offers to escort Guenevere back to her entourage. She makes her decision and elects to stay, quoting his own words from the song "Camelot," and they walk off to their future together.

Richard would say to me, "Tonight I'll make the audience cry when I do the big speech." I would watch as he held the audience so spellbound you could hear a pin drop. Another night he would play the speech for comedy, and the audience would laugh, just as he intended. They were amazing exercises in control. Whatever Richard did onstage was magical. Even on the nights when he had imbibed too much, he managed to pull something out of his bag of theatrical wonders.

It was well known that Richard was a heavy drinker. He seldom drank before a performance, but there were exceptions. One weekend was a case in point. Beginning on a Thursday, he stayed up all night on a bender. After the show on Friday he went and drank all night again. He came in and managed to do the Saturday matinee. With a few more drinks between shows, he could barely lift his sword during the evening's performance.

He worried us all, for he was weaving and a leg would buckle occasionally. But he played Arthur as if he was the most weary king, the weight of the world on his shoulders, and I honestly don't think anyone in the audience was any the wiser.

Goulet was so taken by Richard's acting that he began to emulate his style, enhancing his own role with a Shakespearean tone here, a flourish there. Richard said to me one day, "I've suddenly become aware that Bob is doing my performance, so I've had to change the whole thing." Not entirely true, but it made a good story.

In truth, I suspect all the knights in the play became a little grander, a little more noble, by watching Richard.

Bobby Goulet's singing voice was a phenomenal instrument, and his good looks made him the epitome of a true matinee idol. I would sit onstage every night as he sang to me "If Ever I Would Leave You." He was dressed in a royal blue leotard, tights, and boots, and while trying desperately to concentrate on my role, I found myself thinking, "My God! His legs are *divine*."

*

ALMOST THREE MONTHS to the day that Alan said they would return, he, Fritz, and our beloved Moss came back into our lives. How thrilled we were to see them, and how hard we tried to give the best show possible, knowing that Moss was in the audience once again.

Moss acknowledged that the show still had many imperfections. "But at least it aspires," he said, "and it has quality."

It was announced that we would now go back to rehearsals during the day while performances continued at night. Despite the extra work it meant for everyone, we welcomed the chance to make *Camelot* better. Two songs were cut, one of them mine—a rather hefty ensemble piece that Guenevere sang with the knights, entitled, "Then You May Take Me to the Fair." I was grateful, for I had never truly succeeded in making it work. Alan did some rewriting. Moss managed to cut forty-five minutes from the show, so that it finally ran just over two hours. To my knowledge, it was the first time a Broadway show had been so substantially reworked after it had already opened on the Great White Way.

It so happened that *My Fair Lady* was celebrating its fifth anniversary, and Ed Sullivan decided to devote a full hour of his famed television show to Lerner and Loewe. Richard and I appeared in it, and after several songs from their other shows were performed, a seventeen-minute excerpt from *Camelot* closed the televised evening. This coincided with the new changes that had just gone into the show, and there was a palpable electricity that night. The following morning, there was a line of people outside the theater and around the block, queuing for tickets. Sales rocketed skyward, and *Camelot* was, at last, a big hit. It was such vindication for our patience and hard work.

Although the production was incredibly improved, I still feel it was never quite the show it could have been. So many evenings, long after we had reworked the play, members of the company would gather for a drink afterward and someone would say, "Do you think if I did this here, it would help? Or if I stressed this line . . . ?" I've never known a company so in love with the potential of a piece. With Richard as our leader, we were fanatical about it, and, of course, we had Tim to thank for the magical book that inspired it all in the first place.

RICHARD ATTRACTED HORDES of fans every night after the show, and there were always screams as he came out of the stage door. Mike Nichols and Elaine May were performing in the Golden Theater next to us, and late one night, Mike joined Richard backstage for a drink. When they finally exited together, the fans began surging toward Richard. One young lady was so overstimulated that she looked across at Mike and screamed, "Oh! Oh! I love him! *I love him!* . . . Who *is* he?"

There were many hilarious moments during the run. My first entrance in the show was a beauty. I was dressed in a pale blue gown, with a long red chiffon cape on my shoulders and a small sparkling crown on my head. Because Guenevere is escaping from her escort, I ran onto the stage as fast as I could. The space in the wings was narrow, and I had to ensure that my costume never became caught, for it would tear instantly. I also had to gauge that there was nothing in my path that might cause me to trip. As I dashed across the stage, the red chiffon cape billowed out behind me, fluttering like a bright moth.

The last thing I took into consideration was what might happen to me vocally when I stopped running and launched into my song. One evening I flew onto the set, managing everything quite perfectly, opened my mouth to sing, and on the first intake of breath, something caught in my throat and I choked. I sang the entire melody, desperate to cough, tears filling my eyes, but I got through it somehow.

There were two dogs in the show that alternated the role of Horrid, King Pellinore's old English sheepdog. You can imagine how Robert Coote milked his role with this dog in tow! One animal was not as smart as the other, and was more a standby. The smarter animal, used more often, was terribly neurotic. Almost every week he developed a nervous tummy. Cooter delighted in teasing me, popping his head around my dressing room door before the curtain went up, whispering, "Just thought you'd like to know . . . Horrid has the squitters again!"

Our medieval costumes had swaths of material, long sleeves, capes, trains. Whenever Horrid relieved himself onstage, Richard, Cooter, and Goulet would have a fine time, winding their long cloaks over their arms and pointedly stepping over the difficult spots, knowing full well I would giggle at their antics. One night, Horrid chose to squat just before I sang "The Lusty Month of May." The chorus boys were swinging me in their arms, and the ladies were dancing gaily with garlands and hoops. I could see my lyrics coming at me as clear as could be. May—the month when "everyone throws self-control away." I simply couldn't finish the line, and the boys nearly dropped me, we were all laughing so hard. If nothing else, Horrid was a master of timing.

Bobby Goulet was a bit of a prankster. Lancelot and Guenevere never exchange a kiss in the play, but one night he grabbed me and kissed me passionately, simultaneously transferring a throat lozenge from his mouth to mine with great glee. I was furious with him for stepping out of character and doing something so unprofessional in front of an audience. The minute I got offstage I chased him all over the theater and down into the basement, saying, "How could you?" and whacked him as hard as I could. He loved every second of it and, truthfully, so did I.

Roddy was, needless to say, always adorable. He loved to hold big soirees at his apartment. He had always wanted a piano, so Sybil Burton organized an evening party and every chum contributed the vast sum of $25 to buy him a lovely little upright. We all arrived early: Judy Garland, Noël Coward, Richard and Syb, Tony and me, Goulet, Tammy Grimes, Anthony Perkins, and so many other people who loved Roddy. He was just bowled over.

There was a pianist for the evening, so everyone sang something. We sat around on the floor, having been sated with food and wine, and at some point, Judy got up to sing. I'll never forget it. In that quiet setting, she was mesmerizing.

After she finished, someone extended a hand to Noël Coward. He hesitated, then said, "I just completed the score of my new musical, *Sail Away*," and he sat at the piano and played and sang songs from his brand-new show.

Tony and I managed to obtain seats for the legendary Judy Garland concert in April at Carnegie Hall. She was everything we could have imagined—and more. A lot of her orchestrations were by the great Nelson Riddle, and when she finished his arrangement of "Come Rain or

Come Shine," I rose up out of my seat to applaud, as did everyone in the audience. At the end of the evening, she sat on the edge of the stage and quietly sang "Over the Rainbow." It was a historic night.

MY FAMILY CAME over to visit that summer. First Dad and Win, then Auntie and my mother. I had a good time showing them the city, getting them tickets for shows, and taking them on the boat cruise that circles Manhattan.

One night, it was so hot that there was a power outage throughout New York. The elevators in our building ceased to function, and I had to walk down seventeen flights to get a cab to the theater, and climb back up again when I returned home. We had emergency power at the theater, but there were very few lights—we performed virtually in the dark, with no air-conditioning, and in our medieval costumes, were soaking wet within the first five minutes onstage. But the heroic audience remained with us throughout, fanning themselves noisily with their programs.

Occasionally Tony and I entertained at our apartment on York Avenue. One night, Richard and his pals got so drunk that they went into our kitchen and, unbeknownst to me, competed with each other as to who could urinate the farthest distance. I didn't notice it until the following morning, when I discovered the kitchen floor and ceiling saturated with beer and urine. I remember saying to Richard later, "You are *disgusting*. Sophomoric."

Fortunately, I had help from our sweet Lily Mae. She was a buxom, sassy lady, and she loved to dress up for the Sabbath. She asked Tony and me if we would do her the honor of coming to her church one day. It was a Baptist gospel church, way uptown, and we had one of the best Sunday afternoons of our lives. The pastor gave an inspiring sermon, members of the congregation shouting their endorsement of his words, and when the choir sang, the place rocked.

ABOUT NINE MONTHS into the run, Richard suddenly began to behave in a very odd way. Up until this point, ours had been a good relationship—easy, friendly, both of us sharing the stage with joy, giving strength to each other. Our families were often social, and I never once sensed anything between us that was the least bit unpleasant.

One evening, his demeanor onstage changed completely. He flinched when I touched him; he withdrew from me as if I were acutely distasteful to him. I was utterly thrown by his manner. I slammed on my brakes, so to speak, and continued the performance observing this strange attitude, puzzling as to what his problem might be. Had he had a row at home? Was he tipsy? Was he trying some new characterization to keep himself fresh? Was he just in a foul mood? But his behavior was almost calculatingly deliberate, and I became very angry, and deeply hurt. I felt demeaned in front of the audience, and embarrassed, for there was no mistaking his displeasure with me. I had no idea how to handle the situation. I admit that at that moment I had not the courage to confront him, especially since I didn't know what was going on. As the final curtain came down, I made for my dressing room, and neither of us spoke about it.

When actors work together, there is a tacit understanding that the show and its message are what matters above all else. Personal issues are set aside once the curtain is up. I hadn't felt much trust between Rex and me in the early days, but as the months in *My Fair Lady* passed, we came to a place of mutual respect, and our work together became all about performing the glorious verbal music of George Bernard Shaw.

I didn't say anything to Tony that first evening. Perhaps Richard was just having a rotten night. But when he behaved the same way at the next performance, my anger became icy. I then spoke to Tony, and he came down to the theater to observe the odd phenomenon. He asked me if I would like him to speak to Richard. I replied, "Don't you *dare*! This is between us, and I have to figure it out for myself."

Tony said that for roughly a week, our performances in *Camelot* were quite electric. I realize now I was an idiot not to stop the foolishness. I should have asked Richard what the hell he was up to. But I began to sense something, which was confirmed the following matinee when he knocked at my dressing room door. He was all smiles and tenderness, looking for a hug, asking if I was all right. I suddenly guessed that he had been trying to manipulate me into a state of despair concerning his behavior. I think I was the only woman in the company who hadn't succumbed to his over-whelming allure—and maybe this was supposed to be my moment.

"Piss off, Richard!" I said to him, surprising myself with my venom.

A smile played around his mouth, and he dallied a little longer. But I meant what I said, and he eventually got the message. It didn't help matters, for we then suffered through two more miserable performances. But at the end of the third show, he took my hand as we made our bows and said, cheekily, "Who do you love?" I was staggered by his audacity, and caught off guard. I replied something dumb like "You, I *think*." As the curtain finally settled, he threw up his hands, and said, "*Okay!* I'm sorry." He pinched my bum, I pinched his, and we never had another bad moment after that.

IN SEPTEMBER, RICHARD and Roddy left the cast. They were both heading for Rome to make the film *Cleopatra* with Elizabeth Taylor and Rex Harrison. My last months in the show were much harder without them.

I received a photograph of Rex, Richard, and Roddy, taken on location in their Roman costumes. Each had signed it with a silly personal note, and the photograph means a lot to me. I suspect that sweet Roddy was the instigator of the idea.

Richard's replacement in *Camelot* was William Squires, a talented, decent gentleman. But it was an extremely tall order to match up to the power and charisma of Richard Burton.

ON DECEMBER 21, 1961, almost exactly a year after his second heart attack, Moss suffered another—a massive one. He and Kitty were in Palm Springs, and had been alerted to the possibility of trouble by a toothache, which always seemed to presage Moss's attacks. He collapsed in his driveway while heading for the hospital, and died instantly.

It was simply devastating. He was only fifty-seven years old.

Before I departed for California, Moss had visited the theater several times, and one night he came to my dressing room and presented me with his own copy of *Lady in the Dark*. He asked if I would be interested in doing a new production of it onstage, and I said I would read it. Fool that I was, I thought it a little dated. Gertrude Lawrence had starred in it with such success, but I was frightened, and didn't trust that Moss could pull it off again with me, though I was incredibly flattered that he asked me. At the time of his death, I had not yet returned his copy of the play, and when I eventually asked Kitty if she would like it back, she said, "No, you keep it. I'd like you to have it."

FORTY-SEVEN

TONY AND I ushered in the New Year sadly and quietly. We asked a few lonesome Brits stranded in New York to join us for Christmas Day. One was Paul Scofield, the wonderful actor who was brilliantly portraying Sir Thomas More in *A Man for All Seasons* on Broadway.

Paul was very shy and modest, and I had asked him to arrive at our apartment at roughly eleven o'clock Christmas morning. Our doorbell rang exactly on the hour, and although showered and ready, I was still in my dressing gown. As I opened the door, Paul's face became ashen. In a mortified voice he said, "Did you mean eleven P.M.? Have I made a *dreadful* mistake?" I assured him we were anticipating his arrival and welcomed him in.

In spite of the quiet beginning, 1962 turned out to be a very busy year.

BACK IN EARLY 1960, Lou Wilson had said to me, "There's a young girl on Broadway I want you to meet. Her name is Carol Burnett. She's starring in a show called *Once Upon a Mattress,* and she's wonderful. I'm going to get tickets for you to see her."

I'm not sure why Lou was so insistent. Maybe he already had conscious—or unconscious—plans for us both. But I went along with his enthusiasm, and, in due course, I saw Carol's show. I just loved it; loved all that she was, all that she exuded. Her performance was completely original and wonderfully funny.

Lou and a friend of his, the producer Bob Banner, took us to supper after the show, and from then on the poor guys never got a word in edgeways. Lou and Bob just sat back, bemused smiles on their faces, as Carol and I chatted on and on. It was as if we suddenly discovered we were living on the same block. We bonded instantly.

Though Carol and I are from very different parts of the world, our childhoods were somewhat similar. We also seem to have an instinct, one for the other, as to how our brains work, our thoughts, feelings. It's always been understood that we are chums: we probably were in a past life, as well. Unhappily, Carol and I don't visit each other as much as we'd like to. Sometimes we're both too busy, or distance separates us, but when we do get together, we always pick up where we left off and never stop talking.

After that first supper, I didn't see Carol again for some months, but once *Camelot* was up and running in New York, I received an invitation to appear on *The Garry Moore Show*, a weekly television series on which Carol was a regular. It was coproduced by Lou's friend Bob Banner and a tall, rangy-looking gentleman by the name of Joe Hamilton. Joe was an endearing rogue, full of dry humor and camaraderie, and he always sported a pair of bright red socks, no matter what his outfit. He and Carol were dating, and eventually they married.

I was intrigued by the invitation, and wondered what on earth I would do on the show. How would I fit in? Ken Welch, a talented gentleman who wrote all the musical material for *Garry Moore*, asked me if there was anything I had always wanted to try but had never been able to. Any fantasy? Any silly dream? Facetiously, I replied, "I've always wanted to do a Western. Be a cowgirl, an English sheriff; turn it on its head somehow. I never could, of course."

The next thing I knew, he came up with the idea of Carol and me doing the song "Big D" from the musical *Most Happy Fella*. It was sublime fun. Because Carol is brave, and willing to take a crack at anything, I lost my own inhibitions and felt free beside her, teaming with her to perform this riotous number staged by the choreographer Ernie Flatt. Dressed in outrageous cowboy chaps and large Stetsons, we flung our lot together with gusto, and the result was a resounding success and a big rating for *Garry Moore*. He later told Carol that it was the first time he had ever known a studio audience rise to give a standing ovation.

A few months later, I was invited back to join Carol on another *Garry Moore Show*. I did four in all, three of them in 1961, and one in early 1962. In February of '62, I also taped a terrific television special entitled *The Broadway of Lerner and Loewe*. Bobby Goulet, Stanley Holloway, and Maurice Chevalier were in it, and Richard Burton came over from Rome and performed the scene from the magnificent Great Hall at the end of Act I in *Camelot*. It was a lovely and successful telecast.

Meanwhile, Lou Wilson's agile mind was churning. Having some clout with CBS (they had funded both *My Fair Lady* and *Camelot*), he and Bob Banner came up with the crazy idea that Carol and I should do a televised concert evening at prestigious Carnegie Hall. To put two young musical comedy ladies in such a legitimate, classical setting seemed wildly improbable, yet no one else was the least bit daunted. Ken Welch again went to work. Most of the production team from *The Garry Moore Show* came aboard, including Ernie Flatt. Joe Hamilton coproduced and directed the show.

Carol and I both knew Mike Nichols fairly well. From time to time, Tony and I would go over to Mike's apartment and spend a lazy Sunday with him. We'd bring smoked salmon and bagels for lunch, and Mike would make bullshots, a potent combination of bouillon and vodka. Mike would lie full length on his sofa while we stretched out on the floor, and we'd listen to Callas, who was the rage at the time, or talk about theater and read all the Sunday papers.

Carol and I took a deep breath and asked Mike if he would consider writing some extra material for our show, especially some voice-over sketches that would keep our audience happy while we girls were changing our costumes between numbers. Mike consented, but being so well known, he preferred to use a pseudonym on the credits, calling himself Igor Peschkowsky . . . which was in fact his real name.

Everything seemed to fall into place, to be serendipitous. Ethel Merman and Mary Martin had once teamed together for a television special, and that had been very successful. Carol and I called ourselves "The B-Team"—the poor man's Ethel and Mary.

I took a week off from *Camelot*, except for one performance when Colonel John Glenn came to see the show. To honor his remarkable achievement in space, it seemed important to have the full company present, and I went back to perform that night.

We filmed *Julie and Carol at Carnegie Hall* on March 5, 1962. We rehearsed on stage and blocked the day before, then taped a dress rehearsal the following afternoon in case of accidents, and played the real show to a packed house in the evening.

Just before we made our first entrance, I recall standing in the wings on one side of the stage, looking across at Carol on the other. We were both nervous, excited, and wound up like racehorses at the starting gate. Our eyes met, we smiled, nodded, indicating we were there for each other, and blew a kiss before entering to meet center stage.

After an introductory number entitled "Together," we did a send-up of *The Sound of Music*, called *The Swiss Family Pratt*. I portrayed the mother, Carol was "Cynthia," the last child and only girl in a family of twelve boys, played by our wonderful dancers. It was great fun, and I had no idea at the time that I would later be asked to play Maria in that beautiful film.

There was another musical skit in our show, based on the Russian dance troupe the Moiseyev—we were called "The Nausiev." We also each sang a solo, and performed a huge twelve-minute medley together featuring the greatest songs of the decade. We repeated our "Big D" number at the end of the show, having enlarged and improved it to make it even better.

It poured with rain that day, and Carol later said that rain was our lucky omen, for it rained when we did a subsequent show together a decade later, and even during one a decade after that. All three shows were hugely successful, the bulk of them written by Ken Welch and his wife, Mitzie, who have both remained friends to this day.

Wherever we go, Carol and I are asked if we are ever going to do another show together. Our friendship hasn't changed over the years, but it has evolved. The first time we worked with each other, it was all about "Who are you dating?" or "How's married life?" The next time, it was "Sorry, gotta dash for a parent/teacher conference" or "I've got to take the kids to the dentist." The last time, it was more "How are your joints holding up?" and "Do you take Metamucil?"

We hoped to do a series of these specials—*Julie and Carol at the London Palladium, Julie and Carol in Paris, Julie and Carol at the Kremlin, Julie and Carol at the Great Wall of China*—but they all proved to be too expensive. We vowed that our final show, should we ever do another, would be *Julie and Carol in the Swimming Pool of the YMCA.*

TWO AND A half weeks after our Carnegie Hall outing, I received the joyous news that I was pregnant. The first person I told was Carol. I had tipped her off earlier that I was going for a pregnancy test.

"Oh, Jools!" she said. "I'm working at CBS, but whatever you do, call me. Leave a message if I can't come to the phone."

In those days a pregnancy test involved the use of a little mouse. If the poor creature died from an injection of one's urine, it confirmed you were pregnant.

When I received the news, I tried to reach Carol, but was told she was locked in rehearsals. The operator asked if I wished to leave a message.

"Could you please tell Miss Burnett that Miss Andrews called," I said. "Just simply say 'the mouse died.'"

I imagined that the message would be delivered to Carol privately, but apparently the operator paged her over the P.A. system, her voice echoing through the halls of CBS. "Miss Burnett, Miss Burnett . . . telephone message for you. Miss Andrews called to say, 'The mouse died.'"

At the end of the Pratt Family sketch on the *Julie and Carol* show, the choreography called for Carol to whack me "accidentally" in the stomach, and for me to double over. When Carol found out I was pregnant, she was horrified to think back on that moment.

"If I'd known you were pregnant, I never would have touched you!" she exclaimed. Then she added, laughing, "But I bet that's when it connected!"

I told Tony the great news that same day, of course. I wanted to shout it to the world. Tony was designing sets and costumes for *A Funny Thing Happened on the Way to the Forum*. It had an amazing cast: Zero

Mostel, David Burns, Jack Gilford, John Carradine. Tony was attending rehearsals in the theater, and I rushed there to find him, but the first person I bumped into was Stephen Sondheim, who was walking up the aisle. I blurted out my great news to him. Tony still occasionally chastises me for telling Steve before I told him, but then he smiles, so I don't think he really minded.

FORTY-EIGHT

ALTHOUGH I HAD stolen a few days from *Camelot* in order to do Carnegie Hall, I still had five weeks in the show before my contract expired. I suddenly received word that Walt Disney was coming to see us, and had asked if he could come backstage afterward to meet me. I was flattered, and thought it very polite of him.

When Walt appeared in my dressing room, he exuded natural charm and friendliness. After the formalities, he told me and Tony about a combination live action/animated film that he was planning to make, based on the *Mary Poppins* books by P. L. Travers. I was familiar with the title, but had never read the books.

Walt described it a little, and said that his staff at the studio were in the preproduction process. He asked if I might be interested in playing the role of Mary, the English nanny, and whether, after I was finished with *Camelot*, I would like to come out to Hollywood to hear the songs and see the designs that had been created thus far.

Apparently the co-producer and co-screenwriter of *Mary Poppins*, a dear man called Bill Walsh, had recommended me to Walt. He had suggested that Walt come and see the show, and Walt must have felt sure enough about my performance to make an immediate offer. I was overwhelmed by this sudden turn of events, but had to tell him that I was pregnant, and therefore it would not be possible for me to do the film.

Walt gently explained that his team wouldn't be ready to commence shooting until some time after our baby was born. He turned to Tony and said, "And what is it that you do, young man?" Tony explained that he was a scenic and costume designer.

"Then when you come to California, you should bring your portfolio with you," Walt replied.

MY FINAL PERFORMANCE of *Camelot* was on Saturday April 14, 1962. Mum and Dad Walton were in New York and attended that night.

I bid a loving farewell to the company. I had never missed a performance due to sickness through the entire eighteen months of the run, and my faith in my ability to survive the rigors of Broadway had been restored. Now that my tonsils were no longer poisoning my system, I discovered what it was like to actually feel healthy.

I spent the following week in midnight sessions with my chum Carol, recording the album of *Julie and Carol at Carnegie Hall* for Columbia Records. I then traveled to Washington to join Tony and see *A Funny Thing Happened on the Way to the Forum* in previews there. What a wonderful, joyous show *Forum* is! I still rank it among my six favorite musicals—*West Side Story, Carousel, Guys and Dolls, Gypsy* . . . and *My Fair Lady*, of course. But those are just the first favorites, for I have many, many more.

Tony's designs were a riot of marvelous color. There was one curtain in the show that was a radiant, translucent red—almost a signature of his work. Burnt oranges, reds, and corals are particular palettes Tony loves to use, as well as midnight blues, aquamarines, and ocean colors. No one can equal his eye for mixing the tones so uniquely, not to mention his ability for creating drawings that appear utterly facile and free.

It's a rare talent that makes everything seem so easy that it belies the dedication and hard work behind it. Astaire had it, Rubinstein, Baryshnikov, Segovia, certain painters, writers, and poets—the ones who convey the feeling that there's so much strength and energy left unused. It's a quality supremely to be desired.

Forum opened on Broadway on May 8, and received great notices. Two days later, on our third wedding anniversary, Tony and I flew to California to meet with Walt Disney, as arranged.

We stayed once again at the Beverly Hills Hotel, and had a quiet, celebratory dinner there that first evening. The following day, we were driven to the Disney Studios in Burbank. Walt proudly hosted us. We had lunch in the Disney commissary, famous in those days for its good food. People were on the lawn playing table tennis; there were trees everywhere; the streets were neatly signposted.

Walt had a grand office at one end of the animation building. On the walls of his inner sanctum, lacquered plaques told of his many films. There were awards everywhere, plus a huge board showing the grosses of every single movie he had ever made. It was mind-boggling to see the numbers.

Walt was a workaholic, arriving at the studios around six A.M., long before anyone else. He'd roam the animation building, checking the designs on people's desks to see what was being accomplished. Nothing could escape Walt's eagle eye.

The first day was all about meeting everyone, being shown the studio, seeing the storyboards of *Mary Poppins*. These were sketches of every scene in the movie, pinned around the office walls, so we were able to get a very clear idea of what Walt had in mind for this production.

The next day, a Saturday, Walt took us to the races. He was an investor in the Hollywood Park racetrack, and he invited Tony and me to join him and his diminutive wife, Lillian, in his private box. We could not have been more spoiled.

We were informed that there was a horse running that day called "Little Walt." Because he had just been blessed with a new grandson who had been named after him, Walt put a lot of money on this horse, a rank outsider. Tony and I didn't have much between us, but thought we ought to appear willing, so we put everything we had on it, crossed our fingers, and prayed. Amazingly, the horse romped home and we all made a bundle!

Sunday was Mother's Day, and Walt took us to Disneyland, which had been attracting massive crowds since it opened, and was flourishing.

Seeing Disneyland for the first time is a riveting experience, but seeing it with Walt Disney as your guide was nothing less than extraordinary. He and Lillian had their own private apartment overlooking the town square of Main Street. It was a tiny replica of a Victorian residence, with a bedroom, kitchen, and offices, all in perfect scale, the furniture in proportion, pretty fringed velvet lamps strategically placed throughout. Apparently Lillian had wanted it that way, and Walt had humored her. Occasionally, for a special function or gala evening, they would gather with the family there, or perhaps even stay overnight in the early days. Nobody else ever used it. It was the Disneys' private hideaway.

Walt took us on a tour of the park in his golf cart. People recognized him, and waved or ran up to touch his sleeve. "God bless you, Walt!" or "We love you, Walt!" they cried. He had the kind of celebrity that rock groups now have. I suppose his *is* one of the most famous and beloved names in the world. Has anyone, anywhere, *not* heard of Disney?

Walt took us on almost every attraction, including Twenty Thousand Leagues Under the Sea, a submarine ride which was quite phenomenal. It closed in 1998, but happily re-opened in 2007, and was renamed Finding Nemo. We drove through Tomorrowland and Fantasyland. We went on the Jungle Boat Cruise and into the Tiki Room. We ate a great lunch in a private restaurant called "Club 33," which was for special clients and friends. Then Walt escorted us to his newest creation, the Swiss Family Robinson Tree House.

It was huge and completely man-made. Walt proudly told us how many leaves and blossoms it had. Children were scrambling all over it, climbing ladders, crossing bridges, and exploring the many little rooms.

With a twinkle in his eye, Walt said, ". . . and they say only God can make a tree!"

Later, we were invited back to the Disneys' home, where Walt had a miniature steam train in the garden for his children and grandchildren. It was amazing to see the tiny railway line weaving in and out of the flower beds and to hear the shriek of the little engine, which Walt rode with enthusiasm. He always exhibited the delight of a child.

The day after Disneyland, we returned to the studios and listened to all the terrific songs for *Mary Poppins,* written by the Sherman brothers, Robert and Richard. The latter played the piano enthusiastically. I recognized in the songs a kind of "rum-ti-tum" vaudeville quality, and, in a flash, the value of my early years in music hall fell into place.

"Oh! I think I might know how to do this!" I thought. I suddenly realized that all the endless touring and hard work had *not* been wasted after all.

Concerning his request that Tony bring his portfolio to Hollywood, Walt took one look at his work and signed him on the spot, commissioning him to design the film sets for Cherry Tree Lane and the interior of the Banks household, plus all the costumes, for which Tony ultimately received an Oscar nomination.

Walt had an infallible gift for spotting talent in people. I should add the word "decency" as well. Down to the lowliest go-fer in his vast organization, I never met one soul who wasn't kind, enthusiastic, and generous. The Disney aura touched everyone on the studio lot in those days, and anyone who didn't have these qualities didn't last long.

It was very easy to gasp a grateful thank-you to Walt and to accept his invitation to be in the film.

FORTY-NINE

A T THE END of May, we flew home to London. Alexa had left the
U.S. the previous autumn. She had taken Shy with her, depositing
her at our English vet's country home to serve out her quarantine and to
be mated once again. Three weeks after we returned to Britain, we
departed for Alderney, and spent a grand and glorious summer there in
our little cottage. Though we had owned it for over a year, we hadn't yet
claimed it as our own, and it seemed the perfect place to enjoy the days
of my pregnancy.

From time to time, I popped back over to the mainland for checkups
with my obstetrician, and to interview prospective nannies, but for the
most part we spent the next two months cleaning, painting, buying furniture and necessaries, and generally playing house on the island.

Because Alderney is so small, it does not have many trees, and there is
often a biting wind that cuts like a knife. If you survive the first three days
there, you end up feeling fresh, cleansed, and rudely healthy. I never felt
better—and I loved being pregnant.

My dad had been over to the island prior to our arrival, and he had
supervised on our behalf the painting throughout of our tiny cottage, and
had done a few extra things, like putting up towel rails and making sure
the lights worked and the beds didn't collapse when we used them.

Our first day there we shopped for a mass of food items, bath mats,
Kleenex, toilet paper, paraffin, aprons, tins for storage, clothes hangers,
and shelf paper. I cooked brunch for Tim and Tony—eggs and bacon,
tomatoes and toast. Even though we hadn't unpacked, we took a quick

drive around the island with Tim and his ever-present and rambunctious red setter, Jenny. In contrast, our little Shy was a model of good behavior. We stopped to admire the stone arch that Tim had built in my honor next to the little outdoor stage in his garden. He said it was a Roman triumphal arch, and in the cement, at the top of the curve, were the words, "DIVA IULIA."

We returned to our fresh, clean cottage to discover that the propane gas wasn't working properly. The men fiddled with it, and I kept fearing they were going to blow us up. I panicked at the thought of the roast lamb I was planning to cook on Sunday. Having never cooked one before, I figured that in our tiny and ancient oven, it was going to need about nine hours' cooking time, which almost turned out to be the case.

Alderney was quaint, and seemed untouched by the passage of time. The milkman still delivered foaming, creamy milk in an old tin churn every morning. If we wanted more, we just left him a note. We had no phone, so we had to use Tim's or the airport's to make any calls. The weekly supply boat was often delayed by fog or rough seas, which resulted in produce sometimes being hard to come by. And that summer, there was a drought on the island, so the water was switched off every night between 10:00 P.M. and 7:00 A.M. None of this bothered us at all.

The Royal Engineers were visiting, building a slipway in the harbor, putting up radar, repairing broken steps. Their brass band played in Connaught Square each afternoon outside Tim's house, and the islanders, especially the children, loved to come and watch. The engineers played appallingly, and offered excruciating arrangements of Cole Porter, Gershwin, and Irving Berlin. One day, they played a selection from *My Fair Lady*. It was hilarious, and so incongruous to hear the music on that tiny island, so far from Broadway. I thought I should write Alan to say, "Now, that's *real* fame!"

We rented a tiny car, a Morris Minor. Tony did not drive, since during his stint in the Royal Air Force, a memo had been issued, stating, "This man is not equipped with a proper sense of danger," and he had been deemed too "absentminded and reckless" to operate a moving vehicle. I therefore chauffeured us all over the island, across the fields and up the steep cliffs, bouncing along dirt roads and doing three- and four-point turns on the hairpin bends. Once, I got stuck in the mud and had to be towed out.

Tony and I sunbathed on quiet beaches. I exposed my enlarging belly to the skies, hoping that our baby would somehow benefit from the air and sun. My upper torso was now sporting "*une belle poitrine,*" and I had the bra size I'd always longed for.

Tony had been commissioned to design two book jackets. He commandeered our small dining table, and the pile of papers and sketches began to spread across the entire room. In spare moments, we read J. D. Salinger, made papier coupés, and wrote ridiculous limericks.

Tim was expecting company, and when it came to preparation, he always left things until the last minute. He stomped about rather sulkily, wondering who was going to put him in good order. I don't know where kind Maisie was, but, armed with a pair of rubber gloves, and wearing one of my new aprons, I marched down the lane to his house and swept, dusted, polished, and cleaned his tiny kitchen and downstairs bathroom. Everything was hopelessly dusty.

We, too, had a constant stream of visitors—Dad, Win, Johnny, Celia, Mum, Auntie, Donald and Chris, all the Waltons, my old chum Sue Barker, and Sudi, to mention just a few. The latter was hilarious, shooting endless photographs and cine film to share with Svetlana, who was working in London. His voice boomed up and down the high street as he shopped in every store, apologizing to everyone he inconvenienced. Showing him our island, we had to stop every few seconds for photo opportunities, Sudi calling, "Julis! Please get out of the car! Make a pretty picture—talk to me—hallo! Wave! That's it!" Stephen Sondheim came for a brief weekend, and we had great fun together. I worried that perhaps Alderney was too bare, too cold and wet for him, but he declared that it suited his brooding personality very well, and that he couldn't be happier.

In August, when Dad came, we joined in the celebrations of Alderney Week, and went down to the village to watch the three-legged race and the quoits competition.

The summer flew by. Tim began drinking again, and was occasionally irrational and verbally abusive. One evening, he took Tony and me to dinner at a fancy restaurant on the island. Dressed appallingly, he insisted on having Jenny in the "No Dogs Allowed" dining room, whereas we had left Shy in his car. He was so rude to the waiter and in such a foul temper that I finally called him on it. He stomped off in a huff before dessert, driving away, leaving little Shy to run around the parking lot, and us to foot the bill and get a cab.

Tony was always more than ready to forgive his transgressions, but I felt that this time Tim had gone too far. He was irritating, thoughtless, behaving like a spoiled child. I was pretty far along in my pregnancy, and not inclined to be tolerant. I pulled back from Tim for the rest of the holiday, and I regret it deeply, for though we patched it up, it was never quite the same again.

Tony and I traveled back to England. We enrolled in National Childbirth Trust classes, and I studied the Lamaze technique of childbirth. Tony learned what was expected of him on the big day. We hired a very qualified baby nurse, a New Zealander named Vel McConnell, to help me with the baby for the first few weeks. We purchased baby clothes and bedding. My mother bought a beautiful, classic pram and gave it to us. Tony moved his mess of designs out of our little guest bedroom, and stuffed them all over the small apartment, under our bed, behind the curtains. We made a nursery of the guest room, with a bed for the nanny and a pretty crib for the baby.

We spent some lovely evenings with Svetlana and Sudi, going to their apartment in Hans Crescent to socialize, since there was no room in ours. Our friend, the photographer Zoë Dominic, was there often, as was Rudolf Nureyev, newly arrived in England and now the toast of London. One evening, he sported a huge Russian overcoat and I climbed into the sleeves with him. Zoë snapped a photo of us both, snuggled together inside.

Sudi gave me D. W. Winnicott's wonderful book on pregnancy, childbirth, and the first stages of infancy. It was all about trusting one's instincts. I pored over it, took comfort from it, and shared some of it with Tony. I read Dr. Spock cover to cover, as well.

I was becoming a little nervous, eating too much, and feeling heavy and unpretty. I went to Harrods, and though I only had a couple of weeks before my due date and my old clothes would soon be in use again (the larger ones, anyway), I purchased a lovely, burnt orange silk shantung maternity dress, which helped boost my morale.

Four weeks passed and there was still no sign that our baby was ready to come into the world. I went into the London Clinic and the baby was induced. Tony sat on the bed, and rubbed my back during my labor, and I railed at him for bouncing about too much.

I did not know until later that Svetlana had come to the hospital and had kept vigil in the hall all evening. She refused to come in lest she disturb me. As I was being wheeled to the delivery room, I sensed her presence beside me for a moment, and heard her soft voice, whispering, "Good luck, Julis." I was deeply touched that she was there.

Emma Katherine Walton was born a few minutes before 1:00 A.M., on Tuesday November 27, 1962.

The next morning, as I was recuperating in my hospital room, the phone rang. Thinking it would be a family member, I somewhat groggily picked it up. A voice at the other end of the line said, "Hello? This is P. L. Travers."

"Oh, hello, Miss Travers!" I stammered, gathering my wits as best I could. "How nice of you to call . . ."

"Well, talk to me!" she said brusquely.

"Oh—well—I've just had a baby and I'm feeling a bit exhausted . . ."

"Yes, yes," she interrupted, "but you're going to be playing Mary Poppins?"

"Yes, Miss Travers."

"Well, you're much too pretty, of course. But you've got the nose for it!"

Later, we met in person when I went to tea with her, and once Tony and I had settled in Los Angeles, we corresponded, because she wanted to be kept in the loop. She became a bit of a thorn in Disney's side, and Walt had to ultimately tell her, rather firmly, that she didn't have the right to dictate how he should make a film. Apparently she was not that thrilled with the movie, but it became a huge annuity for her.

Three days after Emma was born, Tony had to leave for America to prepare for his work on *Poppins*. Sudi happened to visit me just after he departed, and found me weeping copiously.

"Oh, my dear Julis," he kept saying, "You have the baby blues. Poor Julie-gee!"

"But he's *gone*," I sobbed, feeling utterly abandoned, and with the responsibility of a new baby and no idea how to take care of her weighing heavily upon me.

Emma and I stayed in the clinic for two weeks (one did, in those days). We bonded quickly, and, as I nursed her, the wonder of motherhood flooded over me. Her birth coincided with a monstrous smog that blacked out London and killed many elderly people. The clinic closed its doors and insulated the windows, but still the yellow crud seeped and curled into the room. I feared our lovely daughter would suffer dreadful complications; she never did, and it was the last pea souper that London ever had.

Tony and I were late deciding our baby's name. I had Sarah, Joanna, Emily, Emma, and Susan on our list for girls. An Irish nurse brought her to me from the nursery one evening, crooning, "Come along, Emma, it's time for your feed."

"How do you know she's an Emma?" I asked in surprise.

"Well, the newspapers printed the list, didn't they? I've always called her Emma."

So Emma she was—and it suited her.

My mother came to visit, and Auntie, Dad, Win—even some of the great aunts came up to London to peek at the new arrival. It was a sweet time, with so much love spread around. Charlie Tucker visited. Alan and other friends from America sent telegrams and cards. Carol Burnett became Emma's godmother, Svetlana also; Lou Wilson, her godfather.

Tony phoned me every day while he was in Hollywood, and he returned home two days after we moved back from the hospital to our little flat in Eaton Square.

Vel McConnell, the baby nurse, was the greatest help, and I was so grateful to her. She looked a bit Mary Poppins–ish herself, thin and tall, with dark hair. She stayed two weeks with us, and when she left, I was nervous coping with Emma all by myself.

Tony and I would stand in the nursery by Emma's crib as she slept, and we'd do the classic new parent thing of checking to make sure she was still breathing. I managed to take her out for daily walks in the huge pram, which was ridiculously difficult to get up and down the two flights of stairs to our apartment, and I would sit with her in the winter sun in the little park in Eaton Square.

Just before Christmas, Emma and I had our first photo session together with Zoë. Who could possibly have guessed then that one of those photos would end up, forty-something years later, gracing the cover of a little book Emma and I wrote together?

We hired a sweet young nanny from Alderney named Wendy, whose parents ran one of the local hotels. Our apartment soon began to feel far too small. I remember being in the only bathroom, which I now shared with Tony, Emma, and Wendy. On the bathtub was a plastic V-shaped laundry stand, with all Emma's clothes hanging on it. Under the wash-basin was a huge diaper pail (no disposables in those days!). In the foyer was the enormous pram, and of course, Tony's artwork continued to spread everywhere.

It was all suddenly overwhelming, and I felt the intense need for some privacy. So I locked the bathroom door. Seconds later, Tony rattled the knob, wanting to come in.

"Why did you lock the door?" he inquired in a hurt voice.

"Because there's nowhere else I can go to be on my own!"

Soon after that, we found and bought a big, airy apartment on the edge of Wimbledon Common. Alas, we never moved into it. Life had other plans for us.

Svetlana and Sudi visited often in the days before we left for America. Sudi was sweetly gentle, with me and with Emma.

"Julie-gee," he said, "be sure to give the baby time every day to kick and be free, without clothes. It is important that she feel the air on her skin—to learn who she is." So every evening, Emma would lie naked on a big bath towel on our living room couch by the warm fire. She obviously enjoyed the experience—kicking, punching, gurgling, and happily doing her calisthenics. We made sure that Shy still felt an important part of the family.

Tony and I became hopelessly weary, awake every night with our hungry baby. We suffered through this for what seemed like an age, and one day, in desperation, I called my mother.

"Mum," I wailed, "we feed her as late as we can, hoping that she'll sleep all night, but still it doesn't work."

My mother, who had raised four children, lovingly explained that I was going about it the wrong way. "By delaying her evening feed, she's getting her longest sleep before you even go to bed," she said. "Wake her up every four hours, no matter what, and give her something to eat, and she will soon adjust to your schedule."

That's exactly what happened.

On February 24, 1963, we held a christening for Emma at St. Mary's, Oatlands, the church where we were married. The Reverend Keeping did the honors, Emma behaved beautifully, and all the Waltons, Wellses, and Andrewses gathered at The Meuse afterward for a small celebration. Three days later we left for Hollywood.

TONY, WENDY, EMMA, and I flew first-class, sitting in the bulkhead at the front of the plane. The airline had installed a bassinet against the wall, and Emma traveled comfortably.

Disney Studios had rented and furnished a house for us in Toluca Lake, but I had not seen it. As before, when I first headed to Broadway, I was once again venturing into a totally new world. I could not know that life would turn me inside out and upside down several times in the years ahead. I only knew that at this moment, all was serene and happy, and I felt supremely blessed. Tony and I were going to work together, we had a beautiful baby daughter who was the love of our lives, and Walt Disney beckoned with kind, creative hands.

As it turned out . . . I was going home.

ACKNOWLEDGMENTS

W HEN I FIRST began this memoir, I had no idea how many people would come forward to help and share in my journey of rediscovery. My gratitude and thanks go to them all.

Without my daughter Emma, there would be no memoir. I had established an extensive timeline and, working from that, she interviewed and recorded me, researched, and ultimately correlated all the information so that I could begin writing. She then used her good editorial skills to advise and reinforce my instincts. Her encouragement, enthusiasm, and interest in the history of my early years were ever present. A mother with her own family and career, she embraced this project unreservedly, and was patient, understanding, and generous of heart throughout it all. I could not have been given a greater gift.

My deep gratitude goes to Bob Miller and Ellen Archer of Hyperion. Ten years ago, Bob approached me about writing a memoir and, to my amazement, never lost faith. With a "day job" that took up so much of my time, I missed every deadline and even offered to return my advance payment—but he always politely refused.

Leslie Wells, my trusted editor at Hyperion, in New York, and Ion Trewin, of Weidenfeld & Nicolson, in England, contributed so much to the final shape of the book, and I am indebted to them.

Francine Taylor, my longtime friend and assistant, tirelessly took my notes, transcribed my recordings and those of my family, and put up with my pleas for "just one more insert" at all hours of the day and night.

My deepest thanks go to her and to our dear friend, Jim Brennan, who did so much research in England for me concerning vaudeville and my own stage appearances.

Similarly, my thanks go to my Los Angeles assistant and friend, Christine Jardine; her counterpart in our California household, Carmen Garcia; and Eliza Rand, our editorial associate in the Julie Andrews Collection, for their constant help.

Tony Walton and his wife, Gen (who fondly refer to me as "our Ex") were generous in their support, comments, and contribution of letters and photographs. Jen Gosney, Tony's sister, could not have been more contributive, providing memorabilia she had saved of our early lives together, and I have her to thank for introducing me to Peter De Rougemont, whose expertise in archival research turned up valuable and sometimes surprising information.

I extend a thank you to Giles Brearley, whom I have never met, but whose work on the life of my maternal grandfather arrived on my desk, incredibly, the day I began this memoir.

I was able to record my father, Ted Wells, and interview his wife, Win, and my mother's friend, Gladys Barker, while they were alive, and their recollections turned out to be invaluable.

Similarly, my late Aunt Joan wrote many biographical pages, and I have unashamedly borrowed from them.

My brothers, John, Donald, and Christopher, and sister, Celia (Shad), shared many hours with me while we discussed family recollections. For all of us it was a time of stirred feelings and, ultimately, deeper understandings—special moments that I shall always treasure.

I am grateful to dear friends Carol Burnett, Sybil Christopher, Zoë Dominic, and Catherine Ashmore for their love and help.

Special thanks must go to my personal manager, Steve Sauer, for his belief in this project, and for his efforts to facilitate a smooth path, especially during the last hectic months when it was finally coming together.

I extend my gratitude to Ted Chapin for providing research concerning my work with Rodgers and Hammerstein.

To David Lott, production editor, and Linda Lehr, production manager, my thanks for helping to correct and improve the book. Thanks to Beth Gebhard, Jane Comins, Jessica Wiener, and Betsy Spigelman for marketing and publicity; and to Jill Sansone for her work in subsidiary rights. For the many hours spent in photo researching, I would like to acknowledge Ruth Mandel. Fritz Metsch delighted me with his design of the book, and to all the good people behind the scenes at Hyperion, my warm appreciation.

I am deeply touched that our four other children, Jennifer, Geoffrey, Amy, and Joanna, and all the grandchildren, put up with this mum who, though present in love, must have seemed absent when writing occupied her thoughts.

My gratitude also goes to Steve Hamilton, who was ever patient during this period, both with his wife, Emma, and his mother-in-law.

Finally, to my dearest Blackie, husband for the past thirty-eight years and the real writer in our household: bless you for understanding so completely the obligations and needs of a work that consumed so much of my time. Thank you for always being there and for holding the fort.

JA
Sag Harbor, 2007

INDEX

Julie Andrews' career has flourished over seven decades. From her legendary Broadway performances, to her roles in such iconic films as *The Sound of Music, Mary Poppins, Thoroughly Modern Millie, Hawaii, 10,* and *The Princess Diaries,* to her award-winning television appearances, multiple album releases, concert tours, international humanitarian work, best-selling children's books, and championship of literacy, Julie's influence spans generations. Today, she lives with her husband of thirty-nine years, the acclaimed writer/director Blake Edwards; they have five children and seven grandchildren.